Johann Wolfgang von Goethe

"a fiery spirit, soaring with the wings of an eagle."
—HEINRICH HEINE

Poet, novelist, essayist, letter-writer, scientist, statesman and playwright—Goethe's interests encompassed all spheres of human activity and knowledge. A writer of power and sensitivity, he combined a life of poetry with one of action and self-fulfillment.

In this sparkling anthology, Stephen Spender, the renowned poet and critic, presents a brilliant collection of some of Goethe's greatest writings in exciting, modern translations. Letters, poems, autobiographical selections, reflections and maxims, and Part I of Goethe's tragic masterpiece FAUST—here is the work of a man of genius who was the embodiment of 18th century literature.

Stephen Spender, the editor of this remarkable volume, was once described by Herbert Read, the critic, as "another Shelley." He is considered by almost all critics to be one of the greatest poets now writing in English. His literary criticism and fiction have also earned him a world-wide reputation as an artist and scholar. Mr. Spender makes his home in England but spends a great deal of his time traveling throughout the world.

The Mentor Philosophers

A distinguished series of six volumes presenting, in historical order, the basic writings of the outstanding philosophers of the Western world—from medieval times to the present.

The Age of Belief: The Medieval Philosophers
    Anne Fremantle, ed.   (#MQ739—95¢)

The Age of Adventure: The Renaissance Philosophers
    Giorgio de Santillana, ed.   (#MT437—75¢)

The Age of Reason: The 17th Century Philosophers
    Stuart Hampshire, ed.   (#MT367—75¢)

The Age of Enlightenment: The 18th Century Philosophers
    Sir Isaiah Berlin, ed.   (#MQ689—95¢)

The Age of Ideology: The 19th Century Philosophers
    Henry D. Aiken, ed.   (#MQ733—95¢)

The Age of Analysis: 20th Century Philosophers
    Morton White, ed.   (#MT353—75¢)

✣

GREAT WRITINGS OF

GOETHE

Edited and
with an Introduction by
STEPHEN SPENDER

A MENTOR BOOK
Published by THE NEW AMERICAN LIBRARY,
New York and Toronto
The New English Library, Limited

ACKNOWLEDGMENTS

The author wishes to thank the following publishers for their kind permission to reprint from the books indicated below.

EDINBURGH UNIVERSITY PRESS:
   Letters of Goethe, translated by M. von Herzfeld and C. Melvil Sym.

FABER & FABER LIMITED (LONDON):
   Part I, with additions, of Goethe's *Faust*, translated by Louis MacNeice.

G. BELL & SONS LIMITED (LONDON):
   "Elective Affinities" from *Novels and Tales*, translated by James Anthony Froude and R. Dillon Boylan; and *Travels in Italy*, translated by A. J. W. Morrison and Charles Nisbet.

THOMAS NELSON & SONS LIMITED (EDINBURGH AND NEW YORK):
   Letters of Goethe, translated by M. von Herzfeld and C. Melvil Sym.

OXFORD UNIVERSITY PRESS (NEW YORK):
   Part I, with additions, of Goethe's *Faust*, translated by Louis MacNeice. Copyright, 1951, by Louis MacNeice.

WEIDENFELD & NICOLSON LIMITED (LONDON):
   "First Love and the Coronation" from Goethe's *Truth and Fantasy from My Life*, translated by Eithne Wilkins and Ernst Kaiser.

Library of Congress Catalog Card No. 58-12835

MENTOR TRADEMARK REG. U.S. PAT. OFF. AND FOREIGN COUNTRIES
REGISTERED TRADEMARK——MARCA REGISTRADA
HECHO EN CHICAGO, U.S.A.

MENTOR BOOKS are published *in the United States* by
The New American Library, Inc.,
1301 Avenue of the Americas, New York, New York 10019,
in Canada by The New American Library of Canada Limited,
295 King Street East, Toronto 2, Ontario,
in the United Kingdom by The New English Library Limited,
Barnard's Inn, Holborn, London, E.C. 1, England

PRINTED IN THE UNITED STATES OF AMERICA

CONTENTS

❖

INTRODUCTION

Goethe is sometimes described as the last man to have the qualities of a Renaissance genius. He certainly has claims to be universal. He is a poet who could, to the credit of the aristocrat who was ruler of the little state of Weimar, be described as a poet among princes. Besides writing *Faust,* he was statesman, administrator, scholar, and scientist. In his beliefs, he was a humanist, often siding with the pagan as against the Christian world, but with an obsessed preoccupation with Christ and a *pietas* that extended beyond the churches to ancient pagan and modern Oriental religions.

We are inclined to consider anyone who attained his prime before the French Revolution as belonging to an epoch cut off from our own; Goethe was forty in 1789, at the outbreak of the French Revolution. Half his life stands on the side of a barrier of time which separates the old regime from the new. Yet far more than the philosophers of the French Revolution, who conditioned our age for us, Goethe seems a modern writer, dealing with the particular problems of being a poet in modern times. He fascinates those who fall under his spell because he was more successful in the attempt to make a synthesis of contemporary knowledge and thought than anyone has been since. And if we think of him as the "last" universal genius, this may be because he was the last man in a position to attempt such a synthesis. After him, knowledge, invention, and their consequence—specialization—increased so rapidly that no one could bridge the gulf between science and poetry; although, largely as a result of Goethe's influence, to do so remained one of the aims of the "Great Victorians." Rather than the last Renaissance genius, one might say, then, that Goethe was the first, and also the last, complete modern individual: an all-rounder, sane in mind and body, who combined the roles of poet, statesman, and scientist. After him all occupations split up into their separate and special compartments.

Yet his many-sidedness also reveals the limitations which already in the eighteenth century bound the imaginative, faith-determined poetic mind, when faced by methods of detached specialist analytic observation. To study facts and draw whatever conclusions led from them, to look too scientifically into the unknown, to question skeptically the mysterious, was as blasphemous to him as to his very different contemporary William Blake. Goethe "knew" a lot of science but disliked the most advanced scientific approach in his time. Unknown to one another, Goethe and Blake meet in anathematizing Newton. "I discovered light in its purity and truth, and I considered it my duty to fight for it. The opposite party, however, did their utmost to darken the light; for they maintained that shade is a *part of light*." Thus Goethe to Eckermann in 1824, pondering his own theory of colors. There is a feeling here that the Newtonian method of pure inquiry is in itself the work of the devil: that it was the duty of science to search for metaphors in nature illustrating the underlying unity in everything. Goethe expected science as well as religion to confirm his most basic conviction: "All things weave themselves into a whole."

Goethe's attitude to Newton shows that he is far closer to the predicament of the modern poet confronted by the results and methods of scientific specialization than to a Renaissance universal mind like Leonardo. To Leonardo, science was an extension into the world of objects of the same kind of discoveries and inventions that he made in painting. His inventions were closer to the attempts of surrealists in our own time to conquer new areas of experience for the imagination, than to modern researches. It is true that Goethe's industry and imagination led him to

make at least one significant scientific discovery, and to
foreshadow Darwin's theory of evolution. But this only
emphasizes the modern dilemma, which confronts us in
his life, that poetry needs science and science needs poetry.
And yet it is almost impossible to envisage a modern
mind which could combine the utmost poetic faith with
the utmost scientific skepticism.

On the verge of the age of specialization, Goethe saw
the importance of synthesizing and not specializing. He
made the gigantic effort to form a synthesis of all the forces
in his own life, which would be realized in his poetry.
His writing and his life are a reflection of a harmony
achieved in his behavior, responsibility, action, and being.
He expressed this truth when he called his poetry autobiographical and said of the novel *Elective Affinities* that
there was not a line of it which he had not experienced.

By specialization I don't mean just "science," I mean
the centrifugal tendency of all the activities of the modern
mind to concentrate on those particularities which distinguish them from all other activities. That the arts and
intellectual disciplines should split apart seems almost inevitable in an age where men's lives are dominated by
struggle for power in politics, by the newspapers, by scientific inventions. *Life is short and art is long* is a tag that
recurs in Goethe. No one knew better than he that the outward circumstances of the time were developing in ways
unsuitable for the development of art.

Everything in his life, after he was twenty-five, seems
significant in relation to the challenge of circumstances.
The way in which he met this has itself been a challenge
to later writers confronted with the same modern situation.
Thomas Mann is only one great modern writer who felt
challenged by this example. His writings about Goethe
recall the colloquies of Hamlet with his father's ghost.

The fact that later writers have been unable to follow
Goethe's example of combining a life of poetry with one of
action and self-fulfillment, only emphasizes his purposive-
ness. The deliberated choice extends even to his faith in
the necessity of following ways which underlie consciousness; consciously obeying his instincts at times almost

blindly, pursuing byways of his own development, accepting error, and then finally, out in the clear, showing in the resultant work that what seemed wayward, obscure, or erroneous could be resumed within the open rightness of the result. Goethe meets Blake in holding that "what we call evil is only the other side of good." And Blake might have recognized in Mephistopheles the devil as Milton ought to have portrayed him—the Milton who was, in Blake's words, "of the devil's party without knowing it"— an aphorism which would have delighted Goethe.

The change that took place in Goethe's life after he became minister of state, classicist, and objectivist, might well have made a familiar story of a man of genius, after a youth of sowing wild oats, accepting public duties and becoming a public institution, were it not for the respect for what D. H. Lawrence called the "dark gods," which Goethe brought forward into his changed—outwardly respectable yet deeply ironic—Weimar life. The transformation is apparent in the contrast between the first and second parts of *Faust*. The first part is concerned with the subjective world of Faust's self-exploration through magic, the second with the objective world in which the past, religion and art, and the science that can transform nature are greater than subjective preoccupations. Magic is an agent of the subjective Faust in search of himself. The terror, darkness, and mystery of the classical world, the superhuman forces, and the strange "mothers" of the second part of the drama build up a picture of a life greater than individual beings, a mystery which makes the greatest individuals instruments in its high service.

Mephistopheles, a medieval figure, is dwarfed by the terrifying greatness of the inhabitants of the classical Walpurgisnacht. And as in the second half of the play that occupied his whole working life, so in his own later life Goethe surrounded himself with objective forces and banished the devils, witches, and temptations of his first period. He came to regard withdrawal into oneself, subjectivism, romanticism, as symptoms of the modern disease which poets ought to be resisting. Hence his intolerance of the romantics. "All eras in a state of decline and dissolution are subjective," he observed to Eckermann. "On the other hand, all progressive eras have an objective tendency. Our present time is retrograde, for it is subjective; we see this not merely in poetry, but also in painting, and much besides. Every healthy effort, on the contrary, is directed from the inward to the outward world."

Nothing could be further from Goethe's view of poetry than Keats' definition of the "poetical character" as having "no self," "no identity," and the poet being "the most unpoetical of all God's creatures." Nor, even, does Goethe correspond to Keats' exception to his own generalization, the "Wordsworthian or egotistical sublime; which is a thing per se and stands alone." Goethe's egotism was the defense of a disinterestedness, far from egotistic.

Goethe's view of poetry is, then, the opposite of that of the romantic school. But at certain points these opposites do converge. One is where the Keatsian view that the poet, through annihilation of his identity, enters into everything coincides with the Goethean view that "every healthy effort . . . is directed from the inward to the outward world." But in Keats the emphasis is all on receptive personality which, through empathic sensibility, can enter into the nature of sun and moon; in Goethe the emphasis is on positive character which enters into the world but contests it with objective values of moral and poetic worth. Keats subjectifies the objective, Goethe objectifies the subjective.

Goethe's position was, and still is, one of massive isolation in the development of modern poetry. From his own time until our own, the beating of waves of romantic temperament against this rock of the man and the work is painful to witness, and often shows Goethe in an unsympathetic light. A good deal has been made of the manner in which he refused to interest himself in Hölderlin, the coldness of a famous letter to Kleist. Yet it is hardly necessary to defend Goethe as a poet from criticism of him as a man, because he could not extend his sympathy to other poets for attitudes which he had mercilessly rejected in himself. His life is the price he paid for his poetry, and in the end that life itself is his greatest work. Did he not describe his own work as one long autobiography? *Werther* and the early poems were the expression of subjective and romantic living; his life after he was forty was more and more an object of his poetry. At first his life wrote his poetry; after, his greatness wrote his life.

It is inadequate to discuss Goethe simply as a poet. For that which we mean by "Goethe" includes not only his poetry and prose, but also his example and what is called his wisdom. His greatness lies precisely in his achievement of objectifying himself; so that today when one says "Goethe," one means the sum of a great many significances —some of them poetry or prose, some of them in action, some of them hedonistic yet sacrificial acts of sensual living—which add up to an image resembling some great epic written by a man not only out of words, but out of his acts and even his insistent flesh and blood.

For he insisted on making his development the object of the many-sided fullness of his nature. It is this which we find difficult to accept in him; we are accustomed to associate sacrifice with asceticism. That sacrifice can be achieved through self-realization, and not self-abnegation; through insistence on happiness, and not through un-happiness; through self-preservation and not through self-lessness; all this is quite alien to our Puritan Christianized conception of character. We may be repelled when we learn that Goethe disliked seeing corpses or visiting the dead, did his utmost to ignore his wife's suffering on her sickbed, broke off with lovers when the relationship threatened his independence. Yet we have to accept this as the price we pay for "Goethe." And to understand his greatness, we have to see that he himself paid the price and was aware of doing so.

His name is often linked with those of other great poetic geniuses—Shakespeare, Dante, and Goethe is a sequence that falls all too readily from many lips. Yet how little the earlier poets have in common with the later one! Goethe himself took the measure of this gulf, when he observed to Eckermann, speaking of Shakespeare: "That undisturbed, innocent, somnambulatory production, by which alone anything great can thrive, is no longer possible. Our

talents lie before the public. Daily criticisms in fifty different places, and gossip caused by them, prevent the appearance of any sound production. He who does not keep
aloof from all this, and isolate himself by main force, is lost.
Through the bad, chiefly negative aesthetical and critical
tone of the journals, a sort of half-culture finds its way into
the masses; but to productive talent it is a noxious mist, a
dropping poison, which destroys the tree of creative power
—from the ornamental green leaves, to the deepest pith
and the most hidden fibers."

Modern circumstances make the poet self-conscious; a
vigilant and determined acceptance of the poet's situation
is the only answer to these circumstances. Innocence is
impossible. Consciousness becomes everything.

Goethe's own life illustrates the shift in his attitude
from innocent creating to extreme consciousness and to a
kind of willed isolation, which was not an "escape" but
a solitude set up at the center of outside things. No young
man was more spontaneous, impulsive, temperamental,
than the young Goethe "all strength and energy from
crown to toe; a heart filled with emotion, a fiery spirit,
soaring with the wings of an eagle," as Heine described him
(although Herder found him "somewhat light and sparrow-
like"). He struck his contemporaries as the spirit of
genius personified; the center of the "Storm and Stress"
writing of that time, his wonderfully direct and original
lyrics, the pure gold of the *Urfaust,* and the Shakespearean
fire of *Goetz von Berlichingen* still communicate the shock
of the early Goethe—even if we do find it puzzling that
Werther should have set a fashion in youthful suicide.

In his youth Goethe experienced the Romantic sickness,
learned to know it as something which brought him to the
verge of suicide, despair, madness even. The man who,
looking back at his past, at the end of his life, said he had
never known a week in which he had not endured agony,
who despite his health was subject to serious bouts of illness—lived most of his days very close to dissolution under
the surface of his resolution. The force that gave him such
power over himself, such determination to mold his own
life, was, ultimately, despair.

The most important events in Goethe's life were his employment as minister of state by Karl August, "hereditary prince" of Weimar in 1715; eleven years later, his first Italian journey; his love relationship with Charlotte von Stein which belongs to the first twelve years at Weimar, and his friendship with Schiller, begun in 1794, which saved him, until Schiller's death, from poetic isolation. The most important outside event affecting his ideas was, inevitably, the French Revolution.

With his Weimar appointment, the young romantic changed his skin, ceased to be driven before the gales of Storm and Stress, and became the shaper of his destiny which shaped his poetry. With the change, he began to fall in love with the classical ideal. Explaining his unannounced departure for Rome to Charlotte von Stein, he wrote that for years he had not been able to look upon any Latin author or any picture of Italy without suffering and anguish. The Italian journey also enabled him to overcome the spiritual crisis caused by his employment in the court of Weimar. He had accepted responsible and public service in the world, in order to direct his own spirit, but the tasks of courtier and administrator did not provide him with the foundations for a non-romantic poetry. He could discover these only by going to the center of the classical world.

It is above all antiquity—the Rome of Winckelmann and the Rome of Greece—which Goethe discovered on his Italian journey. He was moved by Raphael and Palladio and by the Italian landscape and sky. His *Roman Elegies* wonderfully combine the discovery of the antique world with abandonment to the pagan delights of this one and with acute contemporary social criticism.

It was not only the crisis of his position and tasks at Weimar that the Italian journey enabled him to resolve, but also that of his relationship with the woman who for the past twelve years had been the emotional and spiritual center of his life. Charlotte von Stein, seven years older than Goethe, wife of a court official, and mother of seven children, was the object of Goethe's passionate attention during the years of his ripest manhood. Whether at some point she "yielded" to him is of less importance than the fact that Goethe's flight to Rome was the conclusion to what had remained essentially a frustrated, if exalted, relationship. In Rome, Goethe certainly renounced high-mindedness and began a new life in which sensuality was an unashamed value; there he wrote poems in which Priapus was as important as Eros. A famous line in the *Roemische Elegien* describes him lying in his Italian mistress's arms, while with his free hand he beats out the rhythm of the hexameter on her back. He was refreshing the roots of his poetry by the escape from the abstemiousness of Weimar to the license of Rome.

Charlotte von Stein could not forgive Goethe such a falling off. Indeed, when he returned to Weimar he found himself received there coolly by most of his friends. But true to the voluptuousness which he had put back into his life, he took into his household as mistress a young girl, Christiane Vulpius, who later became his wife.

Goethe is famous for his "wisdom." To some extent the reputation of the "sage of Weimar" overshadows that of the poet. When T. S. Eliot made his famous observation that Goethe should have devoted himself to making aphorisms in the manner of La Rochefoucauld, he only expressed what a good many readers in this century have probably tacitly concluded.

The reputation of wisdom has something about it which blows cold air on that of poet. Yet Goethe's wisdom, which is real, is not that of a privileged observer, one who can afford to be wise. It is much closer to that of the hermit: of the man who has submitted his whole life to the pressure of lived principles which will produce in him a certain detachment from the world. In the midst of his place at the center of the world, Goethe does attain this detachment, which comes from submitting all his actions —his pleasures and his passions even—to the test of their effect on his character and work. Because of what he had made of himself and created, he had the right to claim that during the Napoleonic wars he stood above the struggle and refused to support the German nationalist fervor. He saw in Napoleon an instrument of fate with a historic purpose not entirely different from his own. He stigmatized the French Revolution as the end of the European culture of which he was inseparably part.

Profound as are Goethe's aphorisms, one must distinguish between the kind of wisdom in him which is cleverness, and that which consists of a certain tone of voice, a certain "golden" way of seeing things, which rises superior to the conflicts of the world. This invisible musical and visual wisdom affects the music of his poetry, the line and vision of his prose. It binds up the arguments in his conversations with a greater cause than the causes he may be talking about—with a cause of art, of history, of a struggle of good and evil above transient things. It foreshadows in his work something of which he speaks often—the idea of a world literature. For Goethe world literature would not be a tower of Babel or a Unesco conference; it would be the meeting of minds within the agreements common to literature, above worldly disputes. It would resemble perhaps what André Malraux has called the Musée Imaginaire of all times and cultures meeting within the modern mind.

It is this tone which gives parts of *Wilhelm Meister*, some of the lyrics, and the mythological story entitled simply *Novelle,* a quality that lifts them beyond the literary form, to Mozart's music, to the pastoral landscape of Giorgione. Here the wisdom is not of the aphoristic kind; it is inseparable from the poetic vision, and it suffuses the best of Goethe with a wonderful golden glow.

The wisdom brings us back also to the appropriateness, the inevitability, of Goethe's living. The meeting with Schiller—beginning with a certain coldness because each felt the other poet his "opposite," and continuing like a duet, because each saw the other as his complement in thought and life—is an example of a harmony which was not just good luck. It was part of the great work that wrested virtues out of circumstances.

Goethe's view of life was essentially aristocratic. He believed that the best possible ruler was an enlightened monarch. Nevertheless he also held strongly that monarchs should serve the people, and he was critical of those who did not do so. With the duke he served—Karl August, Duke of Saxe-Weimar-Eisenach—he was often outspoken in advice and criticism. He saw in the French Revolution the doom of the aristocratic class.

Yet he regarded himself as striving on behalf of the people, and complained to Eckermann that in nothing had he been so misunderstood as when he was mockingly named the "Friend of the Established Order." He protested that although he hated revolutions, he regarded them not as faults of peoples, but of governments.

Goethe's political enemies, knowing his hatred of liberals, his support of press censorship, etc., probably would not have been satisfied with these self-explainings. Indeed, they do not lead very far. The poet's politics were partly an expression of his need for the profound roots in tradition which were vital to his work, partly loyalty to the responsibility he had undertaken as a member of a princely government. On a deeper level, in *Faust,* Goethe is an intuitive political thinker who made observations about the struggles of action in life, later quoted and discussed by those whom he would have regarded as his worst opponents—the Marxists. Stronger far than the sense of good and evil in *Faust* is that of dialectic: that action emerges from the conflict between opposed historic forces. As Karl Vietor puts it in his *Goethe the Poet,* "Goethe knows that, while acting, man is basically without conscience. How many of the deeds which history regards as truly great can stand up under moral judgement? One who does not wish to incur guilt may not act. Only the contemplative man can keep his soul pure. This is the inescapable contradiction imposed upon human existence, and most of all upon the activist man of the present. For by throwing all of his strength into plans and actions he simultaneously withdraws farther and farther from the sphere to which he belongs. What passes here for achievement and success is rated over there, before the tribunal of morality, as betrayal and guilt. This is Faust's tragedy too."

In an age when poets are turning to the dogmas of orthodox systems of Christianity as a scaffolding of belief and symbolism on which to build their poems, or when, failing this, they feel it necessary, like W. B. Yeats, to construct and elaborate their own private and involved metaphysical systems—Goethe's poetry may seem to suffer from the spiritual defects of that very liberalism he decried, in its morals and metaphysics. He is lacking in dogma, yet fond of invoking God, pantheistic in the presence of nature, worshipful of beauty, a lover of Greece, and, in affairs, commonsensical. Attempts to found a creed on Goethe's ideas end in some world religious movement like theosophy.

Faust is indisputably a great work, but on what do the claims of Goethe's lyrical poetry rest?

There are several answers to this question. One is that they benefit from the good fortune that here was a poet of tremendous energy, intelligence, and mastery, writing in the German language, which was unique among European languages in the eighteenth century, in having enormous opportunities as yet unexplored by poets. Goethe's language has a freshness and vigor belonging to literature four hundred years before it, in other European countries.

Next, Goethe had sublime vigor, power, and ease of expression. The only one of his contemporaries with whom he compares for strong vivid facility is Byron at his best in *Don Juan*: and Goethe was at his best in a great many more styles and forms than Byron. And his mind was, of course, more interesting, better informed, more cultivated than Byron's, and had time in which to mature.

Next, Goethe foreshadowed some twentieth-century poets (Ezra Pound, for example) in the technical skill with which he improvised free verse and imagist writing to echo classical themes and forms. He is more successful in poems like *Prometheus* and *Grenzen der Menschheit* in entering imaginatively into the classical spirit than in the hexameters of the set classical pieces.

Next, Goethe was stimulated by other cultures to produce incomparable effects in his own language. *West-Oestlicher Divan* is not marvelous bric-a-brac like Fitzgerald's *Omar Khayyam*. It is an escape of the imagination into the spirit of a past culture which still exhales the excitement of a discovered Oriental world; and yet the energy and contemporaneity and pathos of the aging

Goethe enters into this past like a blood transfusion, everywhere bringing it to modern life.

One could go on adding to this list of claims to greatness, mentioning for instance that Goethe can be (and often is) as spontaneous and fresh as Robert Burns, and that his occasional poems add vivid touches to a vast work of autobiographical confession.

This selection cannot claim to do more than arouse the reader's curiosity about Goethe. With this aim, I have begun with one revealing section from Eckermann, and followed this up with some letters. In this way, I hope that the reader will feel that he is, at the outset, confronted by the man.

I have emphasized the autobiographical element in this selection, because autobiography is the clue to Goethe. I have tried to compensate for the inevitable fragmentariness of such a selection by putting in the whole of the first part of *Faust* (which can justly be considered complete in itself without the second part). I have not taken anything from *Wilhelm Meister,* a novel which is so large and leisurely in conception that I think it would require a passage of very considerable length to give an idea of its quality, and which seems to me to suffer in translation. Instead I have put in the late work *Novelle* which illustrates very well the Mozartian music, the Giorgionesque golden glow of Goethe's imaginative prose; and a chapter from *Elective Affinities,* which illustrates strikingly the way in which Goethe put his knowledge of science—in this case, mineralogy—to imaginative use.

In making this selection, I have been extremely fortunate, I think, in persuading Mr. Christopher Middleton, Mr. Michael Hamburger, and Mr. Vernon Watkins to make some entirely new translations of a selection of Goethe's lyrics. The brilliant translation of the first part of *Faust,* made for a broadcast performance, Mr. Louis MacNeice has completed, adding those scenes which he had not translated for the previously published edition.

From

CONVERSATIONS OF GOETHE

with Eckermann and Soret

TRANSLATED BY JOHN OXENFORD

Tuesday, March 11, 1828

"Every *Entelechy** is a piece of eternity, and the few years during which it is bound to the earthly body do not make it old. If this *Entelechy* is of a trivial kind, it will exercise but little sway; the body will predominate, and when this grows old the *Entelechy* will not hold and restrain it. But if the *Entelechy* is of a powerful kind, as is the case with all men of natural genius, then it will, with its animating penetration of the body, not only strengthen and ennoble the organization, but also endeavor with its spiritual superiority to confer the privilege of perpetual youth. Thence it comes that in men of superior endowments, even during their old age, we constantly perceive fresh epochs of singular productiveness; they seem constantly to grow young again for a time, and that is what I call a repeated puberty. Still—youth is youth; and, however powerful an *Entelechy* may prove, it will never become quite master of the corporeal, and it makes a wonderful difference whether it finds in the body an ally or an adversary.

"There was a time when I had to furnish a printed sheet

* If for this Aristotelian word the reader substitutes the popular expression "soul" he will not go far wrong as far as this passage is concerned. J.O.

An Aristotelian *Entelechy* is the condition by which a potentiality becomes an actuality.

21

every day, and I did it easily. I wrote my *Geschwister* [*Brother and Sister*] in three days; my *Clavigo,* as you know, in a week. Now it seems I can do nothing of the kind, and still I can by no means complain of want of productiveness even at my advanced age. But whereas in my youth I succeeded daily and under all circumstances, I now succeed only periodically and under favorable conditions. When, ten or twelve years ago, in the happy time after the war of independence, the poems of the *Divan* had me in their power, I often composed two or three in a day; and it was all the same to me whether I was in the open air, in the chariot, or in an inn. Now, I can only work at the second part of my *Faust* during the early part of the day, when I feel refreshed and revived by sleep and have not been perplexed by the trifles of daily life. And after all, what is it I achieve? In the most favorable circumstances, a page of writing: but generally only so much as could be written in the space of a handbreadth, and often, when in an unproductive humor, still less."

"Are there, then, no means," said I, "to call forth a productive mood, or, if it is not powerful enough, of increasing it?"

"No productiveness of the highest kind," said Goethe, "no remarkable discovery, no great thought that bears fruit and has results, is in the power of anyone; such things are above earthly control. Man must consider them as an unexpected gift from above, as pure children of God which he must receive and venerate with joyful thanks. They are akin to the demon, which does with him what it pleases, and to which he unconsciously resigns himself while he believes he is acting from his own impulse. In such cases, man may often be considered an instrument in a higher government of the world—a vessel worthy to contain a divine influence. I say this when I consider how often a single thought has given a different form to whole centuries, and how individual men have imprinted a stamp upon their age which has remained uneffaced and operated beneficially for generations.

"However, there is a productiveness of another kind: one subject to earthly influences, one that man has more in his power—although here also he finds cause to bow before something divine. In this category I place all that appertains to the execution of a plan, all the links of a chain of thought, the ends of which already shine forth; I also place there all that constitutes the visible body of a work of art.

"Thus, Shakespeare was inspired with the first thought of his *Hamlet* when the spirit of the whole presented itself to his mind as an unexpected impression; and when he surveyed the several situations, characters, and conclusion, in an elevated mood, as a pure gift from above on which he had no immediate influence—although the possibility of such a conception certainly presupposed a mind like his. But the individual scenes, and the dialogue of the characters, he had completely in his power, so that he might produce them daily and hourly and work at them for weeks if he liked. And, indeed, we constantly see in all that he has achieved the same power of production; and in all his plays we never come to a passage of which it could be said, 'This was not written in the proper humor, or with the most perfect faculty.' While we read him, we receive the impression of a man thoroughly strong and healthy in both mind and body.

"Supposing, however, that the bodily constitution of a dramatic poet were not so strong and excellent, and that he were subject to frequent illness and weakness—the productiveness necessary for the daily construction of his scenes would very frequently cease, and would often fail him for days. If now, by alcohol, he tried to force his failing productiveness, the method would certainly answer; but it would be discoverable in all the scenes he had written under such an influence, to their great disadvantage. My counsel is, to force nothing, and rather to trifle and sleep away all unproductive days and hours, than on such days to compose something that will afterwards give no pleasure."

"That," said I, "is what I myself have very often experienced and felt. Still, it appears to me that a person might by natural means heighten his productive mood without exactly forcing it. I have often been unable to arrive at any right conclusion in complicated circumstances; but if I have drunk a few glasses of wine I have at once seen clearly what was to be done, and have come to a resolution on the spot. The adoption of a resolution is, after all, a species of productiveness; and, if a glass or two of wine will bring about this good effect, such means are surely not to be rejected altogether."

"I will not contradict you," said Goethe, "but what I said before is also correct, by which you see that truth may be compared to a diamond, the rays of which dart not to one side, but to many. Since you know my *Divan* so well, you know also that I myself have said:

> When we have drunk
> We know what's right;

and therefore that I perfectly agree with you. Productive-making* powers of a very important kind certainly are contained in wine; still, all depends upon time and circumstance, and what is useful to one is prejudicial to another. Productive-making powers are also contained in sleep and repose; but they are also contained in movement. Such powers lie in the water, and particularly in the atmosphere. The fresh air of the open country is our proper element; it is as if the breath of God were there wafted immediately to men, and a divine power exerted its influence. Lord Byron, who daily passed several hours in the open air—now riding on horseback along the seashore; now sailing or rowing in a boat; now bathing in the sea, and exercising his physical powers in swimming—was one of the most productive men who ever lived."

Goethe had seated himself opposite to me. We again dwelt upon Lord Byron, and the many misfortunes that had embittered his later life—until at last a noble will, but an unhappy destiny, drove him into Greece, and entirely destroyed him.

"You will find," continued Goethe, "that in middle age a man frequently experiences a change; and that, while

* "Productivmachende." Probably he meant "production-stimulating."

in his youth everything has favored him, and has prospered with him, all is now completely reversed, and misfortunes and disasters are heaped one upon another.

"But do you know what I think about it? Man must be ruined again! Every extraordinary man has a certain mission to accomplish. If he has fulfilled it, he is no longer needed upon earth in the same form, and Providence uses him for something else. But as everything here below happens in a natural way, the demons keep tripping him up till he falls at last. Thus it was with Napoleon and many others. Mozart died in his thirty-sixth year. Raphael at the same age. Byron only a little older. But all these had perfectly fulfilled their missions; and it was time for them to depart, that other people might still have something to do in a world made to last a long while."

❧

LETTERS
FROM GOETHE

TRANSLATED BY M. VON HERZFELD AND C. MELVIL SYM

To J. C. KESTNER

> *Frankfort*
> *December 25, 1772*
> *Christmas morning, very early*

It is still dark, dear Kestner. I have got up to write by candlelight on this morning; this brings back happy memories of former days. I have had coffee made in honor of the day, and I will write till it is light. The watchman has sounded his horn already; it woke me up. "Praise be to Thee, Jesus Christ." I love this season and the songs one sings; and the cold that has set in makes me thoroughly cheerful. I had a wonderful day yesterday; I was anxious about today, but it has begun well, too, so I'm not worrying about the end of it. Last night I promised my two silhouettes that I would write to you. The two dear faces hover like angels round my bed. As soon as I got here, I pinned up Lotte's silhouette. They put my bed in while I was in Darmstadt, and Lotte's picture is now above it —such a joy. Lenchen's is on the other side. Many thanks, Kestner, for this dear picture. It is more like what you wrote to me of her than anything I had imagined. It shows what folly it is for us to guess and dream and prophesy.

The watchman has turned this way again; the north wind carries his tune across as if he were blowing just outside my window.

Dear Kestner, I spent yesterday in the country with some fine fellows. We were very noisy and very merry, shouting and laughing the whole time. Usually that isn't good for the following day, but is there anything the high gods cannot turn to good if they choose? They gave me a happy evening; I drank no wine, so I looked on nature with a dispassionate eye. A beautiful evening. Night fell as we came back. It always touches a chord in me, you know, when the sun is already low in the sky and darkness has spread from the east to north and south, and now only a disk of fading light glows low in the west. In flat country, Kestner, it is a most magnificent sight. On my rambles when I was younger and felt more warmly, I used to watch for hours and see the sun sink and fade. I stood awhile on the bridge. The dim town light to right and left, the calm glowing horizon, the reflection on the river —it made a wonderful impression on me, one that I welcomed with open arms. I ran to the Gerocks', asked for pencil and paper and, happy as I was, sketched the whole picture in a warm soft glow, just as it lingered within me. The Gerocks joined in my pleasure, feeling all I had for it, and that gave me confidence too. I suggested tossing for it, but they wouldn't; they wanted me to send it to Merck. It's hanging here on my wall at the moment, and I am as pleased with it today as I was yesterday. We spent a happy evening together like people to whom fortune has brought some great gift, and I fell asleep thanking the saints in Heaven for making our Christmas rich with childlike joy. On my way across the market square I saw all the candles and toys, and thought of you and the dear boys at home. I can see you coming to them like a messenger from Heaven with your blue Bible in your hand and their joy when you open it. If I could have been with you, I should have wanted to light a feast of wax tapers that would have mirrored the glory of Heaven in their little heads.

The city guards are coming from the Mayor's, rattling their keys. The first gray light of dawn is reaching me over my neighbor's roof, and the bells are ringing Christians together.

Yes, I feel uplifted, in my room up here; it hasn't been so dear to me for many a day. It is bright with the happiest of pictures, bidding me a friendly good morning. Seven heads copied from Raphael's, inspired by the spirit of

God. I have made a copy of one of them, and I am satisfied though not really happy. And there are my dear girls' silhouettes too; Lotte's and Lenchen's as well. Tell Lenchen I am as keen to come and kiss her hand as the monsieur who wrote those love letters. He's a mighty poor fish. I would stuff my daughter's coverlet with billets-doux like these, and she will sleep under it as peacefully as a child. My sister laughed and laughed; she has some letters like this from her younger days. That sort of thing must seem as sickening as a rotten egg to any girl with good feeling. I have changed Lotte's comb; this one isn't such a good color or shape as the first, but I hope it will be more useful. Lotte has a little head—what a little head!

Daylight is coming fast; if good fortune comes as quickly, there'll soon be a wedding. I must write one more page; I'll pretend not to notice the daylight.

My love to Kielmansegg. Don't let him forget me.

That miserable hound in Giessen,* fussing about us like the old woman in the Gospel about her lost penny, and spying and rummaging about everywhere in our concerns, whose name ought not to defile any letter with your or Lotte's name on it! The wretch is angry because we don't pay attention to him, and he tries to provoke us into thinking of him. He has been so overhasty in writing about my "Baukunst," obviously it is grist for his mill, and he dashed off a foul review for the *Frankfort Journal;* I've heard about it. He is a real donkey, munching the thistles that grow round my garden, gnawing at the hedge that guards it from creatures like himself, and braying his critical Hee-Haw as if to tell the owner in the arbor: "I am here too."

Adieu now, it is daylight. God be with you; I always am. The day has made a festive beginning. I have to waste the good hours, alas, writing reviews; but I'll do it cheerfully, it is for the last number.

Farewell, and don't forget me, an odd creature, sometimes Dives and sometimes Lazarus.

Love to all the dear ones. And let me have news of you all.

* Professor Schmidt.

To FRAU von STEIN

In the Herrmann's Cave
July 22, 1776

I have begun a sketch on the other side of this, but it's no good; better to write from my beloved cave; I would like to rest and remain here. Dearest, I have done a lot of sketching, but it is only too clear to me that I shall never make an artist. Love gives me everything, and when there is no love, it's like threshing straw, not grain. I can't do a picturesque scene, and a perfectly ordinary one comes out friendly and charming. It is raining hard in the thick woods. If you could only be here, it is beyond description and any sketch. I have made a good many sketches since I came here—all rather childish, alas, from eye to hand, without passing through the heart, so there is very little to show for it. It is always true, what makes the poet, the artist, the man, is to limit oneself, really to need, to love, to cling to one or a few objects, to see them from all sides and to become one with them.

Addio. I will take a look at the cliffs and pines. It's still raining. . . .

To FRAU von STEIN

In the Harz Mountains
September 9, 1780

I have been passive today and got nothing done worth doing, and so I don't feel happy, my dearest. The Duke is still not quite well; first he is careful, then he pretends he is all right, and then he is careless—and so one seems to dawdle away one's life and these good days.

This morning all the murderers, thieves, and receivers

were summoned, questioned, and confronted with each other. At first I didn't want to be present, for I shun anything defiled. It is a great study of human nature and physiognomy, where one likes to lay one's finger to one's lips and leave it all to God, with whom alone is power and wisdom for ever and ever, Amen.

A son who with every detail accuses himself and his father of murder. A father who denies everything his son says to his face. A man who in the agony of famine sees his wife die beside him in the barn and, because nobody will bury her, he has to hide her in the earth himself; and now this misery is counted against him, as if he could have murdered her, for he is under suspicion because of some other denunciations, etc.

After this I went back into the hills; we had a meal there, amused ourselves with some birds of prey, and I kept wanting to write either to you or at my novel, but I never got to either. But I wish I had written out for you a long conversation which I had with the Duke on the subject of delinquents and the value and futility of human actions. In the evening Stein came and sat with me and entertained me delightfully with old tales of the wretchedness of Court life, of children, and women, etc. Goodnight, dearest. I am sorry for this wasted day. It might have been better spent, but we have at least made use of its fragments.

To LAVATER (Extract)

October 4, 1782

I very much enjoyed the first part of your confessions, as I call them. It is always most interesting to read something like this. But I noticed again that the reader has often to make what I might call his own psychological calculations to draw his conclusions from the facts. I cannot at the moment explain more than this; what a man notices and feels about himself seems to me the least part of him. He is more inclined to see what he lacks than what he has, to remark what worries than what delights him and enlarges his mind. Soul and body forget about themselves when things are pleasant and happy, and they are only reminded of themselves again by something unpleasant. A man writing of himself and his past will therefore mostly note what is cramping and painful. As he does so he seems to shrivel up as a person, and we have to put in a tincture of what we have seen of his actions or read of his writings to get a picture of the man as perhaps he really is or was. This is one of my many, many reflections.

To FRIEDRICH JACOBI

Ilmenau
May 5, 1786

I have been reading your little book with interest but not with pleasure. After all it is a polemic, a philosophical one, and I have a great objection to any kind of literary controversy; I shouldn't enjoy this kind of thing, even if Raphael painted it for me or Shakespeare dramatized it. I can't say more than that. I quite see you had to write this pamphlet and I expected it, but I wish you could have given the *species facti* more simply. I don't approve of emotion in this kind of thing, and all these bits, tacked on, only injure your own case. The briefer the better. You will say that's only my style and each has his own. Well, I can't do anything about that. . . .

Self-confidence is bound to become offensive as soon as it leads to contempt of others, even the least important ones. A thoughtless person may mock, humiliate, slight others, for he will expose himself too, but it seems anyone who respects himself has renounced the right to despise others. And what are we after all that we should set ourselves up so high?

To FRAU von STEIN

Weimar
June 8, 1789

I have seldom found any page more difficult to write than my last letter to you, and it was no doubt as disagreeable for you to read as for me to write it. But I have at least opened my lips and I hope that we shall never again close them toward each other. I have never known greater happiness than in confiding in you, as I have always done without reserve; prevented from doing so, I am a different person and must continue to change still more.

I make no complaint about my present situation; I have reconciled myself to it quite well and hope I shall persevere in it although the climate has already begun to affect me again, and sooner or later will render me unfit for much that is good.

When one considers the cold, damp summer season, the severe winters; when the Duke's outward relations and other circumstances deprive and will deprive everything here of consistency and result; when it is well-nigh impossible to name anyone who feels at ease in his position; —it needs strength not to be weighed down, to maintain a certain degree of cheerfulness and activity and not to make a plan by which one could gradually free oneself. But if on top of this an unhappy relationship develops to those nearest, then one really does not know where to turn. I say this as well for *you* as for *myself,* and I assure you it causes me infinite pain to distress you so deeply in these circumstances.

I shall say nothing to excuse myself. Indeed I only want to beg you: let me have your help, so that the connection which is so distasteful to you does not degenerate but remains as it is.

Give me your confidence once more; consider the whole matter from a natural point of view, permit me to speak calmly and frankly about it, and I can then hope that everything between us will become pure and good again.

You have seen my mother and given her great pleasure, to Frau La Roche too. Let me too find warmth in your return.

Arens, the architect, is here at the moment and I am again enjoying the company of an artist. Fritz will learn a great deal in these few days; intelligent as he is he will be quick in noticing what is right.

Herder is unfortunately showing a considerable and almost definite desire for another post in his letters; it will be difficult to retain him in Weimar, and if retained to make him happy.

I have been in Belvedere for a week with the Prince. The child is a great joy to me.

Farewell! Think lovingly of me. *Tasso* is nearly finished. I shall not believe it is finished till I see it in print.

I have not been doing much else. Farewell. Love from Fritz.

To FRIEDRICH SCHILLER

Ettersburg
August 27, 1794

Your letter is the most welcome present I could have had for my birthday, which falls this week. Your friendly hand seems to sum up myself and my work, and your sympathetic interest encourages me to make a more diligent and lively use of my powers.

Genuine pleasure and real usefulness must be mutual, and I shall be glad to show you some day more fully what your conversation has meant to me, and how I too date an epoch in my life from those days. I shall tell you how content I am to have pursued my own way, though without particular encouragement, because now after our unexpected meeting we seem destined to go on together. I have always appreciated the sincere and rare seriousness apparent in everything you have written or done, and I now feel encouraged to ask you to tell me yourself how your mind has been developing, especially during these last few years. We shall be able to work all the more un-interruptedly together once we have made clear to each other the point we have reached at present.

I shall be glad to tell you of everything about me or in my mind. I am most vividly conscious that what I have undertaken to do far exceeds any human powers and their duration on earth. So I am anxious to entrust many things to you to preserve them and even to give new life to them.

You will soon see how much I have to gain from your sympathy. A closer acquaintance will reveal to you a certain obscurity and hesitance in me, which I cannot master, though I am plainly conscious of them. But traits like these are frequent in many of us, yet we tend to allow our nature to rule us unless it grows all too despotic.

I hope to spend some time with you soon, and then we shall discuss a number of things at length.

To J. C. KESTNER

Weimar
July 16, 1798

My dear old friend, if you had sent me a line now and then, I am sure you would have heard from me sooner in return. For it doesn't mean anything if I don't answer a letter and for some time don't let you have any news of me. The days and the years fly past at such a breathless pace that one has hardly time to collect one's thoughts; and downhill the pace seems quicker than ever. If we were to meet again, I hope you would recognize the inner man; as for the outer, they tell me I have grown stout with the years. I'm enclosing a bit of string to show my girth, so that you can measure and see if I am better preserved than you in this respect; for we used to be fairly alike in figure. I am well and busy and as happy as one can expect to be here on earth.

I hope to hear the same of you and yours. My heartiest greetings to them.

To FRIEDRICH SCHILLER (Extract)

Oberrosla (Goethe's farm)
April 3, 1801

As for the questions in your letter, I not only share your view, I would even go further. I hold that whatever genius does as genius is done unconsciously. The man of genius can act according to reason when convinced by reflection, but all that is incidental. No work of genius can be improved or freed from its faults by reflection and its immediate results. But reflection and action may so improve a man of genius that he ends by producing exemplary works. The more the age itself possesses genius, the better for the individual.

I agree with you that the great demands now made on the poet are unlikely to create one. Poetry requires of the man who is to write it a sort of limitation full of kindly love of reality; the Absolute lies hidden behind it. Demands from outside destroy this innocent and productive state, and by sheer poetizing put in the place of poetry something that quite definitely is *not* poetry. Alas, we see this only too well today. And the same is true of the sister-arts, indeed of art in the widest sense.

This is my creed, which, I may add, makes no further claims.

To ZELTER

Weimar
June 1, 1805

I have had few happy days since I wrote last. I thought to lose my own life and lost a friend* and with him half of my own existence. I ought really to make a fresh start, but at my age no way is open for it. So I am just taking

* Schiller; he had died on May 9.

each day as it comes and doing what is nearest, without a thought of anything further.

But people try to derive some entertainment from every loss and misfortune, and the actors and others are pressing me hard to commemorate the deceased in some way on the stage. I don't want to say more than that I have no objection, and I should just like to ask you if you would give me your help with some music? . . .

To HEINRICH von KLEIST

Weimar
February 1, 1808

Dear Sir, I am most grateful to you for the copy of *Phoebus*. I have enjoyed reading the essays in prose very much. I knew some of them already. I have not yet been able to come to terms with your *Penthesilea*. She belongs to such an unusual race and moves in so strange a region that I must take time to get used to both. And allow me to say—for unless one is honest, it would be better to say nothing at all—that it always disturbs and saddens me to see really talented and gifted young men waiting for a theater that is still to be. A Jew waiting for the Messiah, a Christian for the New Jerusalem, a Portuguese for Don Sebastian, is not to my mind a more distressing sight. Before any trestle-stage I would say to the true theatrical genius, *"Hic Rhodus, hic salta!"* On any fair-ground, even on planks put across barrels, I could—*mutatis mutandis*—bring the highest enjoyment to the masses, cultured and uncultured, with Calderon's plays. Forgive my plain speaking, it shows my sincere affection. I realize one might say this kind of thing with friendlier phrases and more attractively. I am content now to have got something off my chest. More soon.

To BEETHOVEN

Carlsbad
June 25, 1811

Honored Sir, your friendly letter, which has reached me through Herr von Oliva, has given me great pleasure. I am deeply grateful to you for the views you express in it, views which I assure you I can heartily reciprocate. For I have never heard either professionals or amateurs play any of your compositions without wishing I could admire your own performance at the pianoforte and rejoice in your outstanding talent. Good Bettina Brentano deserves the interest you have shown her. She speaks of you with delight and the most eager affection and counts the hours spent with you among the happiest of her life.

The music you sent for my *Egmont* will be waiting for me at home; I am grateful for it already. I have heard it praised in several quarters, and I hope to be able to produce it with the play this winter in our theater. It will give great pleasure to me as well as to your numerous admirers in the district. And I trust I have understood Herr Oliva rightly in hoping your projected journey may bring you to us. I hope your visit will come at a time when the Court as well as the entire music-loving public are there. I am certain you will have a reception worthy of your merit and your character. No one, however, can be more keenly interested in this than I am. Let me commend myself to your kind memory and send my good wishes with my sincerest thanks for all the good I already owe you.

To ZELTER (Extract)

Weimar
December 3, 1812

. . . One really cannot wonder nowadays at the misdeeds through which man injures himself and others. There is untold pressure from outside and young people especially yield to their appetites and passions. The sad follies of the age distort and disfigure even what is noble and higher in them; so what should guide to bliss leads to perdition —I could write a new *Werther* that would make people's hair stand on end, even more than the first. And let me add that most young people who feel there is something in them, demand more from themselves than they should. But it is their gigantic surroundings that urge and force them to this. I know half a dozen who are certain to succumb and for whom there is no help, even if one could make their own possibilities clear to them. People often fail to see that reason and courage are given us to keep us not only from evil but also from too much good.

To FRIEDRICH JACOBI (Extract)

Weimar
January 6, 1813

Men are united by their outlook and divided by their opinions. An outlook is something simple in which we can come together; opinions are something complex, where we scatter. The former is the basis of youth's friendships; the latter are to blame for the breaches of later years. If we realized this sooner we should acquire a liberal attitude toward other—even opposite—ways while developing our own way of thinking. We should be considerably more tolerant and we might seek to reassemble through our outlook what had been scattered through our opinions.

One single way of thinking cannot be enough for me with the many sides of my personality. As a poet and an artist I am a polytheist, as a scientist, however, a pantheist; the one is as firm a conviction as the other. And if as a moral being I require a God, that too has been granted.

The things of heaven and earth are so wide a realm that even all created beings together can only begin to grasp it. . . .

. . . I sincerely wish you and yours all happiness. My love to you all! I am glad you had such good luck in that game of Rouge et Noir that decided where you were to live. Fate has done as much for me. . . .

To ZELTER*

Weimar
March 26, 1816

So you have had another severe trial. It is still, alas, the same old story that to live long is to outlive many; and after all we do not even know then what it was all about. The other day I chanced on a first edition of my *Werther,* and this tune that had so long been dead for me, began to play again. One wonders how a man can bear to live another forty years in a world that even when he was young seemed to him so void of meaning.

The answer to part of the riddle is: because we each have something peculiarly our own that we mean to develop by letting it take its course. This strange thing cheats us from day to day, and so we grow old without knowing how or why. When I look at it clearly, I realize it is only the talent in me that helps me through all the predicaments in which I see false steps, chance, and the complications of fate involving me.

In the meantime you will have had another letter from me. I will soon be sending you something. . . .

* Whose youngest son had died of a nervous fever in France, where he was serving with the Prussian Army of Occupation.

To WILHELM von HUMBOLDT*

Weimar
March 17, 1832

After a long involuntary pause I am beginning like this, and yet simply impromptu. The Ancients said that the animals are taught through their organs; let me add to this, so are men, but they have the advantage of teaching their organs in return.

Every action, and so every talent, needs some inborn faculty which acts naturally, and unconsciously carries with it the necessary aptitude, and which, therefore, continues to act in such a way that though its law is implicit in it, its course in the end may be aimless and purposeless.

The earlier man becomes aware that there exists some craft, some art, that can help him toward a controlled heightening of his natural abilities, the happier he is; whatever he may receive from without does not harm his innate individuality. The best genius is that which absorbs everything within itself, knows how to appropriate everything, without this in the least impairing its fundamental dispositions, called its character, but rather enhancing and furthering them throughout as much as possible.

Here begin the manifold relations between the conscious and the unconscious. Take for instance a talented musician, composing an important score; consciousness and unconsciousness will be like warp and weft, a simile I am fond of using.

Through practice, teaching, reflection, success, failure, furtherance and resistance, and again and again reflection, man's organs unconsciously and in a free activity link what he acquires with his innate gifts, so that a unity results which leaves the world amazed.

* Whom Goethe had told that he had recently completed his *Faust* and that this had required a more conscious effort than he had made before in writing that poem. Humboldt, in reply, asked for further explanation of this conscious creative process.

These general remarks may serve as a rapid answer to your question, and as an explanation to the note I return herewith.

For more than sixty years the conception of *Faust* has lain here before my mind with the clearness of youth, though the sequence with less fullness. I have let the idea go quietly along with me through life and have only worked out the scenes that interested me most from time to time. So in the Second Part gaps remained, waiting for this kind of interest before they could be joined to the rest. It was difficult to do through conscious effort and strength of personality something that really should have been the spontaneous work of active nature. But it surely would not be right if this were not possible after my long life of thought and action, and I am not afraid of people being able to pick out the new from the old, the later from the earlier work. We can leave that to future readers.

It would naturally be an infinite joy to me if during my lifetime, too, I could dedicate these serious fantasies to my valued friends everywhere. I have always been grateful for their interest and should like to hear their response. But the present age is so senseless and confused that I know I should only be poorly rewarded for my many years of sincere effort at erecting this strange building. It would be driven like a wrack on the shore and lie there, getting gradually covered by the sands of time. The world is ruled today by bewildering wrong counsel, urging bewildered wrong action. My most important task is to go on developing as much as possible whatever is and remains in me, distilling my own particular abilities again and again. You, my friend, are doing the same up there in your castle.

Tell me about your work, too; as you know, Riemer is still busy on the same sort of studies as we are, and our evening conversations often touch on these subjects. Forgive this long-delayed letter. In spite of my retirement, there is seldom a time when I am in the mood to remind myself of those mysteries of life.

Ever yours,

POEMS

FOUND

TRANSLATED BY MICHAEL HAMBURGER

Once in the forest
I strolled content,
To look for nothing
My sole intent.

I saw a flower,
Shaded and shy,
Shining like starlight,
Bright as an eye.

I went to pluck it;
Gently it said:
Must I be broken,
Wilt and be dead?

Then whole I dug it
Out of the loam
And to my garden
Carried it home,

There to replant it
Where no wind blows.
More bright than ever
It blooms and grows.

GYPSY SONG

(1772)

TRANSLATED BY MICHAEL HAMBURGER

In the foggy drizzle, in the deep snow,
In the wild wood, in the winter night
I heard the howling of hungry wolves,
I heard the brown owl cry.
> Willy wow wow wow!
> Willy wo wo wo!
> Wito who!

One day I shot a cat on the fence,
It was Anne's the witch's darling black cat;
So at night seven werewolves came to me,
There were seven seven hags in the village.
> Willy wow wow wow!
> Willy wo wo wo!
> Wito who!

I knew them all, I knew them well.
There was Kate and Betty and old Anne,
There was Madge and Barbara, Eve and Jane;
They crouched in a circle and howled at me.
> Willy wow wow wow!
> Willy wo wo wo!
> Wito who!

Then I called each one out loud by her name:
What is it, Anne? what is it, Jane?
So they shook themselves and betook themselves
Back home, and howled as they ran:
> Willy wow wow wow!
> Willy wo wo wo!
> Wito who!

AT MIDNIGHT

TRANSLATED BY MICHAEL HAMBURGER

At midnight, far from gladly at that hour,
A small, small boy along the churchyard I
Walked to my father's vicarage; star on star,
Oh how they shone, too richly lit the sky;
      At midnight.

When later I, moved farther though not far,
Must see the loved one, must because she drew me,
Above me stars and northern lights at war,
Going and coming I felt bliss flow through me;
      At midnight.

Until at last the full moon made a rift
So bright, so clear within the dark of me,
And even thought, grown willing, sensuous, swift
Embraced both past and future easily;
      At midnight.

NEARNESS OF THE BELOVED

TRANSLATED BY MICHAEL HAMBURGER

I think of you when from the sea the shimmer
    Of sunlight streams;
I think of you when on the brook the dimmer
    Moon casts her beams.

I see your face when on the distant highway
    Dust whirls and flakes,
In deepest night when on the mountain byway
    The traveler quakes.

I hear your voice when, dully roaring, yonder
   Waves rise and spill;
Listening, in silent woods I often wander
   When all is still.

I walk with you, though miles from you divide me;
   Yet you are near!
The sun goes down, soon stars will shine to guide me.
   Would you were here!

ON ORIGINALITY

TRANSLATED BY MICHAEL HAMBURGER

I

Somebody says: "Of no school I am part,
Never to living master lost my heart;
Nor any more can I be said
To have learned anything from the dead."
That statement—subject to appeal—
Means: "I'm a self-made imbecile."

II

My build from Father I inherit,
His neat and serious ways;
Combined with Mother's cheerful spirit,
Her love of telling stories.
Great-grandfather courted the loveliest,
His ghost won't leave me alone;
Great-grandmother liked fine jewels best,
This twitch I've also known.
If, then, no mortal chemist can
Divide the components from the whole,
What is there in the entire man
You could call original?

REVIEWER

(1776)

TRANSLATED BY MICHAEL HAMBURGER

There was a fellow dropped in for lunch,
Didn't bother me much, I just let him munch,
Had the kind of meal I have every day;
The fellow gorged himself mightily
And for dessert ate up what I'd stored.
But as soon as he'd left my larder cleared,
The devil led him to my neighbor's, where
After this fashion he discussed the fare:
"The soup might have been more piquantly spiced,
The roast more crisp, the wine better iced."
A curse on that damnable knave, that evil-doer!
Put the dog to sleep. He's a book reviewer.

A LIKENESS

TRANSLATED BY VERNON WATKINS

I picked some flowers that I saw bloom
In a field, and thoughtfully carried them home;
But soon their heads, in the warm hand bound,
Had fallen, and limply hung to the ground.
I put them in water, in a fresh glass;
Next, what a wonder came to pass!
The little heads rose up straightway,
And the stems of the leaves in green display;
And altogether so healthy and sound
As if they still stood on their mother-ground.

So it was with me when miracle-sprung
I heard my song in a foreign tongue.

MIGNON

TRANSLATED BY VERNON WATKINS

Know you the land where bloom the lemon trees,
In the dark leaves burn gold the oranges,
There where a soft wind breathes from the blue sky
The myrtle stands there still, the laurel high,
Know you it well?

                          But there, but there,
Might I with you, O my belovéd, fare!

Know you the house? Its roof on pillars rests,
Bright gleams the hall, the room in brilliance feasts,
And marble statues stand and stare me through:
Tell us, poor child, what have they done to you?
Know you it well?

                          But there, but there,
Might I with you, O my protector, fare!

Know you the mountain and its path cloud-kissed?
The mule seeks out its pathway through the mist,
In caverns dwells the dragon's ancient brood,
Plunges the rock and over it the flood;
Know you it well?

                          But there, but there,
Our way being bound, O Father, let us fare!

BUCCANEER

TRANSLATED BY CHRISTOPHER MIDDLETON

(Original in dialect)

My house has no door
My door has no house;
And always my sweetheart
She comes and she goes.

No fire in my kitchen,
No kitchen, you see;
But I fry up and boil for
My pleasure and me.

My bed has no trestle
My trestle no bed;
But no man I know rests
A happier head.

My cellar is high,
My barn, it is deep;
All topsy and turvy
I lay down to sleep.

And sharpish, awaking,
I'm off at a pace;
At no place I'm stopping,
My stopping's no place.

❧

FIRST LOVE AND THE
CORONATION

(From *Truth and Fantasy from My Life*)

TRANSLATED BY EITHNE WILKINS AND ERNST KAISER

Meanwhile, I was quite unexpectedly involved in affairs that nearly got me into very serious trouble, and at least for a time caused me embarrassment and distress. My friendship with the boy whom I have referred to as Pylades* continued into our teens. Although we saw each other less frequently, because our parents were not on the best of terms, whenever we did meet we felt the same old upsurge of friendly warmth. Once we met in those very pleasant leafy walks between the inner and outer St. Gallen Gate. The first thing he said to me when we had shaken hands was: "It's always the same thing with your poems. I read the last ones you gave me to some jolly friends of mine, and they refuse to believe you wrote them." "Never mind," I replied, "we shall go on writing poems for the fun of it. Don't let us worry about what the others may think and say."

"Here comes one of the unbelievers," my friend said.

"Don't let us talk about it," was my reply. "What's the use? We shall not be able to convert them in any case."

"Not a bit of it," my friend said. "I won't let him off so easily."

After a short conversation of no importance, my well-

* A childhood friend.

49

meaning friend could not restrain himself any longer, and said, rather irritably: "This is my friend who wrote the poems that you liked and wouldn't believe he could have written."

"I'm sure he won't be offended by that," the other said. "After all, we are paying him a compliment by thinking that the writing of such verses requires much more learning than he can have at his age."

I made some random answer.

But my friend went on: "It won't be much trouble to prove it. Give him a subject and he'll write you a poem in a twinkling."

As I had no objection, the other asked me if I would try my hand at composing a dainty little love letter in verse from a shy girl, declaring her love to a young man.

"Nothing could be easier," I answered. "If we only had something to write on."

The other produced his pocket book, which had plenty of blank pages, and I sat down on a bench to write. In the meantime they walked back and forth, not taking their eyes off me. I at once began to imagine the situation vividly and thought how nice it would be if some pretty young girl were really in love with me and were to tell me so in verse or prose; and so I set about my declaration without delay, quickly working it out in a meter between that of the ballad and that of the madrigal, and as simply as possible. And when I read the little poem to them, the doubter was overcome by amazement and my friend was quite delighted. I could not very well refuse to let the stranger have the poem, especially as it was written in his notebook, and was quite glad for him to have documentary proof of my abilities. He went away, after repeatedly assuring me of his admiration and friendship, and saying that he hoped to meet us more often. We agreed to go on a trip into the country together soon.

We made the expedition with several other young men of the same sort. Although they belonged to the middle and perhaps even the lower classes, they were by no means without brains, nor, as they had had some schooling, without general knowledge and even a degree of polish. There are many ways of earning a living in a large and wealthy city, and they got along by doing clerical work for lawyers or coaching lower-class children up to a higher standard of education than was provided by the elementary schools. They held confirmation classes for older children, did odd jobs for merchants and brokers, and in the evenings, particularly on Sundays and holidays, indulged in some frugal entertainment.

On the way, while singing the praises of my little love letter, they confessed to me that they had made very amusing use of it. It had been copied out in a disguised handwriting and, with the addition of a few private allusions, slipped into the hands of a conceited young man who was now firmly convinced that a lady whom he had admired from a distance was frantically in love with him and looking for an opportunity to make closer acquaintance. They also told me in confidence that this young man was very eager to reply in verse, but neither he nor they had the necessary skill; so they implored me to compose the desired answer.

Mystifications always have been a source of amusement to idle, and more or less intelligent, people. A taste for mischief or a complacent indulgence in malice amuses those who do not know what to do with themselves and cannot exert any good influence on others. At no age are people entirely free from such temptations. We had often played tricks on each other when we were little boys; indeed, many games are based on such mystifications and hoaxes. The practical joke under discussion did not seem to me to go any further than this, and so I agreed. They gave me a number of details to be worked into the letter, and it was finished by the time we went home.

A short time afterwards, through my friend, I received a pressing invitation to join an evening party with the same people. The party was being given by that amorous young man, who particularly wanted to thank me for having rendered such valuable services as poétic secretary.

We met fairly late; the meal was very simple and the wine drinkable. The talk consisted almost exclusively of jeering at our host, not a very wide-awake sort of man, who, after reading the letter over and over again, was not far from believing he had written it himself.

Being naturally warm-hearted, I did not really enjoy this malicious performance, and I was soon sick of the continuous harping on the same subject. I would certainly have spent a boring evening, if I had not been revived by the unexpected appearance of another person. When we arrived, the table was already neatly laid, with sufficient wine, and we sat down and were left alone, without any need of being waited on. When the wine ran out, one of us shouted for the maid. But, instead of her, an uncommonly beautiful girl came in, a startling contrast to these surroundings.

"What is it you want?" she asked, after having said good evening to us pleasantly. "The maid is ill in bed. Can I do anything?"

"We're short of wine," one of us said. "It would be very nice if you would fetch us a few bottles."

"Do, Gretchen," another said. "It's only over the road."

"Of course," she answered, took a few empty bottles from the table, and hurried away.

Her figure was even prettier from behind. The cap was poised so adroitly on the small head, and the slender neck formed a graceful line with the shoulders. Everything about her was exquisite; and it was easier to look at her now that one's attention was not primarily attracted by the tranquil, clear gaze and lovely mouth. I reproached my drinking companions for having sent the young girl out alone in the dark. They merely laughed at me, and I was reassured when she returned in a few minutes—the tavern was only across the road.

"Now you must sit down and have a drink with us," one of the company said.

She did, but unfortunately not near me. She drank a glass to our health and left soon, advising us not to stay up too long and not to make so much noise, as "Mother" was just going to bed. It was our host's mother whom she meant.

From that moment the vision of this girl haunted me wherever I went. It was the first time any woman had made a real impression on me. As I could not find excuse for going to the house to see her, I began to go to church in order to meet her there and soon discovered where she sat; and so I could gaze at her to my heart's content all through the long Protestant service. On the way out I did not dare to speak to her, and even less to offer to see her home; I was in the seventh heaven that she seemed to notice me and nod in reply to my bow. But soon I was lucky enough to get to know her better.

My friends had succeeded in making that lovesick young man, whose poetic secretary I had become, believe that the letter written in his name had really been sent to the woman concerned, and at the same time worked him up into a state of great suspense about the answer, which was soon to follow; and which, of course, they expected me to write. The mischievous conspirators sent me an urgent message by Pylades to exert all my ingenuity and all my poetic gifts in making a perfect job of it.

In the hope of seeing my fair lady again, I set about it at once, now with everything in mind that I should like to read myself if it were written by her. So deeply did I become absorbed that after a while what I had written seemed to reflect her appearance, manner, and personality to such an extent that I could not help wishing it were really so, and was lost in rapture at the mere possibility of her writing such a letter to me. So I deluded myself, while believing that I was making a fool of somebody else; and this was later to bring me much joy and also much trouble. By the time I was sent a reminder about it, I had finished and promised to come. I was there at the appointed time. Only one of my friends was at home; Gretchen was sitting by the window, spinning, and the mother looked in from time to time. The young man asked me to read it to him, which I did, with some emotion, glancing across the paper at the lovely girl. And as I seemed to notice that she was faintly disturbed, even blushing slightly, I went on reading still more expressively the things that I would have wished to hear from her. Her cousin, who had interrupted me several times with approving remarks, finally asked me to make some alterations.

There were, in fact, some details which applied to Gretchen better than to the lady who was supposed to have written the letter and who was of some social standing, wealthy, well known, and respected in the town. After the young man had pointed out the necessary changes and fetched writing materials, he went out for a short time on an errand. I remained sitting on the bench against the wall, at the large table, trying out the corrections on the big slate which almost covered the table, using the slate-pencil that always lay on the window sill, these things being used for working out sums and making odd notes and for messages left by people coming and going.

After various attempts, scribbling things down and rubbing them out again, I exclaimed impatiently: "I can't do it!" "So much the better," Gretchen said calmly. "I would rather you could not do it at all. You should not become mixed up in such things." She stood up from her spinning wheel and, coming over to the table where I was, she lectured me on the subject sternly and sensibly, though not without friendliness. "It looks like a harmless practical joke. It may be a joke, but it is not harmless. I have known several cases when our young men got into serious trouble as a result of such mischief."

"But what can I do?" I replied. "The letter is written, and they are counting on me to make the alterations."

"Take my advice and do not alter it. Fold it up, put it in your pocket, and go and try to put the matter right through your friend. I am only a poor girl and dependent on these relatives of mine—who certainly don't mean any serious harm, but sometimes do very reckless things for the sake of amusement and profit—when they asked me to copy out the first letter, I refused. They had to write it out themselves in a disguised handwriting, and so far as I am concerned, they can do the same with this one. And why should you, a young man of good family, well off and independent, make yourself a tool for such machinations, from which no good can come—and perhaps even trouble for yourself?" I was delighted to listen to this long speech, for she generally spoke very little. I loved her more than ever. I was overcome by my feelings and said: "I am not so independent as you think. And what is the good of being well off, if I have not got the most precious thing I could wish for?"

She took my draft of the poem and read it through very charmingly, half to herself. "That's rather pretty," she said, stopping at an apparently naïve turn of phrase. "What a pity it is not meant for a better purpose—that it isn't true!"

"Ah, that would be wonderful!" I exclaimed. "How happy one would be to receive such a declaration of affection from a girl one really cared for!"

"That is not the sort of thing that happens every day," she answered. "Yet nothing is impossible."

"For instance," I went on, "if somebody who knows you and thinks a great deal of you, somebody who is very much in love with you, put such a poem in front of you, and pleaded with all his heart and soul—what would you do?" I pushed the sheet of paper toward her again, after she had pushed it back to me. She smiled, hesitated for a moment, then took the pen and put her name to the letter.

Wild with delight, I jumped up to take her in my arms. "Please don't kiss me," she said. "It makes it all so vulgar. But let us love each other if we can."

I had taken the sheet of paper and put it in my pocket. "No one shall have it," I said. "The thing is over and done with. You have saved me."

"You must save yourself a little more," she exclaimed. "Hurry up, and go before the others come! It would be awkward for you." I could hardly tear myself away from her, but she asked me to go, so sweetly, taking my right hand in both of hers and pressing it gently. I was not far from tears and noticed that her eyes were wet, too. I pressed my cheek against her hands and hurried away. Never before in my life had my mind been in such a whirl.

Innocent young people's first love always has a spiritual turn. Nature seems to intend each sex to see the other as the embodiment of the good and the beautiful. So it was with me; this girl's presence and my love for her opened up a new world of beauty and perfection for me. I read my poem through over and over again, gazed at the signature, kissed it and pressed it to my heart, overjoyed by this sweet confession. But the more my delight increased, the sadder I felt at not being able to visit her at once, to see her and talk to her again, for I dreaded her cousins' reproaches and attempts to talk me over. I did not know how to get in touch with my good friend Pylades, who might have settled the matter. So next Sunday I set out for Niederrad, where these young men were in the habit of going, and there I found them. I was most astonished that instead of being annoyed and stand-offish, they welcomed me cheerfully. The youngest one in particular was very friendly, took me by the hand, and said: "You played rather a bad trick on us the other day, and we were thoroughly annoyed with you. But after you had gone off with the poem, we had a better idea, which we might not have thought of otherwise. To show there's no ill will, we shall be delighted to be your guests today and tell you all about what we're so proud of. We are sure you will like it too."

I was somewhat embarrassed by this suggestion, for I had just enough money with me to pay for myself and perhaps one friend, but certainly not to entertain a party, especially one that did not always know where to stop. I was all the more surprised by the proposal, as they usually made a point of honor of each paying for himself. They were amused by my embarrassment, and the same young man went on: "Let's first sit down in the arbor, and then you shall hear the whole story." When we were seated, he explained: "When you took away the love letter the other day, we talked the whole thing over again and came to the conclusion that we were misusing your talent for nothing but to tease other people and perhaps get ourselves into trouble, out of a sheer love of mischief, when we could be using it to everybody's advantage. Look, here I have a commission for a wedding poem and another for a dirge. The latter must be done at once, the former will do in a week. If you will do them—and it's no bother for you—it will be as good as if you treated us twice, and we shall be in your debt for a long time."

I liked this proposal in every way. From childhood I

had been rather envious of those occasional poems that used to circulate every week, even dozens of them appearing in celebration of fashionable weddings, for I thought I could do them just as well as other people, if not better. Here, now, I had the chance to prove my skill and to see myself in print into the bargain. I accepted the offer. They gave me some personal details of the family concerned; then I walked a little way off, made a rough scheme, and wrote some of the verses. But when I rejoined the party and the wine flowed freely, I began to get stuck with the poem and could not deliver it that evening. "Tomorrow evening will do," they said, "and we may as well tell you that the fee that we are receiving for the dirge will be enough to pay for another party tomorrow evening. Come to our house. It's only right that Gretchen should be able to join in, as it was actually she who gave us the idea." I was beside myself with joy. On the way home I thought out the missing verses, wrote the whole thing down before going to bed, and copied it out very beautifully the next morning. The day seemed endlessly long. The moment it was dark I was back in that poky little house, together with my beloved Gretchen.

The young men with whom I became closely acquainted in this way were not exactly rough people, but they were rather common. I admired their energy and liked listening to them talking about the various ways and means of earning a living. They were also very fond of talking about very rich people who had started with nothing. Some of these people who had been shop assistants had made themselves indispensable to their employers and finally rose to become their sons-in-law. Others who had started by peddling matches and the like had worked up their trade until now they were rich merchants. But for a young man who could be up and doing, undoubtedly the best way of earning a living was being an agent for wealthy men without much initiative, and running all kinds of errands for them. We all liked listening to this sort of talk, each of us feeling rather pleased with himself as he imagined, at least for the moment, that he himself had the makings of a man who would not merely get on in the world but even rise to fame and fortune. None of us seemed to take all this more seriously than Pylades, who at last confessed that he was in love with a girl and had actually become engaged to her. His parents' financial position made it impossible for him to go to the university; but he had taken the trouble to develop a good handwriting, as well as a knowledge of bookkeeping and of modern languages, and now, looking forward to setting up a home of his own, he meant to exert himself for all he was worth. Gretchen's cousins applauded him for taking this attitude, although they did not approve of such early engagements; and they went on to say that although he certainly was a decent, good fellow, he was neither energetic nor enterprising enough to achieve anything very remarkable. And when in self-defense he began to explain in detail what he meant to do and how he would set about it, the others were also egged on to give a detailed account of what they had achieved so far, and what they hoped for in the future. At last it was my turn to describe my way of living and my intended career, and while I was thinking it over, Pylades said: "There is just one condition I want to make, in fairness to us. He must not count in his material advantages. Instead, he shall make up a story and tell us how he would set about things if at this moment he had to rely completely on himself, just like us."

Gretchen, who had been spinning all this time, got up and sat down at the end of the table, as she usually did. We had already emptied several bottles, and it was in a thoroughly good humor that I began to tell my imaginary life story.

"First of all, I beg to present my compliments," I said, "and hope that you will continue to favor me with your custom as heretofore. If, in the course of time, you can put me in the way of turning an honest penny by writing all the occasional poems that need writing, and if we do not just squander it on dining and wining, I am sure to get on. Apart from that, you must not mind if I dabble in your own line of work." And then I began to tell them what I had picked up of their occupations, and what I thought I would be capable of doing well if I had to. Each of them had previously given an account of his earnings, and I asked them to help me draw up my own balance sheet. Gretchen had been following the conversation very closely, sitting with her arms folded on the table and her hands clasped over them—a position that suited her very well, whether she was talking or listening. She could sit like this for a long time, only turning her head now and then, when something special caught her attention. She had sometimes put in a word, helping us along when we ran out of ideas, but most of the time she was as quiet as she always was. I did not take my eyes off her, and it can easily be imagined that I worked out my plan with her in mind. My feelings for her made what I was saying seem so true and possible that for a moment I really tricked myself into believing I was quite on my own, without support, just as I was supposed to be in my own story; and the idea of making her my own made me utterly happy. Pylades' account had ended with marriage, and the question for the rest of us was whether our own plans were to take us so far. "I don't doubt it in the least," I said. "For in fact each of us needs a wife to make a home and keep him comfortable on what he scrapes together, out in the world, in such odd ways." I gave a description of the sort of wife that I would like, and it would have been strange if she had not been the image of Gretchen.

Although the fee for the dirge had gone on food and wine, the money from the wedding poem was now hovering pleasantly near. I got the better of all my anxious fears, and as I had many friends, I managed to keep my family from knowing how I really spent my evenings. I had reached a stage where I could not get on without seeing and being near Gretchen. And they had all got so used to me that it became the most natural thing for us to meet almost every day. Now Pylades introduced his sweetheart into the house, and this couple spent many evenings with us. An engaged couple, although still very young and inexperienced, they did not need to conceal their feelings for each other; but Gretchen's behavior seemed only meant to keep me at a distance. She did not give her hand to anyone, not even to me; nor would she let anyone touch her. The most she sometimes did was to sit beside me, especially when I was writing or reading aloud, and then she would affectionately put her arm on my shoulder, looking into the book or paper. But if I tried to be as free with her, she would slip away and not come near me for quite a while. Yet she showed this sign of affection again and again with all the simplicity and appealing charm characteristic of her movements and few gestures. I never saw her be so intimate with anyone else.

Of all the expeditions that I used to make with various parties of young men, one of the most harmless and amusing was this: we would go on board the market boat for Höchst, study the queer passengers crowded on deck, and fool about, teasing one person or another, as various notions occurred to us. We used to get out at Höchst, where the market boat from Mainz came in at the same time. There was an inn where the better-off travelers dined together before continuing their journey; for both boats then went back again. After dining, we used to go back to Frankfort, having been for a sail in the cheapest way possible, together with a great crowd of other people. Once when I went on this trip with Gretchen's cousins, it happened that while we were dining in Höchst we were joined by a young man slightly older than ourselves, whom they knew and introduced me to. There was something very charming about him, although he was not otherwise remarkable. Having come up from Mainz, he now traveled back to Frankfort with us, and he and I talked about all sorts of things to do with municipal government and public appointments and offices; he seemed to know a good deal about it. When we separated, he made a special point of saying good-by to me, adding that he hoped he had made a good impression on me, as he might sometime ask me for a recommendation. I did not know what he meant, but some days later the cousins gave me an explanation; they spoke highly of him and asked me to put in a word for him with my grandfather, as it happened there was a fairly good position vacant, which this friend of theirs was very eager to have. At first I made excuses, because I had never meddled in such things; but they went on urging me

until I decided to do it. As a matter of fact, I had sometimes noticed that when such appointments were being
made, which were unfortunately often regarded as matters
of favor, my grandmother's or an aunt's word had not been
without weight. I felt I was sufficiently grown up to claim
some such influence myself. So to oblige my friends, who
declared they were extremely grateful for my kindness, I
overcame my awe of my grandfather and took it upon
myself to deliver a petition which they gave me.

After dinner one Sunday, when Grandfather was busy in
his garden, where he had a great deal to do now autumn
was coming on, and I was trying to help in every way I
could, after some hesitation I came out with my request
and produced the petition. He looked at it and asked if
I knew the young man. I told him in broad outline what I
knew, and he left it at that, saying: "If he is the right sort
and has good testimonials, I shall consider him favorably
for his own sake and for yours." That was all he said, and
for a long time I heard no more about it.

Recently I had noticed that Gretchen had given up spinning and was always busy with needlework—and indeed
with very fine work, which surprised me all the more, since
the evenings were already drawing in, with the approach
of winter. I gave it no more thought, though I was per-
turbed at not finding her at home as usual several times
when I called in the morning, and at not being able to discover where she had gone without appearing unduly inquisitive. But one day I had a very odd surprise. My sister,
who was getting things ready to go to a ball, asked me to
go to a milliner's and bring her some so-called Italian
flowers—small, dainty things that were made in convents
—myrtle, wild roses—very pretty and quite natural. I went
to the shop, where I had often been before together with
her. I had only just gone in and said good day to the pro-
prietress, when I noticed a girl sitting in the window, wear-
ing a lace cap and silk mantilla, apparently young and
pretty, and with a good figure so far as I could see. It was
obvious that she was an assistant, for she was busy trim-
ming a bonnet with ribbons and feathers. The milliner
brought out the long box with samples of the many kinds
of flowers, and I began looking at them, constantly glanc-

ing across at the girl in the window while I was trying to choose. I was startled to realize that she was amazingly like Gretchen; and after a while, I came to the conclusion that it must be Gretchen herself. And then I had no doubts left, when she gave me a warning glance not to show that I knew her. Now I drove the milliner to despair with my picking and choosing, behaving far worse than any woman. I was really unable to settle on anything, for I was quite bewildered; and, at the same time, I enjoyed the delay because it kept me near Gretchen, whose disguise worried me, although it made her seem even more charming than usual. At last the milliner lost patience and herself picked out a bandboxful of flowers for me to take to my sister, so that she could choose for herself. She sent her errand girl ahead with the box, and so more or less drove me out of the shop.

I had only just got home again when my father sent for me and told me it was now quite certain that the Archduke Joseph would be elected and crowned as King of Rome.* Such a highly important event, he said, must not be allowed to take one unawares nor let pass by while one merely gaped and stared in amazement. So he wanted to go through the diaries of the last two elections and coronations with me, as well as the terms of the last election, in order to see what new ceremonies might be added on this occasion. Getting out the diaries, we spent the whole day and a good part of the night going through them, the vision of the pretty girl, sometimes in her old housedress, sometimes in her new guise, constantly floating before me, in and out among the most majestic concerns of the Holy Roman Empire. It was impossible to see her that evening, and I spent a very restless night, unable to sleep. The next day we went on eagerly with our study of these documents, and it was only toward evening that I had a chance to visit my sweetheart, whom I found once more in her usual housedress. She smiled as she looked at me, but I did not dare to say anything in front of the others. When we had all quietly settled down together, she opened the conversation by saying: "It is not fair to keep our friend in the dark about what we have decided these last few days." She

* And therefore next in succession to the empire of his father.

then went on to describe how, after our recent discussion about getting on in the world, they had come to talk of ways in which a young woman might turn her abilities and energy to account and make good use of her time. One of her cousins had suggested that she should try working for a milliner, who happened to be in need of an assistant. They had come to an agreement with the woman, and now she went there for some hours every day and was well paid; for the sake of appearances, however, she had to wear a special dress, which she always left at the shop because she thought it was quite an unsuitable style for her general way of living. Although reassured by this explanation, I did not really like to think of her, pretty as she was, being in a shop, a public place where fashionable people were always going in and out. But I kept my jealous worries to myself. Besides, I was soon distracted by her younger cousin, who produced another commission for an occasional poem and began to give me the necessary details, insisting that I should set about working it out at once. He had already had several talks with me about how to do such things, and as I was always very ready to talk on this score, he easily got me to the point of explaining the theoretical side of it to him in detail, giving him an idea of the problem and using my own and other people's work as illustrations. This young man was quite intelligent, though without the slightest gift for poetry, and now he went into such details and wanted to know so much that I could not help remarking: "It almost looks as though you meant to poach on my preserves and take away my custom."

"I won't deny it," he said, smilingly, "for I shall not be doing you any damage. It won't be long before you go to the university, and in the meantime you might as well let me learn something from you."

"With the greatest of pleasure," I answered. And I encouraged him to draft out a scheme himself and choose a meter in keeping with the subject, and all the rest of it.

He tackled the job seriously; but he could not make any headway with it. I had to rewrite so much of it myself that I could have done it better all on my own and more easily. But this teaching and learning, with the team-work it involved, kept us amused. Gretchen joined in, providing many good ideas, and so we were all very cheerful, even happy.

By day she worked at the milliner's; we were generally together in the evenings, and our happiness was not disturbed by the fact that commissions for occasional poems finally began to slacken off. What did upset us was having one of them sent back by a dissatisfied patron. However, we consoled ourselves, as we considered it our best piece of work and so felt justified in regarding him as a bad judge. Gretchen's younger cousin, who had set his mind on learning something, insisted on our doing imaginary commissions, which provided us with a great deal of entertainment; but as it did not bring in any money we had to cut down on our little parties quite considerably.

(A description of the bustle and preparations for the Election concludes with the arrival of the Elector of Mainz.)

Let us pass over the arrival of the Elector Emmerich Joseph, incognito, in the Compostello, and return to Gretchen. Just as the crowd was thinning out, I caught sight of her in the midst of all the bustle, together with Pylades and his sweetheart; the three of them seemed to have become inseparable. We exchanged greetings and at once agreed to spend the evening together. I arrived punctually to find the usual gathering, and everyone had some remark, comment, or anecdote about the various things that had struck him most. At last Gretchen said: "All this talk confuses me even more than what actually happened today. I cannot sort out what I have seen, and there are a number of things I should very much like to have explained to me."

I replied that it would be quite easy to do that, if she would just tell me what interested her most. She did so, and as there were several points I wanted to explain, it seemed best to go over the whole thing right from the beginning. I rather neatly compared these pomps and ceremonies to a play on which the curtain was let down at will, while the players still went on acting their parts, and then raised again, the spectators being more or less able to pick up the thread. As I was inclined to be very talkative whenever I had the chance, I gave a chronological account of the whole thing from the beginning to the present day, incidentally making use of the big slate and slate-pencil in order to illustrate what I said. With only some interruptions from the others, asking questions or quibbling, I wound up my lecture to everyone's satisfaction. Gretchen, who had encouraged me a great deal by following what I said with such concentration, afterwards thanked me, saying she envied people who knew all about what went on in the world, and how things were done, and why. She wished she were a boy, and admitted very charmingly that she had already learned a good deal from me. "If I were a boy," she said, "we would go to the university together and study seriously." The conversation continued along these lines; she decided that she must learn French, which her experience at the milliner's had shown her was essential. I asked her why she did not go there any more; for recently, finding it difficult to slip away in the evenings, I had sometimes gone past the shop during the day for her sake, just to see her for a moment. She explained that she had not wanted to run any risks by being in such a public place in these stirring times. But she meant to go back, once the city settled down again to its usual tranquillity.

Then the conversation turned to the impending Election Day. I was able to give a full account of what happened and how it was all done, providing detailed illustrations on the slate. The most vivid of my drawings was that of the conclave room with its altars, thrones, chairs, and seats. The party broke up at a reasonable hour, all of us in a particularly contented frame of mind.

Nothing can make for a more harmonious relationship between two young people who naturally have a good deal in common than if the girl is eager to learn and the young man to teach. The relationship that develops in such a way is both solid and delightful. She sees him as the creator of her intellectual life, and he sees her as a creature owing her perfection not to nature, chance, or one-sided desire, but to the fact that their two minds are bent to one purpose. And this interplay is so sweet that we need not be surprised if such encounters between two minds, from the time of the first Abelard and of the new,* have given rise to overpowering passions and as much happiness as disaster.

* St. Preux in Rousseau's "Nouvelle Heloïse."

❧

FAUST

TRANSLATED BY LOUIS MACNEICE

PART I

Prologue in Heaven

The LORD. *The* HEAVENLY HOSTS. MEPHISTOPHELES
following

The THREE ARCHANGELS *step forward*

RAPHAEL: The chanting sun, as ever, rivals
The chanting of his brother spheres
And marches round his destined circuit—
A march that thunders in our ears.
His aspect cheers the Hosts of Heaven
Though what his essence none can say;
These inconceivable creations
Keep the high state of their first day.

GABRIEL: And swift, with inconceivable swiftness,
The earth's full splendor rolls around,
Celestial radiance alternating
With a dread night too deep to sound;
The sea against the rocks' deep bases
Comes foaming up in far-flung force,
And rock and sea go whirling onward
In the swift spheres' eternal course.

MICHAEL: And storms in rivalry are raging
From sea to land, from land to sea,
In frenzy forge the world a girdle
From which no inmost part is free.

The blight of lightning flaming yonder
Marks where the thunderbolt will play;
And yet Thine envoys, Lord, revere
The gentle movement of Thy day.

CHOIR OF ANGELS: Thine aspect cheers the Hosts of
Heaven
Though what Thine essence none can say,
And all Thy loftiest creations
Keep the high state of their first day.

(*Enter* MEPHISTOPHELES)

MEPHISTOPHELES: Since you, O Lord, once more ap-
proach and ask
If business down with us be light or heavy—
And in the past you've usually welcomed me—
That's why you see me also at your levee.
Excuse me, I can't manage lofty words—
Not though your whole court jeer and find me low;
My pathos certainly would make you laugh
Had you not left off laughing long ago.
Your suns and worlds mean nothing much to me;
How men torment themselves, that's all I see.
The little god of the world, one can't reshape, reshade
him;
He is as strange today as that first day you made him.
His life would be not so bad, not quite,
Had you not granted him a gleam of Heaven's light;
He calls it Reason, uses it not the least
Except to be more beastly than any beast.
He seems to me—if your Honor does not mind—
Like a grasshopper—the long-legged kind—
That's always in flight and leaps as it flies along
And then in the grass strikes up its same old song.
I could only wish he confined himself to the grass!
He thrusts his nose into every filth, alas.

LORD: Mephistopheles, have you no other news?
Do you always come here to accuse?
Is nothing ever right in your eyes on earth?

MEPHISTOPHELES: No, Lord! I find things there as
      downright bad as ever.
I am sorry for men's days of dread and dearth;
Poor things, *my* wish to plague 'em isn't fervent.

LORD: Do you know Faust?

MEPHISTOPHELES: The Doctor?

LORD: Aye, my servant.

MEPHISTOPHELES: Indeed! He serves you oddly enough,
      I think.
The fool has no earthly habits in meat and drink.
The ferment in him drives him wide and far,
That he is mad he too has almost guessed;
He demands of heaven each fairest star
And of earth each highest joy and best,
And all that is new and all that is far
Can bring no calm to the deep-sea swell of his breast.

LORD: Now he may serve me only gropingly,
Soon I shall lead him into the light.
The gardener knows when the sapling first turns green
That flowers and fruit will make the future bright.

MEPHISTOPHELES: What do you wager? You will lose
      him yet,
Provided *you* give *me* permission
To steer him gently the course I set.

LORD: So long as he walks the earth alive,
So long you may try what enters your head;
Men make mistakes as long as they strive.

MEPHISTOPHELES: I thank you for that; as regards the
      dead,
The dead have never taken my fancy.
I favor cheeks that are full and rosy-red;
No corpse is welcome to my house;
I work as the cat does with the mouse.

LORD: Very well; you have my full permission.
Divert this soul from its primal source
And carry it, if you can seize it,
Down with you upon your course—
And stand ashamed when you must needs admit:

A good man with his groping intuitions
Still knows the path that is true and fit.

MEPHISTOPHELES: All right—but it won't last for long.
I'm not afraid my bet will turn out wrong.
And, if my aim prove true and strong,
Allow me to triumph wholeheartedly.
Dust shall he eat—and greedily—
Like my cousin the Snake renowned in tale and song.

LORD: That too you are free to give a trial;
I have never hated the likes of you.
Of all the spirits of denial
The joker is the last that I eschew.
Man finds relaxation too attractive—
Too fond too soon of unconditional rest;
Which is why I am pleased to give him a companion
Who lures and thrusts and must, as devil, be active.
But ye, true sons of Heaven, it is your duty
To take your joy in the living wealth of beauty.
The changing Essence which ever works and lives
Wall you around with love, serene, secure!
And that which floats in flickering appearance
Fix ye it firm in thoughts that must endure.

CHOIR OF ANGELS: Thine aspect cheers the Hosts of
       Heaven
Though what Thine essence none can say,
And all Thy loftiest creations
Keep the high state of their first day.

(Heaven closes)

MEPHISTOPHELES *(alone)*: I like to see the Old One
       now and then
And try to keep relations on the level.
It's really decent of so great a person
To talk so humanely even to the Devil.

Night

(In a high-vaulted narrow Gothic room FAUST, *restless, in a chair at his desk)*

FAUST: Here stand I, ach, Philosophy
Behind me and Law and Medicine too
And, to my cost, Theology—
All these I have sweated through and through
And now you see me a poor fool
As wise as when I entered school!
They call me Master, they call me Doctor,
Ten years now I have dragged my college
Along by the nose through zig and zag
Through up and down and round and round
And this is all that I have found—
The impossibility of knowledge!
It is this that burns away my heart;
Of course I am cleverer than the quacks,
Than master and doctor, than clerk and priest,
I suffer no scruple or doubt in the least,
I have no qualms about devil or burning,
Which is just why all joy is torn from me,
I cannot presume to make use of my learning,
I cannot presume I could open my mind
To proselytize and improve mankind.

Besides, I have neither goods nor gold,
Neither reputation nor rank in the world;
No dog would choose to continue so!
Which is why I have given myself to Magic
To see if the Spirit may grant me to know
Through its force and its voice full many a secret,
May spare the sour sweat that I used to pour out
In talking of what I know nothing about,

May grant me to learn what it is that girds
The world together in its inmost being,
That the seeing its whole germination, the seeing
Its workings, may end my traffic in words.

O couldst thou, light of the full moon,
Look now thy last upon my pain,
Thou for whom I have sat belated
So many midnights here and waited
Till, over books and papers, thou
Didst shine, sad friend, upon my brow!
O could I but walk to and fro
On mountain heights in thy dear glow
Or float with spirits round mountain eyries
Or weave through fields thy glances glean
And freed from all miasmal theories
Bathe in thy dew and wash me clean!

Oh! Am I still stuck in this jail?
This God-damned dreary hole in the wall
Where even the lovely light of heaven
Breaks wanly through the painted panes!
Cooped up among these heaps of books
Gnawed by worms, coated with dust,
Round which to the top of the Gothic vault
A smoke-stained paper forms a crust.
Retorts and canisters lie pell-mell
And pyramids of instruments,
The junk of centuries, dense and mat—
Your world, man! World? They call it that!

And yet you ask why your poor heart
Cramped in your breast should feel such fear,
Why an unspecified misery
Should throw your life so out of gear?
Instead of the living natural world
For which God made all men his sons
You hold a reeking moldering court
Among assorted skeletons.

Away! There is a world outside!
And this one book of mystic art
Which Nostradamus wrote himself,
Is this not adequate guard and guide?
By this you can tell the course of the stars,
By this, once Nature gives the word,
The soul begins to stir and dawn,
A spirit by a spirit heard.
In vain your barren studies here
Construe the signs of sanctity.
You Spirits, you are hovering near;
If you can hear me, answer me!

(*He opens the book and perceives the sign of the Macrocosm*)

Ha! What a river of wonder at this vision
Bursts upon all my senses in one flood!
And I feel young, the holy joy of life
Glows new, flows fresh, through nerve and blood!
Was it a god designed this hieroglyph to calm
The storm which but now raged inside me,
To pour upon my heart such balm,
And by some secret urge to guide me
Where all the powers of Nature stand unveiled around me?
Am I a God? It grows so light!
And through the clear-cut symbol on this page
My soul comes face to face with all creating Nature.
At last I understand the dictum of the sage:
"The spiritual world is always open,
Your mind is closed, your heart is dead;
Rise, young man, and plunge undaunted
Your earthly breast in the morning red."

(*He contemplates the sign*)

Into one Whole how all things blend,
Function and live within each other!
Passing gold buckets to each other
How heavenly powers ascend, descend!

The odor of grace upon their wings,
They thrust from heaven through earthly things
And as all sing so *the* All sings!
What a fine show! Aye, but only a show!
Infinite Nature, where can I tap thy veins?
Where are thy breasts, those well-springs of all life
On which hang heaven and earth,
Towards which my dry breast strains?
They well up, they give drink, but I feel drought and
dearth.

(*He turns the pages and perceives the sign of the* EARTH
SPIRIT)

How differently this new sign works upon me!
Thy sign, thou Spirit of the Earth, 'tis thine
And thou art nearer to me.
At once I feel my powers unfurled,
At once I glow as from new wine
And feel inspired to venture into the world,
To cope with the fortunes of earth benign or malign,
To enter the ring with the storm, to grapple and clinch,
To enter the jaws of the shipwreck and never flinch.
Over me comes a mist,
The moon muffles her light,
The lamp goes dark.
The air goes damp. Red beams flash
Around my head. There blows
A kind of a shudder down from the vault
And seizes on me.
It is thou must be hovering round me, come at my prayers!
Spirit, unveil thyself!
My heart, oh my heart, how it tears!
And how each and all of my senses
Seem burrowing upwards towards new light, new breath!
I feel my heart has surrendered, I have no more defenses.
Come then! Come! Even if it prove my death!

(*He seizes the book and solemnly pronounces the sign
of the* EARTH SPIRIT. *There is a flash of red flame and the*
SPIRIT *appears in it*)

SPIRIT: Who calls upon me?

FAUST: Appalling vision!

SPIRIT: You have long been sucking at my sphere,
Now by main force you have drawn me here
And now—

FAUST: No! Not to be endured!

SPIRIT: With prayers and with pantings you have pro-
        cured
The sight of my face and the sound of my voice—
Now I am here. What a pitiable shivering
Seizes the Superman. Where is the call of your soul?
Where the breast which created a world in itself
And carried and fostered it, swelling up, joyfully quivering,
Raising itself to a level with Us, the Spirits?
Where are you, Faust, whose voice rang out to me,
Who with every nerve so thrust yourself upon me?
Are you the thing that at a whiff of my breath
Trembles throughout its living frame,
A poor worm crawling off, askance, askew?

FAUST: Shall I yield to Thee, Thou shape of flame?
I am Faust, I can hold my own with Thee.

SPIRIT: In the floods of life, in the storm of work,
In ebb and flow,
In warp and weft,
Cradle and grave,
An eternal sea,
A changing patchwork,
A glowing life,
At the whirring loom of Time I weave
The living clothes of the Deity.

FAUST: Thou who dost rove the wide world round,
Busy Spirit, how near I feel to Thee!

SPIRIT: You are like that Spirit which you can grasp,
Not me!

   (*The* SPIRIT *vanishes*)

FAUST: Not thee!
Whom then?

I who am Godhead's image,
Am I not even like Thee!

(*A knocking on the door*)

Death! I know who that is. My assistant!
So ends my happiest, fairest hour.
The crawling pedant must interrupt
My visions at their fullest flower!

(WAGNER *enters in dressing gown and nightcap, a lamp in his hand*)

WAGNER: Excuse me but I heard your voice declaiming—
A passage doubtless from those old Greek plays.
That is an art from which I would gladly profit,
It has its advantages nowadays.
And I've often heard folk say it's true
A preacher can learn something from an actor.

FAUST: Yes, when the preacher is an actor too;
Which is a not uncommon factor.

WAGNER: Ah, when your study binds up your whole
          existence
And you scarcely can see the world on a holiday
Or through a spyglass—and always from a distance—
How can your rhetoric make it walk your way?

FAUST: Unless you feel it, you cannot gallop it down,
Unless it thrust up from your soul
Forcing the hearts of all your audience
With a primal joy beyond control.
Sit there for ever with scissors and paste!
Gather men's leavings for a rehash
And blow up a little paltry flicker
Out of your own little heap of ash!
It will win you claps from apes and toddlers—
Supposing your palate welcome such—
But heart can never awaken a spark in heart
Unless your own heart keep in touch.

WAGNER: However, it is the delivery wins all ears
And I know that I am still far, too far, in arrears.

FAUST: Win your effects by honest means,
Eschew the cap and bells of the fool!
True insight and true sense will make
Their point without the rhetoric school
And, given a thought that must be heard,
Is there such need to chase a word?
Yes, your so glittering purple patches
In which you make cat's cradles of humanity
Are like the foggy wind which whispers in the autumn
Through barren leaves—a fruitless vanity.

WAGNER: Ah God, we know that art
Is long and short our life!
Often enough my analytical labors
Pester both brain and heart.
How hard it is to attain the means
By which one climbs to the fountainhead;
Before a poor devil can reach the halfway house,
Like as not he is dead.

FAUST: Your manuscript, is that your holy well
A draught of which for ever quenches thirst?
You have achieved no true refreshment
Unless you can tap your own soul first.

WAGNER: Excuse me—it is considerable gratification
To transport oneself into the spirit of times past,
To observe what a wise man thought before our days
And how we now have brought his ideas to consummation.

FAUST: Oh yes, consummated in heaven!
There is a book, my friend, and its seals are seven—
The times that have been put on the shelf.
Your so-called spirit of such times
Is at bottom merely the spirit of the gentry
In whom each time reflects itself,
And at that it often makes one weep
And at the first glance run away,
A lumber room and a rubbish heap,
At best an heroic puppet play
With excellent pragmatical Buts and Yets
Such as are suitable to marionettes.

WAGNER: And yet the world! The heart and spirit of
    men!
We all would wish to understand the same.

FAUST: Yes, what is known as understanding—
But who dare call the child by his real name?
The few who have known anything about it,
Whose hearts unwisely overbrimmed and spake,
Who showed the mob their feelings and their visions,
Have ended on the cross or at the stake.
My friend, I beg you, the night is now far gone;
We must break off for this occasion.

WAGNER: I'd have been happy sitting on and on
To continue such a learned conversation.
Tomorrow however, as it is Easter Day,
I shall put you some further questions if I may.
Having given myself to knowledge heart and soul
I have a good share of it, now I would like the whole.

(*Exit* WAGNER)

FAUST (*alone*): To think this head should still bring
    hope to birth
Sticking like glue to hackneyed rags and tags,
Delving with greedy hand for treasure
And glad when it finds an earthworm in the earth!

That such a human voice should here intrude
Where spiritual fullness only now enclosed me!
And yet, my God, you poorest of all the sons
Of earth, this time you have earned my gratitude.
For you have snatched me away from that despair
Which was ripe and ready to destroy my mind;
Beside that gigantic vision I could not find
My normal self; only a dwarf was there.

I, image of the Godhead, who deemed myself but now
On the brink of the mirror of eternal truth and seeing
My rapturous fill of the blaze of clearest Heaven,
Having stripped off my earthly being;
I, more than an angel, I whose boundless urge
To flow through Nature's veins and in the act of creation

To revel it like the gods—what a divination,
What an act of daring—and what an expiation!
One thundering word has swept me over the verge.

To boast myself thine equal I do not dare.
Granted I owned the power to draw thee down,
I lacked the power to hold thee there.
In that blest moment I felt myself,
Felt myself so small, so great;
Cruelly thou didst thrust me back
Into man's uncertain fate.
Who will teach me? What must I shun?
Or must I go where that impulse drives?
Alas, our very actions like our sufferings
Put a brake upon our lives.

Upon the highest concepts of the mind
That grows an alien and more alien mold;
When we have reached what in this world is good
That which is better is labeled a fraud, a blind.
What gave us life, feelings of highest worth,
Go dead amidst the madding crowds of earth.

Where once Imagination on daring wing
Reached out to the Eternal, full of hope,
Now, that the eddies of time have shipwrecked chance on
        chance,
She is contented with a narrow scope.
Care makes her nest forthwith in the heart's deep places,
And there contrives her secret sorrows,
Rocks herself restlessly, destroying rest and joy;
And always she is putting on new faces,
Will appear as your home, as those that you love within it,
As fire or water, poison or steel;
You tremble at every blow that you do not feel
And what you never lose you must weep for every minute.

I am not like the gods—that I too deeply feel—
No, I am like the worm that burrows through the dust
Which, as it keeps itself alive in the dust,
Is annulled and buried by some casual heel.

Is it not dust that on a thousand shelves
Narrows this high wall round me so?
The junk that with its thousandfold tawdriness
In this moth world keeps me so low?
Shall I find here what I require?
Read maybe in a thousand books how men
Have in the general run tortured themselves,
With but a lucky one now and then?
Why do you grin at me, you hollow skull?
To point out that your brain was once, like mine, confused
And looked for the easy day but in the difficult dusk,
Lusting for truth was led astray and abused?
You instruments, I know you are mocking me
With cog and crank and cylinder.
I stood at the door, you were to be the key;
A key with intricate wards—but the bolt declines to stir.
Mysterious in the light of day
Nature lets none unveil her; if she refuse
To make some revelation to your spirit
You cannot force her with levers and with screws.
You ancient gear I have never used, it is only
Because my father used you that I retain you.
You ancient scroll, you have been turning black
Since first the dim lamp smoked upon this desk to stain you.
Far better to have squandered the little I have
Than loaded with that little to stay sweating here.
Whatever legacy your fathers left you,
To own it you must earn it dear.
The thing that you fail to use is a load of lead;
The moment can only use what the moment itself has bred.

But why do my eyes fasten upon that spot?
Is that little bottle a magnet to my sight?
Why do I feel of a sudden this lovely illumination
As when the moon flows round us in a dark wood at night?

Bottle, unique little bottle, I salute you
As now I devoutly lift you down. In you
I honor human invention and human skill.
You, the quintessence of all sweet narcotics,

The extract of all rare and deadly powers,
I am your master—show me your good will!
I look on you, my sorrow is mitigated,
I hold you and my struggles are abated,
The flood tide of my spirit ebbs away, away.
The mirroring waters glitter at my feet,
I am escorted forth on the high seas,
Allured towards new shores by a new day.
A fiery chariot floats on nimble wings
Down to me and I feel myself upbuoyed
To blaze a new trail through the upper air
Into new spheres of energy unalloyed.
Oh this high life, this heavenly rapture! Do *you*
Merit this, you, a moment ago a worm?
Merit it? Aye—only turn your back on the sun
Which enchants the earth, turn your back and be firm!
And brace yourself to tear asunder the gates
Which everyone longs to shuffle past if he can;
Now is the time to act and acting prove
That God's height need not lower the merit of Man;
Nor tremble at that dark pit in which our fancy
Condemns itself to torments of its own framing,
But struggle on and upwards to that passage
At the narrow mouth of which all hell is flaming.
Be calm and take this step, though you should fall
Beyond it into nothing—nothing at all.

And you, you loving cup of shining crystal—
I have not given a thought to you for years—
Down you come now out of your ancient chest!
You glittered at my ancestors' junketings
Enlivening the serious guest
When with you in his hand he proceeded to toast his
            neighbor—
But today no neighbor will take you from my hand.
Here is a juice that makes one drunk in a wink;
It fills you full, you cup, with its brown flood.
It was I who made this, I who had it drawn;
So let my whole soul now make my last drink
A high and gala greeting, a toast to the dawn!

(He raises the cup to his mouth. There is an outburst of bells and choirs)

CHORUS OF ANGELS: Christ is arisen!
Joy to mortality
Whom its own fatally
Earth-bound morality
Bound in a prison.

FAUST: What a deep booming, what a ringing tone
Pulls back the cup from my lips—and with such power!
So soon are you announcing, you deep bells,
Easter Day's first festive hour?
You choirs, do you raise so soon the solacing hymn
That once round the night of the grave rang out from the
seraphim
As man's new covenant and dower?

CHORUS OF WOMEN: With balm and with spices
'Twas we laid him out,
We who tended him,
Faithful, devout;
We wound him in linen,
Made all clean where he lay,
Alas—to discover
Christ gone away.

CHORUS OF ANGELS: Christ is arisen!
The loving one! Blest
After enduring the
Grievous, the curing, the
Chastening test.

FAUST: You heavenly music, strong as you are kind,
Why do you search me out in the dust?
Better ring forth where men have open hearts!
I hear your message, my faith it is that lags behind;
And miracle is the favorite child of faith.
Those spheres whence peals the gospel of forgiving,
Those are beyond what I can dare,
And yet, so used am I from childhood to this sound,
It even now summons me back to living.
Once I could feel the kiss of heavenly love

Rain down through the calm and solemn Sabbath air,
Could find a prophecy in the full-toned bell,
A spasm of happiness in a prayer.
An ineffably sweet longing bound me
To quest at random through field and wood
Where among countless burning tears
I felt a world rise up around me.
This hymn announced the lively games of youth, the lovely
Freedom of Spring's own festival;
Now with its childlike feelings memory holds me back
From the last and gravest step of all.
But you, sweet songs of heaven, keep sounding forth!
My tears well up, I belong once more to earth.

CHORUS OF DISCIPLES: Now has the Buried One,
        Lowliness ended,
        Living in lordliness,
        Lordly ascended;
        He in the zest of birth
        Near to creating light;
        We on the breast of earth
        Still in frustrating night!
        He left us, his own ones,
        Pining upon this spot,
        Ah, and lamenting,
        Master, thy lot.

CHORUS OF ANGELS: Christ is arisen
        From the womb of decay!
        Burst from your prison,
        Rejoice in the day!
        Praising him actively,
        Practicing charity,
        Giving alms brotherly,
        Preaching him wanderingly,
        Promising sanctity,
        You have your Master near,
        You have him here!

Easter Holiday

(*Holidaymakers of all kinds come out through the city gate*)

FIRST STUDENT: Lord, these strapping wenches they go a
    lick!
Hurry up, brother, we must give 'em an escort.
My program for today is a strong ale,
A pipe of shag and a girl who's got up chic.

FIRST GIRL: Look! Will you look at the handsome boys!
Really and truly it's degrading;
They could walk out with the best of us
And they have to run round scullery-maiding!

SECOND STUDENT: Hold on, hold on! There are two
    coming up behind
With a very pretty taste in dress;
One of those girls is a neighbor of mine,
She appeals to me, I must confess.
You see how quietly they go
And yet in the end they'll be taking *us* in tow.

BEGGAR (*singing*): Good gentlemen and lovely ladies,
        Rosy of cheek and neat of dress,
        Be kind enough to look upon me
        And see and comfort my distress.
        Leave me not here a hopeless busker!
        Only the giver can be gay.
        A day when all the town rejoices,
        Make it for me a harvest day.

FIRST BURGHER: I know nothing better on Sundays or
    on holidays
Than to have a chat about war and warlike pother
When far away, in Turkey say,
The peoples are socking one another.
One stands at the window, drinks one's half of mild,
And sees the painted ships glide down the waterways;

Then in the evening one goes happily home
And blesses peace and peaceful days.

    SECOND BURGHER: Yes, indeed, neighbor! That is all
        right with me.
They can break heads if they like it so
And churn up everything topsy-turvy,
But at home let us keep the status quo.

    OLD WOMAN: Eh, but how smart they look! Pretty young
        things!
Whoever saw you should adore you!
But not so haughty! It's all right—
Tell me your wish and I can get it for you.

    FIRST GIRL: Come, Agatha! Such witches I avoid
In public places—it's much wiser really;
It's true, she helped me on St. Andrew's night
To see my future sweetheart clearly.

    SECOND GIRL: Yes, mine she showed me in a crystal,
A soldier type with dashing chaps behind him;
I look around, I seek him everywhere
And yet—and yet I never find him.

    SOLDIERS (*singing*): Castles with towering
                Walls to maintain them,
                Girls who have suitors
                But to disdain them,
                Would I could gain them!
                Bold is the venture,
                Lordly the pay.

                Hark to the trumpets!
                They may be crying
                Summons to gladness,
                Summons to dying.
                Life is a storming!
                Life is a splendor!
                Maidens and castles
                Have to surrender.
                Bold is the venture,
                Lordly the pay;
                Later the soldiers
                Go marching away.

(FAUST *and* WAGNER *are now walking off on the road to the village*)

FAUST: River and brook are freed from ice
By the lovely enlivening glance of spring
And hope grows green throughout the dale;
Ancient winter, weakening,
Has fallen back on the rugged mountains
And launches thence his Parthian shafts
Which are merely impotent showers of hail
Streaking over the greening mead;
But the sun who tolerates nothing white,
Amidst all this shaping and stirring of seed,
Wants to enliven the world with color
And, flowers being lacking, in their lieu
Takes colorful crowds to mend the view.
Turn round and look back from this rise
Towards the town. From the gloomy gate
Look, can you see them surging forth—
A harlequin-colored crowd in fete!
Sunning themselves with one accord
In homage to the risen Lord.
For they themselves today have risen:
Out of the dismal room in the slum,
Out of each shop and factory prison,
Out of the stuffiness of the garret,
Out of the squash of the narrow streets,
Out of the churches' reverend night—
One and all have been raised to light.
Look, only look, how quickly the gardens
And fields are sprinkled with the throng,
How the river all its length and breadth
Bears so many pleasure boats along,
And almost sinking from its load
How this last dinghy moves away.
Even on the furthest mountain tracks
Gay rags continue to look gay.
Already I hear the hum of the village,
Here is the plain man's real heaven—
Great and small in a riot of fun;
Here I'm a man—and dare be one.

WAGNER: Doctor, to take a walk with you
Is a profit and a privilege for me
But I wouldn't lose my way alone round here,
Sworn foe that I am of all vulgarity.
This fiddling, screaming, skittle-playing,
Are sounds I loathe beyond all measure;
They run amuck as if the devil were in them
And call it music, call it pleasure.

(*They have now reached the village*)

OLD PEASANT: Doctor, it is most good of you
Not to look down on us today
And, pillar of learning that you are,
To mill around with folk at play.
So take this most particular jug
Which we have filled for you at the tap,
This is a pledge and I pray aloud
That it quench your thirst and more mayhap:
As many drops as this can give,
So many days extra may you live.

FAUST: Thank you for such a reviving beer
And now—good health to all men here.

(*The people collect round him*)

OLD PEASANT: Of a truth, Doctor, you have done rightly
To appear on this day when all are glad,
Seeing how in times past you proved
Our own good friend when days were bad.
Many a man stands here alive
Whom your father found in the grip
Of a raging fever and tore him thence
When he put paid to the pestilence.
You too—you were a youngster then—
Where any was ill you went your round,
Right many a corpse left home feet first
But you came out of it safe and sound,
From many a grueling trial—Aye,
The helper got help from the Helper on high.

CROWD: Health to the trusty man. We pray
He may live to help us many a day.

FAUST: Kneel to the One on high, our friend
Who teaches us helpers, who help can send.

(FAUST *and* WAGNER *leave the crowd and move on*)

WAGNER: You great man, how your heart must leap
To be so honored by the masses!
How happy is he who has such talents
And from them such a crop can reap!
The father points you out to his boy,
They all ask questions, run and jostle,
The fiddles and the dancers pause
And, as you pass, they stand in rows
And caps go hurtling in the sky;
They almost kneel to you as though
The Eucharist were passing by.

FAUST: Only a few steps more up to that stone!
Here, after our walk, we will take a rest.
Here I have often sat, thoughtful, alone,
Torturing myself with prayer and fast.
Rich in hope and firm in faith,
With tears and sighs to seven times seven
I thought I could end that epidemic
And force the hand of the Lord of Heaven.
But now the crowd's applause sounds to me like derision.
O could you only read in my inmost heart
How little father and son
Merited their great reputation!
My father was a worthy man who worked in the dark,
Who in good faith but on his own wise
Brooded on Nature and her holy circles
With laborious whimsicalities;
Who used to collect the connoisseurs
Into the kitchen and locked inside
Its black walls pour together divers
Ingredients of countless recipes;
Such was our medicine, the patients died
And no one counted the survivors.

And thus we with our hellish powders
Raged more perniciously than the plague
Throughout this district—valley and town.
Myself I have given the poison to thousands;
They drooped away, *I* must live on to sample
The brazen murderers' renown.

WAGNER: How can you let that weigh so heavily?
Does not a good man do enough
If he works at the art that he has received
Conscientiously and scrupulously?
As a young man you honor your father,
What he can teach, you take with a will;
As a man you widen the range of knowledge
And your son's range may be wider still.

FAUST: Happy the man who swamped in this sea of
          Error
Still hopes to struggle up through the watery wall;
What we don't know is exactly what we need
And what we know fulfills no need at all.
But let us not with such sad thoughts
Make this good hour an hour undone!
Look how the cottages on the green
Shine in the glow of the evening sun!
He backs away, gives way, the day is overspent,
He hurries off to foster life elsewhere,
Would I could press on his trail, on his trail for ever—
Alas that I have no wings to raise me into the air!
Then I should see in an everlasting sunset
The quiet world before my feet unfold,
All of its peaks on fire, all of its vales becalmed,
And the silver brook dispersed in streams of gold.
Not the wild peaks with all their chasms
Could interrupt my godlike flight;
Already the bays of the sea that the sun has warmed
Unfurl upon my marveling sight.
But in the end the sungod seems to sink away,
Yet the new impulse sets me again in motion,
I hasten on to drink his eternal light,
With night behind me and before me day,

Above me heaven and below me ocean.
A beautiful dream—yet the sun leaves me behind.
Alas, it is not so easy for earthly wing
To fly on level terms with the wings of the mind.
Yet born with each of us is the instinct
That struggles upwards and away
When over our heads, lost in the blue,
The lark pours out her vibrant lay;
When over rugged pine-clad ranges
The eagle hangs on outspread wings
And over lake and over plain
We see the homeward-struggling crane.

    WAGNER: I myself have often had moments of fanci-
        fulness
But I never experienced yet an urge like this.
Woods and fields need only a quick look
And *I* shall never envy the bird its pinions.
How differently the joys of the mind's dominions
Draw us from page to page, from book to book.
That's what makes winter nights lovely and snug—
The blissful life that warms you through your body—
And, ah, should you unroll a worthwhile manuscript,
You bring all heaven down into your study.

    FAUST: You are only conscious of one impulse. Never
Seek an acquaintance with the other.
Two souls, alas, cohabit in my breast,
A contract one of them desires to sever.
The one like a rough lover clings
To the world with the tentacles of its senses;
The other lifts itself to Elysian fields
Out of the mist on powerful wings.
Oh, if there be spirits in the air,
Princes that weave their way between heaven and earth,
Come down to me from the golden atmosphere
And carry me off to a new and colorful life.
Aye, if I only had a magic mantle
On which I could fly abroad, a-voyaging,
I would not barter it for the costliest raiment,
Not even for the mantle of a king.

WAGNER: Do not invoke the notorious host
Deployed in streams upon the wind,
Preparing danger in a thousand forms
From every quarter for mankind.
Thrusting upon you from the North
Come fanged spirits with arrow tongues;
From the lands of morning they come parching
To feed themselves upon your lungs;
The South dispatches from the desert
Incendiary hordes against your brain
And the West a swarm which first refreshes,
Then drowns both you and field and plain.
They are glad to listen, adepts at doing harm,
Glad to obey and so throw dust in our eyes;
They make believe that they are sent from heaven
And lisp like angels, telling lies.
But let us move! The world has already gone gray,
The air is beginning to cool and the mist to fall.
It's in the evening one really values home—
But why do you look so astonished, standing there, star-
          ing that way?
What's there to see in the dusk that's worth the trouble?

FAUST: The black dog, do you mark him ranging
     through corn and stubble?

WAGNER: I noticed him long ago; he struck me as
     nothing much.

FAUST: Have a good look at the brute. What do you
     take him for?

WAGNER: For a poodle who, as is the way of such,
Is trailing his master, worrying out the scent.

FAUST: But don't you perceive how in wide spirals
     around us
He is getting nearer and nearer of set intent?
And, unless I'm wrong, a running fire
Eddies behind him in his wake.

WAGNER: I can see nothing but a black poodle;
It must be your eyes have caused this mistake.

FAUST: He is casting, it seems to me, fine nooses of
     magic
About our feet as a snare.

WAGNER: *I* see him leaping round us uncertainly, tim-
      idly,
Finding instead of his master two strangers there.

FAUST: The circle narrows; now he is near.

WAGNER: Just a dog, you see; no phantoms here.
He growls and hesitates, grovels on the green
And wags his tail. Pure dog routine.

FAUST: Heel, sir, heel! Come, fellow, come!

WAGNER: He is a real poodle noodle.
Stand still and he'll sit up and beg;
Speak to him and he's all over you;
Lose something and he'll fetch it quick,
He'll jump in the water after your stick.

FAUST: I think you're right, I cannot find a trace
Of a spirit here; it is all a matter of training.

WAGNER: If a dog is well brought up, a wise man even
Can come to be fond of him in such a case.
Yes, he fully deserves your name upon his collar,
He whom the students have found so apt a scholar.

Faust's Study

(*He enters with the poodle*)

FAUST: I have forsaken field and meadow
      Which night has laid in a deep bed,
      Night that wakes our better soul
      With a holy and foreboding dread.
      Now wild desires are wrapped in sleep
      And all the deeds that burn and break,
      The love of Man is waking now,
      The love of God begins to wake.

Poodle! Quiet! Don't run hither and thither!
Leave my threshold! Why are you snuffling there?
Lie down behind the stove and rest.

Here's a cushion; it's my best.
Out of doors on the mountain paths
You kept us amused by running riot;
But as my protégé at home
You'll only be welcome if you're quiet.

> Ah, when in our narrow cell
> The lamp once more imparts good cheer,
> Then in our bosom—in the heart
> That knows itself—then things grow clear.
> Reason once more begins to speak
> And the blooms of hope once more to spread;
> One hankers for the brooks of life,
> Ah, and for life's fountainhead.

Don't growl, you poodle! That animal sound
Is not in tune with the holy music
By which my soul is girdled round.
We are used to human beings who jeer
At what they do not understand,
Who grouse at the good and the beautiful
Which often causes them much ado;
But must a dog snarl at it too?

But, ah, already, for all my good intentions
I feel contentment ebbing away in my breast.
Why must the stream so soon run dry
And we be left once more athirst?
I have experienced this so often;
Yet this defect has its compensation,
We learn to prize the supernatural
And hanker after revelation,
Which burns most bright and wins assent
Most in the New Testament.
I feel impelled to open the master text
And this once, with true dedication
Take the sacred original
And make in my mother tongue my own translation.

    (*He opens a Bible*)

It is written: In the beginning was the Word.
Here I am stuck at once. Who will help me on?

I am unable to grant the Word such merit,
I must translate it differently
If I am truly illumined by the spirit.
It is written: In the beginning was the Mind.
But why should my pen scour
So quickly ahead? Consider that first line well.
Is it the Mind that effects and creates all things?
It *should* read: In the beginning was the Power.
Yet, even as I am changing what I have writ,
Something warns me not to abide by it.
The spirit prompts me, I see in a flash what I need,
And write: In the beginning was the Deed!

Dog! If we two are to share this room,
Leave off your baying,
Leave off your barking!
I can't have such a fellow staying
Around me causing all this bother.
One of us or the other
Will have to leave the cell.
Well?
I don't really like to eject you so
But the door is open, you may go.

But what? What do I see?
Can this really happen naturally?
Is it a fact or is it a fraud?
My dog is growing so long and broad!
He raises himself mightily,
That is not a dog's anatomy!
What a phantom have I brought to my house!
He already looks like a river horse
With fiery eyes and frightful jaws—
Aha! But I can give you pause!
For such a hybrid out of hell
Solomon's Key is a good spell.

(SPIRITS *are heard in the passage*)

SPIRITS: Captured within there is one of us!
Wait without, follow him none of us!

Like a fox in a snare
An old hell-cat's trembling there.
But on the alert!
Fly against and athwart,
To starboard and port,
And he's out with a spurt!
If help you can take him,
Do not forsake him!
For often, to earn it, he
Helped our fraternity.

  FAUST: First, to confront the beast,
Be the Spell of the Four released;
    Salamander shall glow,
    Undine shall coil,
    Sylph shall vanish
    And gnome shall toil.
One without sense
Of the elements,
Of their force
And proper course,
The spirits would never
Own him for master.
    Vanish in flames,
    Salamander!
    Commingle in babble of streams,
    Undine!
    Shine meteor-like and majestic,
    Sylph!
    Bring help domestic,
    Lubber-fiend! Lubber-fiend!
    Step out of him and make an end!
None of the Four
Is the creature's core.
He lies quite quiet and grins at me,
I have not yet worked him injury.
To exorcise you
I'll have to chastise you.
    Are you, rapscallion,
    A displaced devil?
    This sign can level

Each dark battalion;
Look at this sign!
He swells up already with bristling spine.
You outcast! Heed it—
This name! Can you read it?
The unbegotten one,
Unpronounceable,
Poured throughout Paradise,
Heinously wounded one?
Behind the stove, bound by my spells,
Look, like an elephant it swells,
Filling up all the space and more,
It threatens to melt away in mist,
Down from the ceiling! Down before—
Down at your master's feet! Desist!
You see, I have not proved a liar;
I can burn you up with holy fire!
Do not await
The triply glowing light!
Do not await
My strongest brand of necromancy!

(*The mist subsides and* MEPHISTOPHELES *comes forward from behind the stove, dressed like a traveling scholar.*)

MEPHISTOPHELES: What is the noise about? What
    might the gentleman fancy?

FAUST: So that is what the poodle had inside him!
A traveling scholar? That casus makes me laugh.

MEPHISTOPHELES: My compliments to the learned
    gentleman.
You have put me in a sweat—not half!

FAUST: What is your name?

MEPHISTOPHELES: The question strikes me as petty
For one who holds the Word in such low repute,
Who, far withdrawn from all mere surface,
Aims only at the Essential Root.

FAUST: With you, you gentry, what is essential
The name more often than not supplies,
As is indeed only too patent
When they call you Fly-God, Corrupter, Father of Lies.
All right, who are you then?

MEPHISTOPHELES: A part of that Power
Which always wills evil, always procures good.

FAUST: What do you mean by this conundrum?

MEPHISTOPHELES: I am the Spirit which always denies.
And quite rightly; whatever has a beginning
Deserves to have an undoing;
It would be better if nothing began at all.
Thus everything that you call
Sin, destruction, Evil in short,
Is my own element, my resort.

FAUST: You call yourself a part, yet you stand before
    me whole?

MEPHISTOPHELES: This is the unassuming truth.
Whereas mankind, that little world of fools,
Commonly takes itself for a whole—
I am a part of the Part which in the beginning was all,
A part of the darkness which gave birth to light,
To that haughty light which is struggling now to usurp
The ancient rank and realm of its mother Night,
And yet has no success, try as it will,
Being bound and clamped by bodies still.
It streams from bodies, bodies it beautifies,
A body clogs it when it would run,
And so, I hope, it won't be long
Till, bodies and all, it is undone.

FAUST: Ah, now I know your honorable profession!
You cannot destroy on a large scale,
So you are trying it on a small.

MEPHISTOPHELES: And, candidly, not getting far at all.
That which stands over against the Nothing,
The Something, I mean this awkward world,
For all my endeavors up to date
I have failed to get it under foot
With waves, with storms, with earthquakes, fire—

Sea and land after all stay put.
And this damned stuff, the brood of beasts and men,
There is no coming to grips with them;
I've always buried heaps of them!
And always new blood, fresh blood, circulates again.
So it goes on, it's enough to drive one crazy.
A thousand embryos extricate themselves
From air, from water and from earth
In wet and dry and hot and cold
Had I not made a corner in fire
I should find myself without a berth.

FAUST: So you when faced with the ever stirring,
The creative force, the beneficent,
Counter with your cold devil's fist
Spitefully clenched but impotent.
You curious son of Chaos, why
Not turn your hand to something else?

MEPHISTOPHELES: We will give it our serious
        attention—
But more on that subject by and by.
Might I for this time take my leave?

FAUST: Why you ask I cannot see.
I have already made your acquaintance;
When you feel like it, call on me.
Here is the window, here is the door—
And a chimney too—if it comes to that.

MEPHISTOPHELES: I must confess, there's a slight
        impediment
That stops me making my exit pat,
The pentagram upon your threshold—

FAUST: So the witch's foot is giving you trouble?
Then tell me, since you're worried by that spell,
How did you ever enter, child of Hell?
How was a spirit like you betrayed?

MEPHISTOPHELES: You study that sign! It's not well
        made;
One of its corners, do you see,
The outside one's not quite intact.

FAUST: A happy accident in fact!
Which means you're in my custody?
I did not intend to set a gin.

MEPHISTOPHELES: The dog—he noticed nothing,
    jumping in;
The case has now turned round about
And I, the devil, can't get out.

FAUST: Then why not leave there by the window?

MEPHISTOPHELES: It is a law for devils and phantoms
    all:
By the way that we slip in by the same we must take
    our leave.
One's free in the first, in the second one's a thrall.

FAUST: So Hell itself has its regulations?
That's excellent; a contract in that case
Could be made with you, you gentry—and definite?

MEPHISTOPHELES: What we promise, you will enjoy
    with no reservations,
Nothing will be nipped off from it.
But all this needs a little explaining
And will keep till our next heart-to-heart;
But now I beg and doubly beg you:
Let me, just for now, depart.

FAUST: But wait yet a minute and consent
To tell me first some news of moment.

MEPHISTOPHELES: Let me go now! I'll soon be back
To be questioned to your heart's content.

FAUST: It was not I laid a trap for you,
You thrust your own head in the noose.
A devil in the hand's worth two in hell!
The second time he'll be longer loose.

MEPHISTOPHELES: If you so wish it, I'm prepared
To keep you company and stay;
Provided that by my arts the time
Be to your betterment whiled away.

FAUST: I am in favor, carry on—
But let your art be a pleasing one.

MEPHISTOPHELES: My friend, your senses will have
    more
Gratification in this hour
Than in a year's monotony.
What the delicate spirits sing to you
And the beauties that they bring to you
Are no empty, idle wizardry.
You'll have your sense of smell delighted,
Your palate in due course excited,
Your feelings rapt enchantingly.
Preparation? There's no need,
We are all here. Strike up! Proceed!

  (*The* SPIRITS *sing*)

SPIRITS: Vanish, you darkling
        Arches above him,
        That a more witching
        Blue and enriching
        Sky may look in!
        If only the darkling
        Clouds were unraveled!
        Small stars are sparkling,
        Suns are more gently
        Shining within!
        Spiritual beauty
        Of the children of Heaven
        Swaying and bowing
        Floats in the air,
        Leanings and longings
        Follow them there;
        And ribbons of raiment
        The breezes have caught
        Cover the country,
        Cover the arbor
        Where, drowning in thought,
        Lovers exchange their
        Pledges for life.
        Arbor on arbor!
        Creepers run rife!

Grapes in great wreathing
Clusters are poured into
Vats that are seething,
Wines that are foaming
Pour out in rivulets
Rippling and roaming
Through crystalline stones,
Leaving the sight of
The highlands behind them,
Widening to lakes
Amid the delight of
Green-growing foothills.
And the winged creatures
Sipping their ecstasy,
Sunwards they fly,
Fly to discover
The glittering islands
Which bob on the wave tops
Deceiving the eye.
There we can hear
Huzzaing in chorus,
A landscape of dancers
Extending before us,
All in the open
Free as the air.
Some of them climbing
Over the peaks,
Some of them swimming
Over the lakes,
Or floating in space—
All towards existence,
All towards the distance
Of stars that will love them,
The blessing of grace.

MEPHISTOPHELES: He is asleep. That's fine, you airy,
    dainty youngsters
You have sung him a real cradle song.
For this performance I am in your debt.
You are not yet the man to hold the devil for long.
Play round him with your sweet dream trickeries

And sink him in a sea of untruth!
But to break the spell upon this threshold
What I need now is a rat's tooth.
And I needn't bother to wave a wand,
I can hear one rustling already, he'll soon respond.
The lord of rats, the lord of mice,
Of flies, frogs, bugs and lice,
Commands you to come out of that
And gnaw away this threshold, rat,
While he takes oil and gives it a few—
So there you come hopping? Quick on your cue!
Now get on the job! The obstructing point
Is on the edge and right in front.
One bite more and the work's done.
Now, Faust, till we meet again, dream on!

FAUST (*waking*): Am I defrauded then once more?
Does the throng of spirits vanish away like fog
To prove that the devil appeared to me in a dream
But what escaped was only a dog?

(*The same room. Later*)

FAUST: Who's knocking? Come in! *Now* who wants
  to annoy me?

MEPHISTOPHELES (*outside door*): It's I.

FAUST: Come in!

MEPHISTOPHELES (*outside door*): You must say "Come
  in" three times.

FAUST: Come in, then!

MEPHISTOPHELES (*entering*): Thank you; you overjoy
  me.
We two, I hope, we shall be good friends;
To chase those megrims of yours away
I am here like a fine young squire today,
In a suit of scarlet trimmed with gold
And a little cape of stiff brocade,
With a cock's feather in my hat
And at my side a long sharp blade,
And the most succinct advice I can give

Is that you dress up just like me,
So that uninhibited and free
You may find out what it means to live.

FAUST: The pain of earth's constricted life, I fancy,
Will pierce me still, whatever my attire;
I am too old for mere amusement,
Too young to be without desire.
How can the world dispel my doubt?
You must do without, you must do without!
That is the everlasting song
Which rings in every ear, which rings,
And which to us our whole life long
Every hour hoarsely sings.
I wake in the morning only to feel appalled,
My eyes with bitter tears could run
To see the day which in its course
Will not fulfill a wish for me, not one;
The day which whittles away with obstinate carping
All pleasures—even those of anticipation,
Which makes a thousand grimaces to obstruct
My heart when it is stirring in creation.
And again, when night comes down, in anguish
I must stretch out upon my bed
And again no rest is granted me
For wild dreams fill my mind with dread.
The God who dwells within my bosom
Can make my inmost soul react;
The God who sways my every power
Is powerless with external fact.
And so existence weighs upon my breast
And I long for death and life—life I detest.

MEPHISTOPHELES: Yet death is never a wholly welcome
        guest.

FAUST: O happy is he whom death in the dazzle of
        victory
Crowns with the bloody laurel in the battling swirl!
Or he whom after the mad and breakneck dance
He comes upon in the arms of a girl!
O to have sunk away, delighted, deleted,
Before the Spirit of the Earth, before his might!

MEPHISTOPHELES: Yet I know someone who failed to
	drink
A brown juice on a certain night.

FAUST: Your hobby is espionage—is it not?

MEPHISTOPHELES: Oh I'm not omniscient—but I know
	a lot.

FAUST: Whereas that tumult in my soul
Was stilled by sweet familiar chimes
Which cozened the child that yet was in me
With echoes of more happy times,
I now curse all things that encompass
The soul with lures and jugglery
And bind it in this dungeon of grief
With trickery and flattery.
Cursed in advance be the high opinion
That serves our spirit for a cloak!
Cursed be the dazzle of appearance
Which bows our senses to its yoke!
Cursed be the lying dreams of glory,
The illusion that our name survives!
Cursed be the flattering things we own,
Servants and plows, children and wives!
Cursed be Mammon when with his treasures
He makes us play the adventurous man
Or when for our luxurious pleasures
He duly spreads the soft divan!
A curse on the balsam of the grape!
A curse on the love that rides for a fall!
A curse on hope! A curse on faith!
And a curse on patience most of all!

(The invisible SPIRITS *sing again)*

SPIRITS: Woe! Woe!
	You have destroyed it!
	The beautiful world;
	By your violent hand
	'Tis downward hurled!
	A half-god has dashed it asunder!

From under
We bear off the rubble to nowhere
And ponder
Sadly the beauty departed.
Magnipotent
One among men,
Magnificent
Build it again,
Build it again in your breast!
Let a new course of life
Begin
With vision abounding
And new songs resounding
To welcome it in!

MEPHISTOPHELES: These are the juniors
Of my faction.
Hear how precociously they counsel
Pleasure and action.
Out and away
From your lonely day
Which dries your senses and your juices
Their melody seduces.

Stop playing with your grief which battens
Like a vulture on your life, your mind!
The worst of company would make you feel
That you are a man among mankind.
Not that it's really my proposition
To shove you among the common men;
Though I'm not one of the Upper Ten,
If you would like a coalition
With me for your career through life,
I am quite ready to fit in,
I'm yours before you can say knife.
I am your comrade;
If you so crave,
I am your servant, I am your slave.

FAUST: And what have I to undertake in return?

MEPHISTOPHELES: Oh it's early days to discuss what
that is.

FAUST: No, no, the devil is an egoist
And ready to do nothing gratis
Which is to benefit a stranger.
Tell me your terms and don't prevaricate!
A servant like you in the house is a danger.

MEPHISTOPHELES: I will bind myself to your service
    in this world,
To be at your beck and never rest nor slack;
When we meet again on the other side,
In the same coin you shall pay me back.

FAUST: The other side gives me little trouble;
First batter this present world to rubble,
Then the other may rise—if that's the plan.
This earth is where my springs of joy have started,
And this sun shines on me when broken-hearted;
If I can first from them be parted,
Then let happen what will and can!
I wish to hear no more about it—
Whether there too men hate and love
Or whether in those spheres too, in the future,
There is a Below or an Above.

MEPHISTOPHELES: With such an outlook you can risk it.
Sign on the line! In these next days you will get
Ravishing samples of my arts;
I am giving you what never man saw yet.

FAUST: Poor devil, can *you* give anything ever?
Was a human spirit in its high endeavor
Even once understood by one of your breed?
Have you got food which fails to feed?
Or red gold which, never at rest,
Like mercury runs away through the hand?
A game at which one never wins?
A girl who, even when on my breast,
Pledges herself to my neighbor with her eyes?
The divine and lovely delight of honor
Which falls like a falling star and dies?
Show me the fruits which, before they are plucked, decay
And the trees which day after day renew their green!

MEPHISTOPHELES: Such a commission doesn't alarm
     me,
I have such treasures to purvey.
But, my good friend, the time draws on when we
Should be glad to feast at our ease on something good

FAUST: If ever I stretch myself on a bed of ease,
Then I am finished! Is that understood?
If ever your flatteries can coax me
To be pleased with myself, if ever you cast
A spell of pleasure that can hoax me—
Then let *that* day be my last!
That's my wager!

MEPHISTOPHELES: Done!

FAUST: Let's shake!
If ever I say to the passing moment
"Linger a while! Thou art so fair!"
Then you may cast me into fetters,
I will gladly perish then and there!
Then you may set the death bell tolling,
Then from my service you are free,
The clock may stop, its hand may fall,
And that be the end of time for me!

MEPHISTOPHELES: Think what you're saying, we shall
     not forget it.

FAUST: And you are fully within your rights;
I have made no mad or outrageous claim.
If I stay as I am, I am a slave—
Whether yours or another's, it's all the same.

MEPHISTOPHELES: I shall this very day at the College
     Banquet
Enter your service with no more ado,
But just one point—As a life-and-death insurance
I must trouble you for a line or two.

FAUST: So you, you pedant, you too like things in
     writing?
Have you never known a man? Or a man's word? Never?
Is it not enough that my word of mouth
Puts all my days in bond forever?
Does not the world rage on in all its streams

And shall a promise hamper *me*?
Yet this illusion reigns within our hearts
And from it who would be gladly free?
Happy the man who can inwardly keep his word;
Whatever the cost, he will not be loath to pay!
But a parchment, duly inscribed and sealed,
Is a bogey from which all wince away.
The word dies on the tip of the pen
And wax and leather lord it then.
What do you, evil spirit, require?
Bronze, marble, parchment, paper?
Quill or chisel or pencil of slate?
You may choose whichever you desire.

   MEPHISTOPHELES: How can you so exaggerate
With such a hectic rhetoric?
Any little snippet is quite good—
And you sign it with one little drop of blood.

   FAUST: If that is enough and is some use,
One may as well pander to your fad.

   MEPHISTOPHELES: Blood is a very special juice.

   FAUST: Only do not fear that I shall break this contract.
What I promise is nothing more
Than what all my powers are striving for.
I have puffed myself up too much, it is only
Your sort that really fits my case.
The great Earth Spirit has despised me
And Nature shuts the door in my face.
The thread of thought is snapped asunder,
I have long loathed knowledge in all its fashions.
In the depths of sensuality
Let us now quench our glowing passions!
And at once make ready every wonder
Of unpenetrated sorcery!
Let us cast ourselves into the torrent of time,
Into the whirl of eventfulness,
Where disappointment and success,
Pleasure and pain may chop and change
As chop and change they will and can;
It is restless action makes the man.

MEPHISTOPHELES: No limit is fixed for you, no bound;
If you'd like to nibble at everything
Or to seize upon something flying round—
Well, may you have a run for your money!
But seize your chance and don't be funny!

FAUST: I've told you, it is no question of happiness.
The most painful joy, enamored hate, enlivening
Disgust—I devote myself to all excess.
My breast, now cured of its appetite for knowledge,
From now is open to all and every smart,
And what is allotted to the whole of mankind
That will I sample in my inmost heart,
Grasping the highest and lowest with my spirit,
Piling men's weal and woe upon my neck,
To extend myself to embrace all human selves
And to founder in the end, like them, a wreck.

MEPHISTOPHELES: O believe *me,* who have been
        chewing
These iron rations many a thousand year,
No human being can digest
This stuff, from the cradle to the bier.
This universe—believe a devil—
Was made for no one but a god!
He exists in eternal light
But *us* he has brought into the darkness
While *your* sole portion is day and night.

FAUST: I will all the same!

MEPHISTOPHELES: That's very nice.
There's only one thing I find wrong;
Time is short, art is long.
You could do with a little artistic advice.
Confederate with one of the poets
And let him flog his imagination
To heap all virtues on your head,
A head with such a reputation:
Lion's bravery,
Stag's velocity,
Fire of Italy,
Northern tenacity.

Let *him* find out the secret art
Of combining craft with a noble heart
And of being in love like a young man,
Hotly, but working to a plan.
Such a person——*I'd* like to meet him;
"Mr. Microcosm" is how I'd greet him.

FAUST: What am I then if fate must bar
My efforts to reach that crown of humanity
After which all my senses strive?

MEPHISTOPHELES: You are in the end . . . what you are.
You can put on full-bottomed wigs with a million locks,
You can put on stilts instead of your socks,
You remain for ever what you are.

FAUST: I feel my endeavors have not been worth a pin
When I raked together the treasures of the human mind,
If at the end I but sit down to find
No new force welling up within.
I have not a hair's breadth more of height,
I am no nearer the Infinite.

MEPHISTOPHELES: My very good sir, you look at things
Just in the way that people do;
We must be cleverer than that
Or the joys of life will escape from you.
Hell! You have surely hands and feet,
Also a head and you-know-what;
The pleasures I gather on the wing,
Are they less mine? Of course they're not!
Suppose I can afford six stallions,
I can add that horsepower to my score
And dash along and be a proper man
As if my legs were twenty-four.
So good-by to thinking! On your toes!
The world's before us. Quick! Here goes!
I tell you, a chap who's intellectual
Is like a beast on a blasted heath
Driven in circles by a demon
While a fine green meadow lies round beneath.

FAUST: How do we start?

MEPHISTOPHELES: We just say go—and skip.
But please get ready for this pleasure trip.

(*Exit* FAUST)

Only look down on knowledge and reason,
The highest gifts that men can prize,
Only allow the spirt of lies
To confirm you in magic and illusion,
And then I have you body and soul.
Fate has given this man a spirit
Which is always pressing onwards, beyond control,
And whose mad striving overleaps
All joys of the earth between pole and pole.
Him shall I drag through the wilds of life
And through the flats of meaninglessness,
I shall make him flounder and gape and stick
And to tease his insatiableness
Hang meat and drink in the air before his watering lips;
In vain he will pray to slake his inner thirst,
And even had he not sold himself to the devil
He would be equally accursed.

(*A* STUDENT *is announced.* MEPHISTOPHELES *puts on*
FAUST's *cap and gown. The* STUDENT *enters, assuming he
is meeting the master.*)

STUDENT: A freshman, here arrived today,
I come, conditioned to obey,
To meet a man whose reputation
Wins universal veneration.

MEPHISTOPHELES: A most polite and flattering view!
You see a man like quite a few.
Have you been round my colleagues yet?

STUDENT: It's your help, please, I crave to get.
I come endowed with all good traits,
A moderate purse, a heart ablaze;
Mother would hardly consent to college
But I *had* to leave home for the sake of knowledge.

MEPHISTOPHELES: You're in the right place here, don't
        doubt.

STUDENT: Frankly, already I wish I were out.
These lecture rooms, these walls that cramp me,
Are just the sort of thing to damp me.
An unimagined lack of space—
Not a tree, not a green thing in the place!
And in those halls where the students sit
I lose my hearing, sight, and wit.

MEPHISTOPHELES: Habit will cure all that, you'll find.
Just so the child that, at the start,
When offered its mother's breast declined,
Soon feeds itself with all its heart.
So you will discover, day by day,
More joy in Wisdom's milky way.

STUDENT: To hang on Wisdom's neck is my ambition—
But how do I attain that high position?

MEPHISTOPHELES: Inform me, before going on,
What Faculty have you fixed upon?

STUDENT: I wish to reach the heights of learning,
To comprehend what needs discerning
In earth and heaven, each fact and action
Of Nature and the Sciences.

MEPHISTOPHELES: You're on the dead right track in
this—
But be on your guard against distraction.

STUDENT: I'm on the target heart and soul—
Though truly I'd have no aversion
To a few hours off, an occasional stroll
On a lovely summer day's excursion.

MEPHISTOPHELES: Use well your time—so fast the
minutes drain it;
Yet Method teaches how to gain it,
And so one word, friend, in your ear:
Begin by studying Logic here.
That breaks the spirit nicely in,
A hair shirt fitting like a skin,
So that it creeps, with prudence fraught,
Along the arterial roads of thought
And does not zigzag through the mire
A will o' the wisp, a fatuous fire.

Then many a day you needs must learn
That what you lately could discern
Bang off, like swallowing meat or drink,
You now need syllogisms to think.
It's true: the fantasy of thought
Is like a master loom so wrought
One treadle moves a world of thread;
The shuttles forward, backward, going,
The threads unseen keep flowing, flowing;
Press once—a thousand such are wed.
Thus your philosopher, you know,
Steps in to prove it must be so:
The first was so, the second too,
Therefore the third and fourth are true,
But if the first and second were missed—
Third and fourth would not exist.
Students throughout the world believe it
But, given this weft, they cannot weave it.
To know and describe a living thing, endeavor
First to expel its spirit for ever;
Then hold the parts and count the cost—
The spiritual link is lost, is lost.
Chemistry gives this a long Latin name
But unconsciously fools herself all the same.

    STUDENT: This is slightly past my understanding.

    MEPHISTOPHELES: Quite soon you'll find your mind's
        expanding;
Once you have learned that all is reducible
To labels in a semantic crucible.

    STUDENT: All this makes me feel so giddy and dull,
Like a millwheel turning in my skull.

    MEPHISTOPHELES: And next, before all else worth
        mention,
Metaphysics claims your full attention.
And here you must take profoundest pains
To grasp what is not for human brains;
What enters the brain or enters not,
A splendid word will mark the spot.
But, above all, for this half year

Your discipline must be severe.
Five lectures is your daily rule;
When the clock strikes be there in school.
Come well prepared for what comes next
After close study of the text,
To check the better that the sage
Dictates no word that was not on the page;
Then ply your quill, as much engrossed
As if he were the Holy Ghost.

STUDENT: This warning you need not redouble.
I see its usefulness all right,
For what one has in black and white
One can take home—and no more trouble.

MEPHISTOPHELES: Still, you must choose a Faculty.

STUDENT: For Jurisprudence, now, I lack the
    disposition.

MEPHISTOPHELES: I cannot blame you for lacking *that*
    ambition;
I know this branch of methodology.
Both legislation and litigation
Like a disease that haunts a race
Drag down from generation to generation
And softly slink from place to place.
Sense turns to nonsense, gifts to curses;
Alas, you had forebears on this earth.
The debts that were owed you at your birth
Are those that no man reimburses.

STUDENT: My allergy's heightened by your speech.
Happy the pupils whom *you* teach!
Why, I could almost turn theological student.

MEPHISTOPHELES: I wouldn't advise you to be
    imprudent.
This science is a confusing field,
To avoid the path of error needs much labor
And hereabouts much poison lies concealed,
Hardly to be distinguished from the true physic, its
    neighbor.
And here again *one* master's much to be preferred
If you swear only by his word.

Stick on the whole to words, stick fast,
You'll find the safe gate safely past
Into the Temple of Certainty.

STUDENT: Yet the word must have some meaning
        presumably.

MEPHISTOPHELES: Of course. But one must not give
        one's brains too fierce a racking;
It's just when you find a meaning's lacking
That dead on cue a word comes helpfully.
Words make for first-rate disputation,
A system needs the word's foundation,
Words command credence in full quota,
A word cannot be changed by an iota.

STUDENT: Excuse me, I'm taking up your time with
        questions—
But just one more to trouble you:
Would you in regard to Medicine too
Help me with one or two suggestions?
Three years will be too quickly past
And the field, my God, is far too vast.
If one has only a hint, you see,
One can feel one's way where the ground is level.

MEPHISTOPHELES (to himself): This arid accent is
        choking me,
I must revert to my role of devil.
(to student) The spirit of Medicine's quickly apprehended,
The two worlds, great and small, you must peruse,
Then let things go when all is ended
As God may choose.
In vain to ramble round in scientific wise,
Each of us learns no more than learn he can;
Who grasps the moment as it flies,
He is the proper man.
Besides, your figure is pretty good,
Your courage will not need the bellows,
Just trust yourself—it's understood
You will be trusted by your fellows.
Above all learn how women are tended:
All that eternal moan and groan—

One point alone
Is where their thousand ills are mended,
And show respect but not too much,
You'll find they all are in your clutch.
First put some letters after your name and make them
Believe most other crafts degrees in the rear;
Then all those perquisites are yours—so up and take
       them—
For which another flatters many a year;
Learn how to press their pulse and please them
And then, with fiery subtle glances, squeeze them
Boldly around the slender waist
To see how tightly it is laced.

    STUDENT: That sounds like sense. At least one sees the
        where and how.

    MEPHISTOPHELES: Gray, my good friend, gray is all
        theory now
And green is Life's own golden tree.

    STUDENT: I swear to you, it's like a dream to me.
Would you some other time, perhaps, be so kind
As to show me *all* the contents of your mind?

    MEPHISTOPHELES: As far as in me lies, I will.

    STUDENT: I cannot possibly leave you till
I hand you my autograph album here to sign.
Grant me this favor—don't decline!

    MEPHISTOPHELES: With pleasure.

    (*Writes and returns it*)

    STUDENT (*reading*): Eritis sicut Deus, scientes bonum et
        malum.

    (*He closes the book respectfully and takes his leave*)

    MEPHISTOPHELES: Just follow the old saying and follow
        my cousin the Snake—
Some day your likeness to God will certainly cause you to
        quake.

    (*Re-enter* FAUST)

    FAUST: And now, where are we going?

MEPHISTOPHELES: Wherever you please.
The small world, then the great for us.
With what pleasure and what profit
You will roister through the syllabus!

FAUST: But I, with this long beard of mine,
I lack the easy social touch,
I know the experiment is doomed;
Out in the world I never could fit in much.
I feel so small in company
I'll be embarrassed constantly.

MEPHISTOPHELES: My friend, it will solve itself, any
        such misgiving;
Just trust yourself and you'll learn the art of living.

FAUST: Well, then, how do we leave home?
Where are your grooms? Your coach and horses?

MEPHISTOPHELES: We merely spread this mantle wide,
It will bear us off on airy courses.
But do not on this noble voyage
Cumber yourself with heavy baggage.
A little inflammable gas which I'll prepare
Will lift us quickly into the air.
If we travel light we shall cleave the sky like a knife.
Congratulations on your new course of life!

The Witch's Kitchen

*(Every sort of witch prop. A large cauldron hangs over
the fire. Monkeys sit around it, seen through the fumes)*

MEPHISTOPHELES: Look, what a pretty species of
        monkey!
She is the kitchen maid, he is the flunky.
It seems your mistress isn't at home?

MONKEYS;   Out at a rout!
                Out and about!
                By the chimney spout!

MEPHISTOPHELES: How long does she keep it up at
        night?

MONKEYS: As long as we warm our paws at this fire.

MEPHISTOPHELES: How do you like these delicate
    animals?

FAUST: I never saw such an outré sight.
I find it nauseating, this crazy witchcraft!
Do you promise me that I shall improve
In this cesspit of insanity?
Do I need advice from an old hag?
And can this filthy brew remove
Thirty years from my age? O vanity,
If you know nothing better than this!
My hope has already vanished away.
Surely Nature, surely a noble spirit
Has brought some better balm to the light of day?

MEPHISTOPHELES: My friend, you once more talk to
    the point.
There is also a natural means of rejuvenation;
But that is written in another book
And is a chapter that needs some explanation.

FAUST: I want to know it.

MEPHISTOPHELES: Right. There is a means
    requires
No money, no physician, and no witch:
Away with you this moment back to the land,
And there begin to dig and ditch,
Confine yourself, confine your mind,
In a narrow round, ever repeating,
Let your diet be of the simplest kind,
Live with the beasts like a beast and do not think it cheat-
    ing
To use your own manure to insure your crops are weighty!
Believe me, that is the best means
To keep you young till you are eighty.

FAUST: I am not used to it, I cannot change
My nature and take the spade in hand.
The narrow life is not my style at all.

MEPHISTOPHELES: Then it's a job for the witch to
    arrange.

FAUST: The hag—but why do we need just her?
Can you yourself not brew the drink?

MEPHISTOPHELES: A pretty pastime! I'd prefer
To build a thousand bridges in that time.
It is not only art and science
That this work needs but patience too.
A quiet spirit is busy at it for years
And time but fortifies the subtle brew.
And the most wonderful ingredients
Go into it—you couldn't fake it!
The devil taught it her, I admit;
The devil, however, cannot make it.
Tell me, you monkeys, you damned puppets,
What are you doing with that great globe?

HE-MONKEY: This is the world:
                    It rises and falls
                    And rolls every minute;
                    It rings like glass—
                    But how soon it breaks!
                    And there's nothing in it.
                    It glitters here
                    And here still more:
                    I am alive!
                    O my son, my dear,
                    Keep away, keep away!
                    You are bound to die!
                    The shards are sharp,
                    It was made of clay.

(FAUST *has meanwhile been gazing in a mirror*)

FAUST: What do I see in this magic mirror?
What a heavenly image to appear!
O Love, lend me the swiftest of your wings
And waft me away into her sphere!
But, alas, when I do not keep this distance,
If to go nearer I but dare
I can see her only as if there were mist in the air—
The fairest image of a woman!
But can Woman be so fair?
In that shape in the mirror must I see the quintessence
Of all the heavens—reclining there?
Can such a thing be found on earth?

MEPHISTOPHELES: Naturally, when a God works six
    days like a black
And at the end of it slaps himself on the back,
Something should come of it of some worth.
For this occasion look your fill.
I can smell you out a sweetheart as good as this,
And happy the man who has the luck
To bear her home to wedded bliss.

   (*The* WITCH *enters down the chimney—violently*)

WITCH: What goes on here?
             Who are you two?
             What d'you want here?
             Who has sneaked through?
             May the fever of fire
             Harrow your marrow!

MEPHISTOPHELES: Don't you know me, you bag of
    bones? You monster, you!
Don't you know your lord and master?
What prevents me striking you
And your monkey spirits, smashing you up like plaster?
Has my red doublet no more claim to fame?
Can you not recognize the cock's feather?
Have I concealed my countenance?
Must I myself announce my name?

WITCH: My lord, excuse this rude reception.
It is only I miss your cloven foot.
And where is your usual brace of ravens?

MEPHISTOPHELES: I'll forgive you this once, as an
    exception;
Admittedly some time has passed
Since we two saw each other last.
Culture too, which is licking the whole world level,
Has latterly even reached the devil.
The Nordic spook no longer commands a sale;
Where can you see horns, claws or tail?
And as regards the foot, which is my *sine qua non,*
It would prejudice me in the social sphere;
Accordingly, as many young men have done,
I have worn false calves this many a year.

WITCH: Really and truly I'm knocked flat
To see Lord Satan here again!

MEPHISTOPHELES: Woman, you must not call me that!

WITCH: Why! What harm is there in the name?

MEPHISTOPHELES: Satan has long been a myth without
          sense or sinew;
Not that it helps humanity all the same,
They are quit of the Evil One but the evil ones continue.
You may call me the Noble Baron, that should do;
I am a cavalier among other cavaliers,
You needn't doubt my blood is blue—

(*He makes an indecent gesture*)

WITCH: Ha! Ha! Always true to type!
You still have the humor of a guttersnipe!

MEPHISTOPHELES: Observe my technique, my friend—
          not a single hitch;
This is the way to get round a witch.

WITCH: Now tell me, gentlemen, what do you want?

MEPHISTOPHELES: A good glass of your well-known
          juice.
And please let us have your oldest vintage;
When it's been kept it's twice the use.

WITCH: Delighted! Why, there's some here on the
          shelf—
I now and then take a nip myself—
And, besides, this bottle no longer stinks;
You're welcome while I've a drop to give.
(*aside*) But, if this man is unprepared when he drinks,
You very well know he has not an hour to live.

MEPHISTOPHELES: He's a good friend and it should set
          him up;
I'd gladly grant him the best of your kitchen,
So draw your circle and do your witching
And give the man a decent cup.

(*The* WITCH *begins her conjuration*)

FAUST: But, tell me, how will this mend my status?
These lunatic gestures, this absurd apparatus,

This most distasteful conjuring trick—
I've known it all, it makes me sick.

   MEPHISTOPHELES: Pooh, that's just fooling, get it in
      focus,
And don't be such a prig for goodness' sake!
As a doctor she must do her hocus-pocus
So that when you have drunk your medicine it will take.

   WITCH: The lofty power
          That is wisdom's dower,
          Concealed from great and clever,
          Don't use your brain
          And that's your gain—
          No trouble whatsoever.

   FAUST: What nonsense is she saying to us?
My head is splitting; I've the sensation
Of listening to a hundred thousand
Idiots giving a mass recitation.

   MEPHISTOPHELES: Enough, enough, you excellent
      Sibyl!
Give us your drink and fill the cup
Full to the brim and don't delay!
This draught will do my friend no injury;
He is a man of more than one degree
And has drunk plenty in his day.

   (*The* WITCH *gives* FAUST *the cup*)

Now lower it quickly. Bottoms up!
And your heart will begin to glow and perk.
Now out of the circle! You mustn't rest.

   WITCH: I hope the little drink will work.

   MEPHISTOPHELES (*to* WITCH): And you, if there's
      anything you want, all right;
Just mention it to me on Walpurgis Night.
(*to* FAUST) Come now, follow me instantly!
You've got to perspire, it's necessary,
That the drug may pervade you inside and out.
I can teach you later to value lordly leisure
And you soon will learn with intensest pleasure
How Cupid stirs within and bounds about.

FAUST: Just one more look, one quick look, in the
     mirror!
That woman was too fair to be true.

MEPHISTOPHELES: No, no! The paragon of womanhood
Will soon be revealed in the flesh to you.
(*aside*) With a drink like this in you, take care—
You'll soon see Helens everywhere.

In the Street

(FAUST *accosts* GRETCHEN *as she passes*)

FAUST: My pretty young lady, might I venture
To offer you my arm and my escort too?

GRETCHEN: I'm not a young lady nor am I pretty
And I can get home without help from you.

(*She releases herself and goes off*)

FAUST: By heaven, she's beautiful, this child!
I have never seen her parallel.
So decorous, so virtuous,
And just a little pert as well.
The light of her cheek, her lip so red,
I shall remember till I'm dead!
The way that she cast down her eye
Is stamped on my heart as with a die;
And the way that she got rid of me
Was a most ravishing thing to see!

(*Enter* MEPHISTOPHELES)

Listen to me! Get me that girl!

MEPHISTOPHELES: Which one?

FAUST: The one that just went
    past.

MEPHISTOPHELES: She? She was coming from her
        priest,
Absolved from her sins one and all;
I'd crept up near the confessional.
An innocent thing. Innocent? Yes!
At church with nothing to confess!
Over that girl I have no power.

FAUST: Yet she's fourteen if she's an hour.

MEPHISTOPHELES: Why, you're talking like Randy
        Dick
Who covets every lovely flower
And all the favors, all the laurels,
He fancies are for him to pick;
But it doesn't always work out like that.

FAUST: My dear Professor of Ancient Morals,
Spare me your trite morality!
I tell you straight—and hear me right—
Unless this object of delight
Lies in my arms this very night,
At midnight we part company.

MEPHISTOPHELES: Haven't you heard: more haste less
        speed?
A fortnight is the least I need
Even to work up an occasion.

FAUST: If I had only seven hours clear,
I should not need the devil here
To bring *this* quest to consummation.

MEPHISTOPHELES: It's almost French, your line of talk;
I only ask you not to worry.
Why make your conquest in a hurry?
The pleasure is less by a long chalk
Than when you first by hook and by crook
Have squeezed your doll and molded her,
Using all manner of poppycock
That foreign novels keep in stock.

FAUST: I am keen enough without all that.

MEPHISTOPHELES: Now, joking apart and without
        aspersion,

You cannot expect, I tell you flat,
This beautiful child in quick reversion.
Immune to all direct attack—
We must lay our plots behind her back.

FAUST: Get me something of my angel's!
Carry me to her place of rest!
Get me a garter of my love's!
Get me a kerchief from her breast!

MEPHISTOPHELES: That you may see the diligent
        fashion
In which I shall abet your passion,
We won't let a moment waste away,
I will take you to her room today.

FAUST: And I shall see her? Have her?

MEPHISTOPHELES: No!
She will be visiting a neighbor.
But you in the meanwhile, quite alone,
Can stay in her aura in her room
And feast your fill on joys to come.

FAUST: Can we go now?

MEPHISTOPHELES: It is still too soon.

FAUST: Then a present for her! Get me one!

(*Exit* FAUST)

MEPHISTOPHELES: Presents already? Fine. A certain
        hit!
I know plenty of pretty places
And of long-buried jewel cases;
I must take stock of them a bit.

Gretchen's Room

GRETCHEN (*alone, doing her hair*): I'd give a lot to be
        able to say
Who the gentleman was today.
He cut a fine figure certainly

And is sprung from the nobility;
His face showed that—Besides, you see,
He'd otherwise not have behaved so forwardly.

(*She goes out; then* MEPHISTOPHELES *and* FAUST *enter*)

MEPHISTOPHELES: Come in—very quietly—Only come
in!

FAUST (*after a silence*): I ask you: please leave me
alone!

MEPHISTOPHELES: Not all girls keep their room so
clean.

FAUST (*looking around*): Welcome, sweet gleaming of
the gloaming
That through this sanctuary falls aslope!
Seize on my heart, sweet fever of love
That lives and languishes on the dews of hope!
What a feeling of quiet breathes around me,
Of order, of contentedness!
What fullness in this poverty,
And in this cell what blessedness!

Here I could while away hour after hour.
It was here, O Nature, that your fleeting dreams
Brought this born angel to full flower.
Here lay the child and the warm life
Filled and grew in her gentle breast,
And here the pure and holy threads
Wove a shape of the heavenliest.

And you! What brought you here today?
Why do I feel this deep dismay?
What do you want here? Why is your heart so sore?
Unhappy Faust! You are Faust no more.

Is this an enchanted atmosphere?
To have her at once was all my aim,
Yet I feel my will dissolve in a lovesick dream.
Are we the sport of every current of air?

And were she this moment to walk in,
You would pay for this outrage, how you would pay!
The big man, now, alas, so small,
Would lie at her feet melted away.

MEPHISTOPHELES: Quick! I can see her coming below.

FAUST: Out, yes out! I'll never come back!

MEPHISTOPHELES: Here is a casket, it's middling heavy,
I picked it up in a place I know.
Only put it at once here in the cupboard,
I swear she won't believe her eyes;
I put some nice little trinkets in it
In order to win a different prize.
Still child is child and a game's a game.

FAUST: I don't know; shall I?

MEPHISTOPHELES: You ask? For shame!
Do you perhaps intend to keep the spoil?
Then I advise Your Lustfulness
To save these hours that are so precious
And save me any further toil.
I hope you aren't avaricious.
After scratching my head so much and twisting my
        hands—

(*He puts the casket in the cupboard*)

Now quick! We depart!
In order to sway the dear young thing
To meet the dearest wish of your heart;
And *you* assume
A look that belongs to the lecture room,
As if Physics and Metaphysics too
Stood gray as life in front of you!
Come on!

(*They go out; then* GRETCHEN *reappears*)

GRETCHEN: It is so sultry, so fusty here,
And it's not even so warm outside.
I feel as if I don't know what—

I wish my mother would appear.
I'm trembling all over from top to toe—
I'm a silly girl to get frightened so.

(*She sings as she undresses*)

> There was a king in Thule
> Was faithful to the grave,
> To whom his dying lady
> A golden winecup gave.
>
> He drained it at every banquet—
> A treasure none could buy;
> Whenever he filled and drank it
> The tears o'erflowed his eye.
>
> And when his days were numbered
> He numbered land and pelf;
> He left his heir his kingdom,
> The cup he kept himself.
>
> He sat at the royal table
> With his knights of high degree
> In the lofty hall of his fathers
> In the castle on the sea.
>
> There stood the old man drinking
> The last of the living glow,
> Then threw the sacred winecup
> Into the waves below.
>
> He saw it fall and falter
> And founder in the main;
> His eyelids fell, thereafter
> He never drank again.

(*She opens the cupboard to put away her clothes and sees the casket*)

How did this lovely casket get in here?
I locked the cupboard, I'm quite sure.
But what can be in it? It's very queer.

Perhaps someone left it here in pawn
And my mother gave him a loan on it.
Here's a little key tied on with tape—
I've a good mind to open it.
What is all this? My God! But see!
I have never come across such things.
Jewels—that would suit a countess
At a really grand festivity.
To whom can these splendid things belong?

(*She tries on the jewels and looks in the looking glass*)

If only the earrings belonged to me!
They make one look quite differently.
What is the use of looks and youth?
That's all very well and fine in truth
But people leave it all alone,
They praise you and pity you in one;
Gold is their sole
Concern and goal.
Alas for us who have none!

(*Elsewhere and later*. MEPHISTOPHELES *joins* FAUST)

MEPHISTOPHELES: By every despised love! By the
    elements of hell!
I wish I knew something worse to provide a curse as well!

FAUST: What's the trouble? What's biting you?
I never saw such a face in my life.

MEPHISTOPHELES: I would sell myself to the devil this
    minute
If only I weren't a devil too.

FAUST: What is it? Are you mad? Or sick?
It suits you to rage like a lunatic!

MEPHISTOPHELES: Imagine! The jewels that Gretchen
    got,
A priest has gone and scooped the lot!
Her mother got wind of it and she

At once had the horrors secretly.
That woman has a nose beyond compare,
She's always snuffling in the Book of Prayer,
And can tell by how each object smells
If it is sacred or something else;
So the scent of the jewels tells her clear
There's nothing very blessed here.
"My child," she cries, "unrighteous wealth
Invests the soul, infects the health.
We'll dedicate it to the Virgin
And *she'll* make heavenly manna burgeon!"
Gretchen's face, you could see it fall;
She thought: "It's a gift horse after all,
And he *can't* be lacking in sanctity
Who brought it here so handsomely!"
The mother had a priest along
And had hardly started up her song
Before he thought things looked all right
And said: "Very proper and above board!
Self-control is its own reward.
The Church has an excellent appetite,
She has swallowed whole countries and the question
Has never arisen of indigestion.
Only the Church, my dears, can take
Ill-gotten goods without stomach-ache!"

FAUST: That is a custom the world through,
A Jew and a king observe it too.

MEPHISTOPHELES: So brooch, ring, chain he swipes
     at speed
As if they were merely chicken feed,
Thanks them no more and no less for the casket
Than for a pound of nuts in a basket,
Promises Heaven will provide
And leaves them extremely edified.

FAUST: And Gretchen?

MEPHISTOPHELES: Sits and worries there,
Doesn't know what to do and doesn't care,
Thinks day and night on gold and gem,
Still more on the man who presented them.

FAUST: My sweetheart's grief distresses me.
Get her more jewels instantly!
The first lot barely deserved the name.

MEPHISTOPHELES: So the gentleman thinks it all a
              nursery game!

FAUST: Do what I tell you and get it right;
Don't let her neighbor out of your sight.
And don't be a sloppy devil; contrive
A new set of jewels. Look alive!

(*Exit* FAUST)

MEPHISTOPHELES: Yes, my dear sir, with all my heart.
This is the way that a fool in love
Puffs away to amuse his lady
Sun and moon and the stars above.

Martha's House

MARTHA (*alone*): My dear husband, God forgive him,
His behavior has *not* been without a flaw!
Careers away out into the world
And leaves me alone to sleep on straw.
And yet I never trod on his toes,
I loved him with all my heart, God knows. (*Sobs*)
Perhaps he is even dead—O fate!
If I'd only a death certificate!

(GRETCHEN *enters*)

GRETCHEN: Frau Martha!
MARTHA: Gretchen! What's up?
GRETCHEN: My legs are sinking under me,
I've just discovered in my cupboard
Another casket—of ebony,
And things inside it, such a store,
Far richer than the lot before.

MARTHA: You musn't mention it to your mother;
She'd take it straight to the priest—like the other.

GRETCHEN: But only look! Just look at this!

MARTHA: O you lucky little Miss!

GRETCHEN: I daren't appear in the street, I'm afraid,
Or in church either, thus arrayed.

MARTHA: Just you visit me often here
And put on the jewels secretly!
Walk up and down for an hour in front of my glass
And that will be fun for you and me;
And then an occasion may offer, a holiday,
Where one can let them be seen in a gradual way;
A necklace to start with, then a pearl earring; your mother
Most likely won't see; if she does one can think up
        something or other.

GRETCHEN: But who brought these two cases, who
        could it be?
It doesn't seem quite right to me.

(*Knocking*)

My God! My mother? Is that her?

MARTHA: It is a stranger. Come in, sir!

(*Enter* MEPHISTOPHELES)

MEPHISTOPHELES: I have made so free as to walk
        straight in;
The ladies will pardon me? May I begin
By inquiring for a Frau Martha Schwerdtlein?

MARTHA: That's me. What might the gentleman want?

MEPHISTOPHELES (*aside to Martha*):
Now I know who you are, that's enough for me;
You have very distinguished company.
Forgive my bursting in so soon;
I will call again in the afternoon.

MARTHA: Imagine, child, in the name of Piety!
The gentleman takes you for society.

GRETCHEN: I'm a poor young thing, not at all refined;
My God, the gentleman is too kind.
These jewels and ornaments aren't my own.

MEPHISTOPHELES: Oh, it's not the jewelry alone;
She has a presence, a look so keen—
How delighted I am that I may remain.

MARTHA: What is your news? I cannot wait—

MEPHISTOPHELES: I wish I'd a better tale to relate.
I trust this will not earn me a beating:
Your husband is dead and sends his greeting.

MARTHA: Dead? The good soul? Oh why! Oh why!
My husband is dead! Oh I shall die!

GRETCHEN: Oh don't, dear woman, despair so.

MEPHISTOPHELES: Listen to my tale of woe!

GRETCHEN: Now, while I live, may I never love;
Such a loss would bring me to my grave.

MEPHISTOPHELES: Joy must have grief, grief must
          have joy.

MARTHA: How was his end? Oh tell it me.

MEPHISTOPHELES: He lies buried in Padua
At the church of Holy Anthony,
In properly consecrated ground
Where he sleeps for ever cool and sound.

MARTHA: Have you nothing else for me? Is that all?

MEPHISTOPHELES: Yes, a request; it's heavy and fat.
You must have three hundred masses said for his soul.
My pockets are empty apart from that.

MARTHA: What! Not a trinket? Not a token?
What every prentice keeps at the bottom of his bag
And saves it up as a souvenir
And would sooner starve and sooner beg—

MEPHISTOPHELES: Madam, you make me quite heart-
          broken.
But, really and truly, he didn't squander his money
And, besides, he repented his mistakes,
Yes, and lamented still more his unlucky breaks.

GRETCHEN: Alas that men should be so unlucky!
Be assured I shall often pray that he may find rest above.

MEPHISTOPHELES: *You* deserve to be taken straight to
the altar;
You are a child a man could love.

GRETCHEN: No, no, it's not yet time for that.

MEPHISTOPHELES: Then, if not a husband, a lover
will do.
It's one of the greatest gifts of Heaven
To hold in one's arms a thing like you.

GRETCHEN: That is not the custom of our race.

MEPHISTOPHELES: Custom or not, it's what takes place.

MARTHA: But tell me!

MEPHISTOPHELES: His deathbed, where I stood,
Was something better than a dungheap—
Half-rotten straw; however, he died like a Christian
And found he had still a great many debts to make good.
How thoroughly, he cried, I must hate myself
To leave my job and my wife like that on the shelf!
When I remember it, I die!
If only she would forgive me here below!

MARTHA: Good man! I have forgiven him long ago.

MEPHISTOPHELES: All the same, God knows, she was
more at fault than I.

MARTHA: That's a lie! To think he lied at the point
of death!

MEPHISTOPHELES: He certainly fibbed a bit with his
last breath,
If I'm half a judge of the situation.
I had no need, said he, to gape for recreation;
First getting children, then getting bread to feed 'em—
And bread in the widest sense, you know—
And I couldn't even eat my share in peace.

MARTHA: So all my love, my loyalty, went for naught,
My toiling and moiling without cease!

MEPHISTOPHELES: Not at all; he gave it profoundest
thought.
When I left Malta—that was how he began—

I prayed for my wife and children like one demented
And Heaven heard me and consented
To let us capture a Turkish merchantman,
With a treasure for the Sultan himself on board.
Well, bravery got its due reward
And I myself, as was only fit,
I got a decent cut of it.

MARTHA: Eh! Eh! How? Where? Has he perhaps
buried it?

MEPHISTOPHELES: Who knows where the four winds
now have carried it?
As he lounged round Naples, quite unknown,
A pretty lady made him her friend,
She was so fond of him, so devoted,
He wore her colors at his blessed end.

MARTHA: The crook! The robber of his children!
Could no misery, no poverty,
Check the scandalous life he led!

MEPHISTOPHELES: You see! That is just why he's dead.
However, if I were placed like you,
I would mourn him modestly for a year
While looking round for someone new.

MARTHA: Ah God! My first one was so dear,
His like in this world will be hard to discover.
There could hardly be a more sweet little fool than mine.
It was only he was too fond of playing the rover,
And of foreign women and foreign wine,
And of the God-damned gaming table.

MEPHISTOPHELES: Now, now, he might have still got by
If he on his part had been able
To follow your suit and wink an eye.
With that proviso, I swear, I too
Would give an engagement ring to you.

MARTHA: The gentleman is pleased to be witty.

MEPHISTOPHELES (aside): I had better go while the
going's good;
She'd hold the devil to his word, she would!
And how is it with *your* heart, my pretty?

GRETCHEN: What does the gentleman mean?

MEPHISTOPHELES (*aside*): Good, innocent child!
Farewell, ladies!

GRETCHEN: Farewell!

MARTHA: O quickly! Tell me;
I'd like to have the evidence filed
Where, how and when my treasure died and was buried.
I have always liked things orderly and decent
And to read of his death in the weeklies would be
    pleasant.

MEPHISTOPHELES: Yes, Madam, when two witnesses
    are agreed,
The truth, as we all know, is guaranteed;
And I have a friend, an excellent sort,
I'll get him to swear you this in court.
I'll bring him here.

MARTHA: Oh yes! Please do!

MEPHISTOPHELES: And the young lady will be here too?
He's an honest lad. He's been around,
His politeness to ladies is profound.

GRETCHEN: I'll be all blushes in his presence.

MEPHISTOPHELES: No king on earth should so affect
    you.

MARTHA: Behind the house there—in my garden—
This evening—both of you—we'll expect you.

In the Street

FAUST: How is it? Going ahead? Will it soon come
    right?

MEPHISTOPHELES: Excellent! Do I find you all on fire?
Gretchen is yours before many days expire.
You will see her at Martha's, her neighbor's house tonight
And that's a woman with a special vocation,
As it were, for the bawd-cum-gipsy occupation.

FAUST: Good!

MEPHISTOPHELES: But there is something *we* must do.

FAUST: One good turn deserves another. True.

MEPHISTOPHELES: It only means the legal attesting
That her husband's played-out limbs are resting
At Padua in consecrated ground.

FAUST: Very smart! I suppose we begin by going to
Padua!

MEPHISTOPHELES: There's no need for that. What a
simple lad you are!
Only bear witness and don't ask questions.

FAUST: The scheme's at an end if you have no better
suggestions.

MEPHISTOPHELES: Oh there you go! What sanctity!
Is this the first time in your life
You have committed perjury?
God and the world and all that moves therein,
Man and the way his emotions and thoughts take place,
Have you not given downright definitions
Of these with an iron breast and a brazen face?
And if you will only look below the surface,
You must confess you knew as much of these
As you know today of Herr Schwerdtlein's late decease.

FAUST: You are and remain a sophist and a liar.

MEPHISTOPHELES: Quite so—if that is as deep as you'll
inquire.
Won't you tomorrow on your honor
Befool poor Gretchen and swear before her
That all your soul is set upon her?

FAUST: And from my heart.

MEPHISTOPHELES: That's nice of you!
And your talk of eternal faith and love,
Of one single passion enthroned above
All others—will that be heartfelt too?

FAUST: Stop! It will! If I have feeling, if I
Feel this emotion, this commotion,
And can find no name to call it by;
If then I sweep the world with all my senses casting
Around for words and all the highest titles

And call this flame which burns my vitals
Endless, everlasting, everlasting,
Is that a devilish game of lies?

   MEPHISTOPHELES: I'm right all the same.

   FAUST: Listen! Mark this well,
I beg you, and spare me talking till I'm hoarse:
The man who *will* be right, provided he has a tongue,
Why, he'll be right of course.
But come, I'm tired of listening to your voice;
You're right, the more so since I have no choice.

Martha's Garden

   (*They are walking in pairs:* MARTHA *and* MEPHISTOPH-
ELES, GRETCHEN *on* FAUST'S *arm*)

   GRETCHEN: The gentleman's only indulging me, I feel,
And condescending, to put me to shame.
You travelers are all the same,
You put up with things out of sheer good will.
I know too well that my poor conversation
Can't entertain a person of your station.

   FAUST: One glance from you, one word, entertains me
      more
Than all this world's wisdom and lore.

   (*He kisses her hand*)

   GRETCHEN: Don't go to such inconvenience! How could
      you kiss my hand?
It is so ugly, it is so rough.
I have had to work at Heaven knows what!
My mother's exacting, true enough.

   (*They pass on*)

   MARTHA: And you, sir, do you always move round
      like this?

MEPHISTOPHELES: Oh, business and duty keep us up
    to the minute!
With what regret one often leaves a place
And yet one cannot ever linger in it.

MARTHA: That may go in one's salad days—
To rush all over the world at random;
But the evil time comes on apace
And to drag oneself to the grave a lonely bachelor
Is never much good in any case.

MEPHISTOPHELES: The prospect alarms me at a distant
    glance.

MARTHA: Then, worthy sir, be wise while you have the
    chance.

(*They pass on*)

GRETCHEN: Yes, out of sight, out of mind!
You are polite to your finger-ends
But you have lots of clever friends
Who must leave *me* so far behind.

FAUST: Believe me, dearest, what the world calls clever
More often is vanity and narrowness.

GRETCHEN: What?

FAUST: Alas that simplicity, that innocence,
Cannot assess itself and its sacred value ever!
That humility, lowliness, the highest gifts
That living Nature has shared out to men—

GRETCHEN: Only think of *me* one little minute,
I shall have time enough to think of you again.

FAUST: You are much alone, I suppose?

GRETCHEN: Yes, our household's only small
But it needs running after all.
We have no maid; I must cook and sweep and knit
And sew and be always on the run,
And my mother looks into every detail—
Each single one.
Not that she has such need to keep expenses down;
We could spread ourselves more than some others do;

My father left us a decent property,
A little house with a garden outside town.
However, my days at the present are pretty quiet;
My brother's in the army,
My little sister is dead.
The child indeed had worn me to a thread;
Still, all that trouble, I'd have it again, I'd try it,
I loved her so.

    FAUST: An angel, if she was like you!

    GRETCHEN: I brought her up, she was very fond of me.
She was born after my father died,
We gave my mother up for lost,
Her life was at such a low, low tide,
And she only got better slowly, bit by bit;
The poor little creature, she could not even
Think for a minute of suckling it;
And so I brought her up quite alone
On milk and water; so she became my own.
On my own arm, on my own knee,
She smiled and kicked, grew fair to see.

    FAUST: You felt, I am sure, the purest happiness.

    GRETCHEN: Yes; and—be sure—many an hour of
        distress.
The little one's cradle stood at night
Beside my bed; she could hardly stir
But I was awake,
Now having to give her milk, now into my bed with her,
Now, if she went on crying, try to stop her
By getting up and dandling her up and down the room,
And then first thing in the morning stand at the copper;
Then off to the market and attend to the range,
And so on day after day, never a change.
Living like that, one can't always feel one's best;
But food tastes better for it, so does rest.

    (*They pass on*)

    MARTHA: No, the poor women don't come out of it
        well,
A *vieux garçon* is a hard nut to crack.

MEPHISTOPHELES: It only rests with you and your like
To put me on a better tack.

MARTHA: Tell me, sir: have you never met someone
    you fancy?
Has your heart been nowhere involved among the girls?

MEPHISTOPHELES: The proverb says: A man's own
    fireside
And a good wife are gold and pearls.

MARTHA: I mean, have you never felt any inclination?

MEPHISTOPHELES: I've generally been received with all
    consideration.

MARTHA: What I wanted to say: has your heart never
    been serious?

MEPHISTOPHELES: To make a joke to a woman is
    always precarious.

MARTHA: Oh you don't understand me!

MEPHISTOPHELES: Now *that* I really mind!
But I do understand—that you are very kind.

(*They pass on*)

FAUST: You knew me again, you little angel,
As soon as you saw me enter the garden?

GRETCHEN: Didn't you see me cast down my eyes?

FAUST: And the liberty that I took you pardon?
The impudence that reared its head
When you lately left the cathedral door.

GRETCHEN: I was upset; it had never happened before;
No one could ever say anything bad of me—
Oh can he, I thought, have seen in my behavior
Any cheekiness, any impropriety?
The idea, it seemed, had come to you pat:
"I can treat this woman just like that."
I must admit I did not know what it was
In my heart that began to make me change my view,
But indeed I was angry with myself because
I could not be angrier with you.

FAUST: Sweet love!

GRETCHEN: Wait a moment!

(*She plucks a flower and starts picking off the petals*)

FAUST: What is that? A
    bouquet?

GRETCHEN: No, only a game.

FAUST: A what?

GRETCHEN: You will laugh at
    me. Go away!

(GRETCHEN *murmurs*)

FAUST: What are you murmuring?

GRETCHEN: Loves me—Loves me
    not—

FAUST: You flower from Heaven's garden plot!

GRETCHEN: Loves me—Not—Loves me—not—
Loves me!

FAUST: Yes, child. What this flower has told you
Regard it as God's oracle. He loves you!
Do you know the meaning of that? He loves you!

(*He takes her hand*)

GRETCHEN: Oh I feel so strange.

FAUST: Don't shudder. Let this look,
Let this clasp of the hand tell you
What mouth can never express:
To give oneself up utterly and feel
A rapture which must be everlasting.
Everlasting! Its end would be despair.
No; no end! No end!

(*She breaks away from him and runs off. After a
    moment's thought he follows her*)

MARTHA (*approaching*): The night's coming on.

MEPHISTOPHELES: Yes—and we must go.

MARTHA: I would ask you to remain here longer
But this is a terrible place, you know.
It's as if no one were able to shape at
Any vocation or recreation
But must have his neighbor's comings and goings to
      gape at
And, whatever one does, the talk is unleashed, unfurled.
And our little couple?

MEPHISTOPHELES: Carefree birds of summer!
Flown to the summerhouse.

MARTHA: He seems to like her.

MEPHISTOPHELES: And vice versa. That is the way of
    the world.

A Summerhouse

(GRETCHEN *comes in and hides behind the door*)

GRETCHEN: He comes!

FAUST (*entering*):   You rogue! Teasing me so!
I've caught you!

(*He kisses her*)

GRETCHEN: Dearest! I love you so!

(MEPHISTOPHELES *knocks*)

FAUST: Who's there?

MEPHISTOPHELES: A friend.

FAUST: A brute!

MEPHISTOPHELES: It is
    time to part, you know.

MARTHA (*joining them*): Yes, it is late, sir.

FAUST: May I not
    see you home?

GRETCHEN: My mother would—Farewell!

FAUST: I must go then.
Farewell!

MARTHA: Adieu!

GRETCHEN: Let us soon meet again!

(FAUST *and* MEPHISTOPHELES *leave*)

Dear God! A man of such a kind,
What things must go on in his mind!
I can only blush when he talks to me;
Whatever he says, I must agree.
Poor silly child, I cannot see
What it is he finds in me.

Forest and Cavern

FAUST (*alone*):   Exalted Spirit, you gave me, gave me
    all
I prayed for. Aye, and it is not in vain
That you have turned your face in fire upon me.
You gave me glorious Nature for my kingdom
With power to feel her and enjoy her. Nor
Is it a mere cold wondering glance you grant me
But you allow me to gaze into her depths
Even as into the bosom of a friend.
Aye, you parade the ranks of living things
Before me and you teach me to know my brothers
In the quiet copse, in the water, in the air.
And when the storm growls and snarls in the forest
And the giant pine falls headlong, bearing away
And crushing its neighbors, bough and bole and all,
With whose dull fall the hollow hill resounds,
Then do you carry me off to a sheltered cave
And show me myself, and wonders of my own breast
Unveil themselves in their deep mystery.

And now that the clear moon rises on my eyes
To soften things, now floating up before me
From walls of rock and from the dripping covert
Come silver forms of the past which soothe and temper
The dour delight I find in contemplation.

That nothing perfect falls to men, oh now
I feel that true. In addition to the rapture
Which brings me near and nearer to the gods
You gave me that companion whom already
I cannot do without, though cold and brazen
He lowers me in my own eyes and with
One whispered word can turn your gifts to nothing.
He is always busily fanning in my breast
A fire of longing for that lovely image.
So do I stagger from desire to enjoyment
And in enjoyment languish for desire.

(MEPHISTOPHELES *enters*)

MEPHISTOPHELES: Haven't you yet had enough of this
        kind of life?
How can it still appeal to you?
It is all very well to try it once,
Then one should switch to something new.

    FAUST: I wish you had something else to do
On my better days than come plaguing me.

    MEPHISTOPHELES: Now, now! I'd gladly leave you
        alone;
You needn't suggest it seriously.
So rude and farouche and mad a friend
Would certainly be little loss.
One has one's hands full without end!
One can never read in the gentleman's face
What he likes or what should be left alone.

    FAUST: That is exactly the right tone!
He must be thanked for causing me ennui.

MEPHISTOPHELES: Poor son of earth, what sort of life
Would you have led were it not for me?
The flim-flams of imagination,
I have cured you of those for many a day.
But for me, this terrestrial ball
Would already have seen you flounce away.
Why behave as an owl behaves
Moping in rocky clefts and caves?
Why do you nourish yourself like a toad that sips
From moss that oozes, stone that drips?
A pretty pastime to contrive!
The doctor in you is still alive.

FAUST: Do you comprehend what a new and vital power
This wandering in the wilderness has given me?
Aye, with even an inkling of such joy,
You would be devil enough to grudge it me.

MEPHISTOPHELES: A supernatural gratification!
To lie on the mountaintops in the dark and dew
Rapturously embracing earth and heaven,
Swelling yourself to a godhead, ferreting through
The marrow of the earth with divination,
To feel in your breast the whole six days of creation
To enjoy I know not what in arrogant might
And then, with the Old Adam discarded quite,
To overflow into all things in ecstasy;
After all which your lofty intuition (*he makes a gesture*)
Will end—hm—unmentionably.

FAUST: Shame on you!

MEPHISTOPHELES: Am I to blame?
You have the right to be moral and cry shame!
One must not mention to the modest ear
What the modest heart is ever agog to hear.
And, in a word, you are welcome to the pleasure
Of lying to yourself in measure;
But this deception will not last.
Already overdriven again,
If this goes on you must collapse,
Mad or tormented or aghast.

Enough of this! Back there your love is sitting
And all her world seems sad and small;
You are never absent from her mind,
Her love for you is more than all.
At first your passion came overflowing
Like a brook that the melted snows have bolstered high;
You have poured your passion into her heart
And now your brook once more is dry.
I think, instead of lording it here above
In the woods, the great man might think fit
In view of that poor ninny's love
To make her some return for it.
She finds the time wretchedly long;
She stands at the window, watches the clouds
As over the old town walls they roll away.
"If I had the wings of a dove"—so runs her song
Half the night and all the day.
Now she is cheerful, mostly low,
Now has spent all her tears,
Now calm again, it appears,
But always loves you so.

FAUST: You snake! You snake!

MEPHISTOPHELES (*aside*): Ha! It begins to take!

FAUST: You outcast! Take yourself away
And do not name that lovely woman.
Do not bring back the desire for her sweet body
Upon my senses that are half astray.

MEPHISTOPHELES: Where's this to end? She thinks you
      have run off,
And so you have—about half and half.

FAUST: I am still near her and, though far removed,
Her image must be always in my head;
I already envy the body of the Lord
When her lips rest upon the holy bread.

MEPHISTOPHELES: Very well, my friend, I have often
      envied you
Those two young roes that are twins, I mean her two—

FAUST: Pimp! Get away!

MEPHISTOPHELES: Fine! So you scold? I must
    laugh.
The God who created girl and boy
Knew very well the high vocation
Which facilitates their joy.
But come, this is a fine excuse for gloom!
You should take the road to your sweetheart's room,
Rather than that to death, you know.

    FAUST: What is the joy of heaven in her arms?
Even when I catch fire upon her breast
Do I not always sense her woe?
Am I not the runaway? The man without a home?
The monster restless and purposeless
Who roared like a waterfall from rock to rock in foam
Greedily raging towards the precipice?
And she on the bank in childlike innocence
In a little hut on the little alpine plot
And all her little household world
Concentrated in that spot.
And I, the loathed of God,
I was not satisfied
To seize and crush to powder
The rocks on the riverside!
Her too, her peace, I must undermine as well!
This was the sacrifice I owed to Hell!
Help, Devil, to shorten my time of torment!
What must be, must be; hasten it!
Let her fate hurtle down with mine,
Let us go together to the pit!

    MEPHISTOPHELES: How it glows again, how it boils
    again!
Go in and comfort her, my foolish friend!
When such a blockhead sees no outlet
He thinks at once it is the end.
Long live the man who does not flinch!
But you've a devil in you, somewhere there.
I know of nothing on earth more unattractive
Than your devil who feels despair.

Gretchen's Room

(GRETCHEN *is alone, singing at the spinning wheel*)

GRETCHEN: My peace is gone,
My heart is sore,
I shall find it never
And never more.

He has left my room
An empty tomb,
He has gone and all
My world is gall.

My poor head
Is all astray,
My poor mind
Fallen away.

My peace is gone,
My heart is sore,
I shall find it never
And never more.

'Tis he that I look through
The window to see,
He that I open
The door for—he!

His gait, his figure,
So grand, so high!
The smile of his mouth
The power of his eye.

And the magic stream
Of his words—what bliss!

The clasp of his hand
And, ah, his kiss!

My peace is gone,
My heart is sore,
I shall find it never
And never more.

My heart's desire
Is so strong, so vast;
Ah, could I seize him
And hold him fast

And kiss him for ever
Night and day—
And on his kisses
Pass away!

Martha's Garden

GRETCHEN: Promise me, Heinrich!

FAUST: If I can!

GRETCHEN: Tell me: how do you stand in regard to
religion?
You are indeed a good, good man
But I think you give it scant attention.

FAUST: Leave that, my child! You feel what I feel for
you;
For those I love I would give my life and none
Will I deprive of his sentiments and his church.

GRETCHEN: That is not right; one must believe thereon.

FAUST: Must one?

GRETCHEN: If only I had some influence!
Nor do you honor the holy sacraments.

FAUST: I honor them.

GRETCHEN: Yes, but not with any zest.

When were you last at mass, when were you last con-
     fessed?
Do you believe in God?

   FAUST: My darling, who dare say:
I believe in God?
Ask professor or priest,
Their answers will make an odd
Mockery of you.

   GRETCHEN: You don't believe, you mean?

   FAUST: Do not misunderstand me, my love, my queen!
Who can name him?
Admit on the spot:
I believe in him?
And who can dare
To perceive and declare:
I believe in him not?
The All-Embracing One,
All-Upholding One,
Does he not embrace, uphold,
You, me, Himself?
Does not the Heaven vault itself above us?
Is not the earth established fast below?
And with their friendly glances do not
Eternal stars rise over us?
Do not my eyes look into yours,
And all things thrust
Into your head, into your heart,
And weave in everlasting mystery
Invisibly, visibly, around you?
Fill your heart with *this,* great as it is,
And when this feeling grants you perfect bliss,
Then call it what you will—
Happiness! Heart! Love! God!
I have no name for it!
Feeling is all;
Name is mere sound and reek
Clouding Heaven's light.

   GRETCHEN: That sounds quite good and right;
And much as the priest might speak,
Only not word for word.

FAUST: It is what all hearts have heard
In all the places heavenly day can reach,
Each in his own speech;
Why not I in mine?

GRETCHEN: I could almost accept it, you make it sound
        so fine,
Still there is something in it that shouldn't be;
For you have no Christianity.

FAUST: Dear child!

GRETCHEN: It has long been a grief to me
To see you in such company.

FAUST: You mean?

GRETCHEN: The man who goes about with you,
I hate him in my soul, right through and through.
And nothing has given my heart
In my whole life so keen a smart
As that man's face, so dire, so grim.

FAUST: Dear poppet, don't be afraid of him!

GRETCHEN: My blood is troubled by his presence.
All other people, I wish them well;
But much as I may long to see you,
He gives me a horror I cannot tell,
And I think he's a man too none can trust.
God forgive me if I'm unjust.

FAUST: Such queer fish too must have room to swim.

GRETCHEN: I wouldn't live with the like of him!
Whenever that man comes to the door,
He looks in so sarcastically,
Half angrily,
One can see he feels no sympathy;
It is written on his face so clear
There is not a soul he can hold dear.
I feel so cozy in your arms,
So warm and free from all restraint,
And his presence ties me up inside.

FAUST: You angel, with your wild alarms!

GRETCHEN: It makes me feel so ill, so faint,
That, if he merely happens to join us,
I even think I have no more love for you.

Besides, when he's there, I could never pray,
And that is eating my heart away;
You, Heinrich, you must feel it too.

FAUST: You suffer from an antipathy.

GRETCHEN: Now I must go.

FAUST: Oh, can I never rest
One little hour hanging upon your breast,
Pressing both breast on breast and soul on soul?

GRETCHEN: Ah, if I only slept alone!
I'd gladly leave the door unlatched for you tonight;
My mother, however, sleeps so light
And if she found us there, I own
I should fall dead upon the spot.

FAUST: You angel, there is no fear of that.
Here's a little flask. Three drops are all
It needs—in her drink—to cover nature
In a deep sleep, a gentle pall.

GRETCHEN: What would I not do for your sake!
I hope it will do her no injury.

FAUST: My love, do you think that of me?

GRETCHEN: Dearest, I've only to look at you
And I do not know what drives me to meet your will
I have already done so much for you
That little more is left me to fulfill.

(*She goes out—and* MEPHISTOPHELES *enters*)

MEPHISTOPHELES: The monkey! Is she gone?

FAUST: Have you
    been spying again?

MEPHISTOPHELES: I have taken pretty good note of it,
The doctor has been catechized—
And much, I hope, to his benefit;
The girls are really keen to be advised
If a man belongs to the old simple-and-pious school.
"If he stand that," they think, "he'll stand *our* rule."

FAUST: You, you monster, cannot see
How this true and loving soul
For whom faith is her whole
Being and the only road
To beatitude, must feel a holy horror
Having to count her beloved lost for good.

MEPHISTOPHELES: You supersensual, sensual buck,
Led by the nose by the girl you court!

FAUST: O you abortion of fire and muck!

MEPHISTOPHELES: And she also has skill in physi-
        ognomy;
In my presence she feels she doesn't know what,
She reads some hidden sense behind my little mask,
She feels that I am assuredly a genius—
Maybe the devil if she dared to ask.
Now: tonight—

FAUST: What is tonight to you?

MEPHISTOPHELES: I have my pleasure in it too.

At the Well

(GRETCHEN *and* LIESCHEN *with pitchers*)

LIESCHEN: Haven't you heard about Barbara? Not
        what's passed?

GRETCHEN: Not a word. I go out very little.

LIESCHEN: It's true, Sibylla told me today:
She has made a fool of herself at last.
So much for her fine airs!

GRETCHEN: Why?

LIESCHEN: It stinks!
Now she feeds two when she eats and drinks.

GRETCHEN: Ah!

LIESCHEN: Yes; she has got her deserts in the end.
What a time she's been hanging on her friend!

Going the rounds
To the dances and the amusement grounds,
She had to be always the first in the line,
He was always standing her cakes and wine;
She thought her looks so mighty fine,
She was so brazen she didn't waver
To take the presents that he gave her.
Such cuddlings and such carryings on—
But now the pretty flower is gone.

GRETCHEN: Poor thing!

LIESCHEN: Is that the way you feel?
When we were at the spinning wheel
And mother kept us upstairs at night,
She was below with her heart's delight;
On the bench or in the shady alley
They never had long enough to dally.
But now she must grovel in the dirt,
Do penance in church in a hair shirt.

GRETCHEN: But surely he will marry her.

LIESCHEN: He'd be a fool! A smart young chap
Has plenty of other casks to tap.
Besides he's gone.

GRETCHEN: That's not right.

LIESCHEN: If she hooks him she won't get off light!
The boys will tear her wreath in half
And we shall strew her door with chaff.

(LIESCHEN goes off)

GRETCHEN (going home): What scorn I used to pour
        upon her
When a poor maiden lost her honor!
My tongue could never find a name
Bad enough for another's shame!
I thought it black and I blackened it,
It was never black enough to fit,
And I blessed myself and acted proud—
And now I too am under a cloud.
Yet, God! What drove me to this pass,
It was all so good, so dear, alas!

Ramparts

(In a niche in the wall is an image of the Mater Dolorosa. In front of it GRETCHEN *is putting fresh flowers in the pots)*

GRETCHEN: Mary, bow down,
Beneath thy woeful crown,
Thy gracious face on me undone!

The sword in thy heart,
Smart upon smart,
Thou lookest up to thy dear son;

Sending up sighs
To the Father which rise
For His grief and for thine own.

Who can gauge
What torments rage
Through the whole of me and how—
How my poor heart is troubled in me,
How fears and longings undermine me?
Only thou knowest, only thou!

Wherever I may go,
What woe, what woe, what woe
Is growing beneath my heart!
Alas, I am hardly alone,
I moan, I moan, I moan
And my heart falls apart.

The flower-pots in my window
I watered with tears, ah me,

When in the early morning
I picked these flowers for thee.

Not sooner in my bedroom
The sun's first rays were shed
Than I in deepest sorrow
Sat waking on my bed.

Save me from shame and death in one!
Ah, bow down
Thou of the woeful crown,
Thy gracious face on me undone.

Night Scene at Gretchen's Door

VALENTINE: When I was at some drinking bout
Where big talk tends to blossom out,
And my companions raised their voice
To praise the maidens of their choice
And drowned their praises in their drink,
Then I would sit and never blink,
Propped on my elbow listening
To all their brags and blustering.
Then smiling I would stroke my beard
And raise the bumper in my hand
And say: "Each fellow to his taste!
But is there one in all the land
To hold a candle to my own
Dear sister, Gretchen? No, there's none!"
Hear! Hear! Kling! Klang! It went around;
Some cried: "His judgment is quite sound,
She is the pearl of womanhood!"
That shut those boasters up for good.
And now! It would make one tear one's hair
And run up walls in one's despair!
Each filthy fellow in the place

Can sneer and jeer at my disgrace!
And I, like a man who's deep in debt,
Every chance word must make me sweat.
I could smash their heads for them if I tried—
I could not tell them that they lied.

(FAUST *and* MEPHISTOPHELES *enter*)

Who comes there, slinking? Who comes there?
If I mistake not, they're a pair.
If it's he, I'll scrag him on the spot;
He'll be dead before he knows what's what!

FAUST: How from the window of the sacristy there
The undying lamp sends up its little flicker
Which glimmers sideways weak and weaker
And round it presses the dark air.
My heart too feels its night, its noose.

MEPHISTOPHELES: And I feel like a tomcat on the loose,
Brushing along the fire escape
And round the walls, a stealthy shape;
Moreover I feel quite virtuous,
Just a bit burglarious, a bit lecherous.
You see, I'm already haunted to the marrow
By the glorious Walpurgis Night.
It returns to us the day after tomorrow,
Then one knows why one's awake all right.

FAUST: I'd like some ornament, some ring,
For my dear mistress. I feel sad
To visit her without anything.

MEPHISTOPHELES: It's really nothing to regret—
That you needn't pay for what you get.
Now that the stars are gems on heaven's brocade,
You shall hear a real masterpiece.
I will sing her a moral serenade
That her folly may increase.

(*He sings to the guitar*)

Catherine, my dear,
What? Waiting here
At your lover's door
When the stars of the night are fading?
Oh don't begin!
When he lifts the pin,
A maid goes in—
But she won't come out a maiden.
So think aright!
Grant him delight
And it's good night,
You poor, poor things—Don't linger!
A girl who's wise
Will hide her prize
From robber's eyes—
Unless she's a ring on her finger.

(VALENTINE *comes forward*)

VALENTINE: Damn you! Who're you seducing here?
You damned pied piper! You magician!
First to the devil with your guitar!
Then to the devil with the musician!

MEPHISTOPHELES: The guitar is finished. Look, it's
      broken in two.

VALENTINE: Now then, to break your heads for you!

MEPHISTOPHELES: Doctor! Courage! All you can
      muster!
Stick by me and do as I say!
Quick now, draw your feather duster!
I'll parry his blows, so thrust away!

VALENTINE: Then parry that!

MEPHISTOPHELES: Why not, why not?

VALENTINE: And that!

MEPHISTOPHELES: Of course.

VALENTINE: Is he the devil or
      what?
What's this? My hand's already lamed.

MEPHISTOPHELES: Strike, you!

VALENTINE: Oh!

(VALENTINE *falls*)

MEPHISTOPHELES: Now the lout is tamed!
But we must go! Vanish in the wink of an eye!
They're already raising a murderous hue and cry.

MARTHA (*at the window*): Come out! Come out!

GRETCHEN (*at the window*): Bring a light!

MARTHA (*as before*): There's a row and a scuffle,
      they're having a fight.

MAN: Here's one on the ground; he's dead.

MARTHA (*coming out*): The murderers, have they gone?

GRETCHEN (*coming out*): Who's here?

MAN: Your mother's
      son.

GRETCHEN: O God! What pain! O God!

VALENTINE: I am dying—that's soon said
And sooner done, no doubt.
Why do you women stand howling and wailing?
Come round and hear me out.

(*They all gather round him*)

Look, my Gretchen, you're young still,
You have not yet sufficient skill,
You bungle things a bit.
Here is a tip—you need no more—
Since you are once for all a whore,
Then make a job of it!

GRETCHEN: My brother? O God! Is it I you blame!

VALENTINE: Leave our Lord God out of the game!
What is done I'm afraid is done,
As one starts one must carry on.
You began with one man on the sly,
There will be more of them by and by,
And when a dozen have done with you
The whole town will have you too.

When Shame is born, she first appears
In this world in secrecy.
And the veil of night is drawn so tight
Over her head and ears;
Yes, people would kill her and forget her.
But she grows still more and more
And brazenly roams from door to door
And yet her appearance grows no better.
The more her face creates dismay,
The more she seeks the light of day.
Indeed I see the time draw on
When all good people in this town
Will turn aside from you, you tart,
As from a corpse in the plague cart.
Then your heart will sink within you,
When they look you in the eye!
It's good-by to your golden chains!
And church-going and mass—good-by!
No nice lace collars any more
To make you proud on the dancing floor!
No, in some dark and filthy nook
You'll hide with beggars and crippled folk
And, if God pardon you, he may;
You are cursed on earth till your dying day.

MARTHA: Commend your soul to the mercy of God!
Will you add slander to your load?

VALENTINE: If I could get at your withered body
You bawd, you sinner born and hardened!
Then I should hope that all my sins
And in full measure might be pardoned.

GRETCHEN: My brother! O hell's misery!

VALENTINE: I tell you: let your weeping be.
When you and your honor came to part,
It was you that stabbed me to the heart.
I go to God through the sleep of death,
A soldier—brave to his last breath.

(*He dies*)

Cathedral

(*Organ and anthem.* GRETCHEN *in the congregation. An*
EVIL SPIRIT *whispers to her over her shoulder*)

EVIL SPIRIT: How different it all was
Gretchen, when you came here
All innocent to the altar,
Out of the worn-out little book
Lisping your prayers,
Half a child's game,
Half God in the heart!
Gretchen!
How is your head?
And your heart—
What are its crimes?
Do you pray for your mother's soul, who thanks to you
And your sleeping draught overslept into a long, long pain?
And whose blood stains your threshold?
Yes, and already under your heart
Does it not grow and quicken
And torture itself and you
With its foreboding presence?

GRETCHEN: Alas! Alas!
If I could get rid of the thoughts
Which course through my head hither and thither
Despite me!

CHOIR: Dies irae, dies illa
          Solvet saeclum in favilla.

(*The organ plays*)

EVIL SPIRIT: Agony seizes you!
                The trumpet sounds!
                The graves tremble
                And your heart
                From its ashen rest
                To fiery torment
                Comes up recreated
                Trembling too!

161

GRETCHEN: Oh to escape from here!
I feel as if the organ
Were stifling me,
And the music dissolving
My heart in its depths.

CHOIR: Judex ergo cum sedebit,
                Quidquid latet adparebit,
                Nil inultum remanebit.

GRETCHEN: I cannot breathe!
The pillars of the walls
Are round my throat!
The vaulted roof
Chokes me!—Air!

EVIL SPIRIT: Hide yourself! Nor sin nor shame
Remains hidden.
Air? Light?
Woe to you!

CHOIR: Quid sum miser tunc dicturus?
                Quem patronum rogaturus?
                Cum vix justus sit securus.

EVIL SPIRIT: The blessed turn
Their faces from you.
The pure shudder
To reach out their hands to you.
Woe!

CHOIR: Quid sum miser tunc dicturus?

GRETCHEN: Neighbor! Help! Your smelling bottle!

(*She faints*)

Walpurgis Night

(FAUST *and* MEPHISTOPHELES *making their way through
the Harz Mountains*)

MEPHISTOPHELES: A broomstick—don't you long for
          such a conveyance?
I'd find the coarsest he-goat some assistance.
Taking this road, our goal is still in the distance.

FAUST: No, so long as my legs are not in abeyance,
I can make do with this knotted stick.
What is the use of going too quick?
To creep along each labyrinthine valley,
Then climb this scarp, downwards from which
The bubbling spring makes its eternal sally,
This is the spice that makes such journeys rich.
Already the spring is weaving through the birches,
Even the pine already feels the spring;
Should not our bodies too give it some purchase?

MEPHISTOPHELES: Candidly—I don't feel a thing.
In my body all is winter,
I would prefer a route through frost and snow.
How sadly the imperfect disk
Of the red moon rises with belated glow
And the light it gives is bad, at every step
One runs into some rock or tree!
Permit me to ask a will-o'-the-wisp.
I see one there, he's burning heartily.
Ahoy, my friend! Might I call on you to help us?
Why do you blaze away there to no purpose?
Be so good as to light us along our road.

WILL O' THE WISP: I only hope my sense of your might-
iness
Will control my natural flightiness;
A zigzag course is our accustomed mode.

MEPHISTOPHELES: Ha! Ha! So it's men you want to
imitate.
In the name of the Devil you go straight
Or I'll blow out your flickering, dickering light!

WILL O' THE WISP: You're the head of the house, I can
see that all right,
You are welcome to use me at your convenience.
But remember, the mountain is magic-mad today
And, if a will-o'-the-wisp is to show you the way,
You too must show a little lenience.

FAUST, MEPHISTOPHELES, WILL-O'-THE-WISP *(singing
successively)*:Into realms of dreams and witchcraft
We, it seems, have found an ingress.
Lead us well and show your woodcraft,

That we may make rapid progress
Through these wide and desert spaces.

Trees on trees—how each one races,
Pushing past—how each one hastens!
And the crags that make obeisance!
And the rocks with long-nosed faces—
Hear them snorting, hear them blowing!

Through the stones and lawns are flowing
Brook and brooklet, downward hustling.
Is that song—or is it rustling?
Sweet, sad notes of love—a relic—
Voices from those days angelic?
Thus we hope, we love—how vainly!
Echo like an ancient rumor
Calls again, yes, calls back plainly.

Now—Tu-whit!—we near the purlieu
Of—Tu-whoo!—owl, jay and curlew;
Are they all in waking humor?
In the bushes are those lizards—
Straggling legs and bloated gizzards?
And the roots like snakes around us
Coil from crag and sandy cranny,
Stretch their mad and strange antennae
Grasping at us to confound us;
Stretch from gnarled and living timber
Towards the passer-by their limber
Polyp-suckers!
                    And in legions
Through these mossy, heathy regions
Mice, all colors, come cavorting!
And above, a serried cohort,
Fly the glowworms as our escort—
More confusing than escorting.

Tell me what our real case is!
Are we stuck or are we going?

Rocks and trees, they all seem flying
Round and round and making faces,
And the will-o'-the-wisps are blowing
Up so big and multiplying.

MEPHISTOPHELES: Hold my coattails, hold on tight!
Standing on this central height
Marveling see how far and wide
Mammon lights the peaks inside.

FAUST: How strangely through the mountain hollows
A sad light gleams as of morning-red
And like a hound upon the scent
Probes the gorges' deepest bed!
Here fumes arise, there vapors float,
Here veils of mist catch sudden fire
Which creeps along, a flimsy thread,
Then fountains up, a towering spire.
Here a whole stretch it winds its way
With a hundred veins throughout the glen,
And here in the narrow neck of the pass
Is suddenly one strand again.
There, near by, are dancing sparks
Sprinkled around like golden sand.
But look! The conflagration climbs
The crags' full height, hand over hand.

MEPHISTOPHELES: Does not Sir Mammon light his
     palace
In splendid style for this occasion?
You are lucky to have seen it;
Already I sense the noisy guests' invasion.

FAUST: How the Wind Hag rages through the air!
What blows she rains upon the nape of my neck!

MEPHISTOPHELES: You must clamp yourself to the
     ancient ribs of the rock
Or she'll hurl you into this gorge, to find your grave down
     there.
A mist is thickening the night.
Hark to the crashing of the trees!
The owls are flying off in fright.

And the ever-green palaces—
Hark to their pillars sundering!
Branches moaning and breaking!
Tree trunks mightily thundering!
Roots creaking and yawning!
Tree upon tree in appalling
Confusion crashing and falling,
And through the wreckage on the scarps
The winds are hissing and howling.
Do you hear those voices in the air?
Far-off voices? Voices near?
Aye, the whole length of the mountainside
The witch-song streams in a crazy tide.

WITCHES (*in chorus*): The witches enter the Brocken
        scene,
  The stubble is yellow, the corn is green.
  There assembles the mighty horde,
  Urian sits aloft as lord.
  So we go—over stock and stone—
  Farting witch on stinking goat.

A VOICE: But ancient Baubo comes alone,
  She rides on a mother sow—take note.

CHORUS: So honor to whom honor is due!
  Let Mother Baubo head the queue!
  A strapping sow and Mother on top
  And we'll come after, neck and crop.

  The way is broad, the way is long,
  How is this for a crazy throng?
  The pitchfork pricks, the broomstick pokes,
  The mother bursts and the child chokes.

VOICE FROM ABOVE: Come along, come along, from
        Felsensee!

VOICES FROM BELOW: We'd like to mount with you
        straight away.
  We wash ourselves clean behind and before
  But we are barren for evermore.

CHORUS: The wind is silent, the star's in flight,
  The sad moon hides herself from sight.

The soughing of the magic choir
Scatters a thousand sparks of fire.

VOICE FROM BELOW: Wait! Wait!

VOICE FROM ABOVE: Who calls there from the cleft in
the rock?

VOICE FROM BELOW: Don't leave me behind! Don't
leave me behind!
Three hundred years I've been struggling up
And I can never reach the top;
I want to be with my own kind.

CHORUS: Ride on a broom or ride on a stick,
Ride on a fork or a goat—but quick!
Who cannot tonight achieve the climb
Is lost and damned till the end of time.

HALF-WITCH: So long, so long, I've been on the trot;
How far ahead the rest have got!
At home I have neither peace nor cheer
And yet I do not find it here.

CHORUS: Their ointment makes the witches hale,
A rag will make a decent sail
And any trough a ship for flight;
You'll never fly, if not tonight.
Once at the peak, you circle round
And then you sweep along the ground
And cover the heath far and wide—
Witchhood in swarms on every side.

(*The* WITCHES *land*)

MEPHISTOPHELES: What a push and a crush and a rush
and a clatter!
How they sizzle and whisk, how they babble and batter!
Kindle and sparkle and blaze and stink!
A true witch-element, I think.
Only stick to me or we shall be swept apart!
Where are you?

FAUST: Here!

MEPHISTOPHELES: What! Carried so far already!
I must show myself the master on this ground.

Room! Here comes Voland! Room, sweet rabble! Steady!
Here, Doctor, catch hold of me. Let's make one bound
Out of this milling crowd and so get clear.
Even for the likes of me it's *too* mad here.
There's something yonder casting a peculiar glare,
Something attracts me towards those bushes.
Come with me! We will slip in there.

FAUST: You spirit of contradiction! Go on though! I'll
follow.
You have shown yourself a clever fellow. Quite!
We visit the Brocken on Walpurgis Night
To shut ourselves away in this lonely hollow!

MEPHISTOPHELES: Only look—what motley flames!
It's a little club for fun and games
One's not alone with a few, you know.

FAUST: I'd rather be above there though.
Already there's fire and whorls of smoke.
The Prince of Evil is drawing the folk;
Many a riddle must there be solved.

MEPHISTOPHELES: And many a new one too evolved.
Let the great world, if it likes, run riot;
We will set up here in quiet.
It is a custom of old date
To make one's own small worlds within the great.
I see young witches here, bare to the buff,
And old ones dressed—wisely enough.
If only for my sake, do come on;
It's little trouble and great fun.
I hear some music being let loose too.
What a damned clack! It's what one must get used to.
Come along! Come along! You have no choice.
I'll lead the way and sponsor you
And you'll be obliged to me anew.
What do you say? This milieu isn't small.
Just look! You can see no end to it at all.
A hundred fires are blazing in a row;
They dance and gossip and cook and drink and court—
Tell me where there is better sport!

FAUST: Do you intend, to introduce us here,
To play the devil or the sorcerer?

MEPHISTOPHELES: I am quite accustomed to go in-
        cognito
But one wears one's orders on gala days, you know.
I have no garter for identification
But my cloven foot has here some reputation.
See that snail? Creeping up slow and steady?
Her sensitive feelers have already
Sensed out something odd in me.
Here I could *not* hide my identity.
But come! Let us go the round of the fires
And I'll play go-between to your desires.

COSTER-WITCH: Gentlemen, don't pass me by!
Don't miss your opportunity!
Inspect my wares with careful eye;
I have a great variety.
And yet there is nothing on my stall
Whose like on earth you could not find,
That in its time has done no small
Harm to the world and to mankind.
No dagger which has not drunk of blood,
No goblet which has not poured its hot and searing
Poison into some healthy frame,
No gewgaw which has not ruined some endearing
Woman, no sword which has not been used to hack
A bond in two and stab a partner in the back.

MEPHISTOPHELES: Auntie! You are behind the times.
Past and done with! Past and done!
You must go in for novelties!
You'll lose our custom if you've none.

FAUST: I mustn't go crazy unawares!
This is a fair to end all fairs.

MEPHISTOPHELES: The whole crowd's forcing its way
        above;
You find you're shoved though you may think you shove.

FAUST: Who then is that?

MEPHISTOPHELES: Look well at Madam;
That's Lilith.

FAUST: Who?

MEPHISTOPHELES: First wife of Adam.
Be on your guard against her lovely hair,
That shining ornament which has no match;
Any young man whom those fair toils can catch,
She will not quickly loose him from her snare.

FAUST: Look, an old and a young one, there they sit.
They have already frisked a bit.

MEPHISTOPHELES: No rest tonight for 'em, not a chance.
They're starting again. Come on! Let's join the dance.

(FAUST *dances with a young witch*)

FAUST: A lovely dream once came to me
In which I saw an apple tree,
On which two lovely apples shine,
They beckon me, I start to climb.

YOUNG WITCH: Those little fruit you long for so
Just as in Eden long ago.
Joy runs through me, through and through;
My garden bears its apples too.

(FAUST *breaks away from the dance*)

MEPHISTOPHELES: Why did you let that lovely maiden
    go
Who danced with you and so sweetly sang?

FAUST: Ugh, in the middle of it there sprang
Out of her mouth a little red mouse.

MEPHISTOPHELES: Why complain? That's nothing out of
    the way;
You should be thankful it wasn't gray.
In an hour of love! What a senseless grouse!

FAUST: And then I saw—

MEPHISTOPHELES: What?

FAUST: Mephisto, look over
    there!

Do you see a girl in the distance, pale and fair?
Who drags herself, only slowly, from the place?
And seems to walk with fetters on her feet?
I must tell you that I think I see
Something of dear Gretchen in her face.

MEPHISTOPHELES: That can do no one good! Let it
  alone! Beware!
It is a lifeless phantom, an image of air.
It is a bad thing to behold;
Its cold look makes the blood of man run cold.
One turns to stone almost upon the spot;
You have heard of Medusa, have you not?

FAUST: Indeed, they are the eyes of one who is dead,
Unclosed by loving hands, left open, void.
That is the breast which Gretchen offered me,
And that is the sweet body I enjoyed.

MEPHISTOPHELES: That is mere magic, you gullible fool!
  She can
Appear in the shape of his love to every man.

FAUST: What ravishment! What pain! Oh stay!
That look! I cannot turn away!
How strange that that adorable neck
In one red thread should be arrayed
As thin as the back of a knife blade.

MEPHISTOPHELES: You are quite correct! I see it too.
She can also carry her head under her arm,
Perseus has cut it off for her.
Always this love of things untrue!

(*A* CHOIR *is heard, pianissimo*)

CHOIR: Drifting cloud and gauzy mist
    Brighten and dissever.
    Breeze on the leaf and wind in the reeds
    And all is gone for ever.

Dreary Day—Open Country

FAUST: In misery! In despair! Long on the earth a wretched wanderer, now a prisoner! A criminal cooped in a dungeon for horrible torments, that dear and luckless creature! To end so! So! Perfidious, worthless spirit—and this you have kept from me! Stand! Just stand there! Roll your devilish eyes spitefully round in your head!

Stand and brave me with your unbearable presence! A prisoner! In irremediable misery! Abandoned to evil spirits, to judging, unfeeling man! And I in the meantime—you lull me with stale diversions, you hide her worsening plight from me, you abandon her to perdition!

MEPHISTOPHELES: She is not the first.

FAUST: Dog! Loathsome monster! Change him, Thou eternal Spirit! Change this serpent back to his shape of a dog, in which he often delighted to trot before me at night —to roll about at the feet of the harmless wanderer and, as he tripped, to sink his teeth in his shoulders. Change him back to his fancy-shape that he may crouch in the sand on his belly before me, that I may trample over his vileness!

Not the first, you say! O the pity of it! What human soul can grasp that more than one creature has sunk to the depth of this misery, that the first did not pay off the guilt of all the rest, writhing and racked in death before the eyes of the Ever-Pardoning! It pierces me to my marrow and core, the torment of this one girl—and you grin calmly at the fate of thousands!

MEPHISTOPHELES: Now we're already back at our wits' end—the point where your human intelligence snaps. Why do you enter our company, if you can't carry it through? So you want to fly—and have no head for heights? Did we force ourselves on you—or you on us?

FAUST: Do not bare at me so those greedy fangs of yours! You sicken me! O great and glorious Spirit, Thou

who didst deign to appear to me, Thou who knowest my
heart and my soul, why fetter me to this odious partner
who grazes on mischief and laps up destruction?

MEPHISTOPHELES: Have you finished?

FAUST: Save her! Or woe to you! The most withering
curse upon you for thousands of years!

MEPHISTOPHELES: I cannot undo the avenger's bonds,
his bolts I cannot open. Save her! Who was it plunged her
into ruin? I or you?

(FAUST *looks wildly around*)

Are you snatching at the thunder? Luckily, that is forbidden you wretched mortals. To smash to pieces his innocent critic, that is the way the tyrant relieves himself when
in difficulties.

FAUST: Bring me to her! She shall be free!

MEPHISTOPHELES: And what of the risk you will run?
Let me tell you; the town is still tainted with blood guilt
from your hand. Over the site of the murder there float
avenging spirits who await the returning murderer.

FAUST: That too from *you*? Murder and death of a world
on your monstrous head! Take me to her, I tell you; set
her free!

MEPHISTOPHELES: I will take you, and what I *can* do—
listen! Am I omnipotent in heaven and earth? I will cast a
cloud on the gaoler's senses; do you get hold of the keys
and carry her out with your own human hands. I meanwhile wait, my magic horses are ready, I carry you off.
That much I can manage.

FAUST: Away! Away!

Night

(FAUST *and* MEPHISTOPHELES *fly past on black horses*)

FAUST: What do they weave round the Gallows Rock?
MEPHISTOPHELES: Can't tell what they're cooking and
    hatching.
FAUST: Floating up, floating down, bending, descending.
MEPHISTOPHELES: A witch corporation.
FAUST: Black mass, black water.
MEPHISTOPHELES: Come on! Come on!

Dungeon

(FAUST *with a bunch of keys and a lamp, in front of an iron door*)

FAUST: A long unwonted trembling seizes me,
The woe of all mankind seizes me fast.
It is here she lives, behind these dripping walls,
Her crime was but a dream too good to last!
And *you*, Faust, waver at the door?
You fear to see your love once more?
Go in at once—or her hope of life is past.

(*He tries the key.* GRETCHEN *starts singing inside*)

GRETCHEN: My mother, the whore,
    Who took my life!
    My father, the rogue,
    Who ate my flesh!
    My little sister
    My bones did lay
    In a cool, cool glen;
    And there I turned to a pretty little wren;
    Fly away! Fly away!

(FAUST *opens the lock*)

FAUST: She does not suspect that her lover is listening—
To the chains clanking, the straw rustling.

(*He enters*)

GRETCHEN: Oh! They come! O death! It's hard! Hard!
FAUST: Quiet! I come to set you free.

(*She throws herself at his feet*)

GRETCHEN: If you are human, feel my misery.
FAUST: Do not cry out—you will wake the guard.

(*He takes hold of the chains to unlock them*)

GRETCHEN (*on her knees*): Who has given you this
        power,
Hangman, so to grieve me?
To fetch me at this midnight hour!
Have pity! Oh reprieve me!
Will tomorrow not serve when the bells are rung?

(*She gets up*)

I am still so young, I am still so young!
Is my death so near?
I was pretty too, that was what brought me here.
My lover was by, he's far today;
My wreath lies torn, my flowers have been thrown away.
Don't seize on me so violently!
What have I done to you? Let me be!
Let me not vainly beg and implore;
You know I have never seen you before.
    FAUST: Can I survive this misery?
    GRETCHEN: I am now completely in your power.
Only let me first suckle my child.
This night I cherished it, hour by hour;

To torture me they took it away
And now I murdered it, so they say.
And I shall never be happy again.
People make ballads about me—the heartless crew!
An old story ends like this—
Must mine too?

(FAUST *throws himself on the ground*)

FAUST: Look! At your feet a lover lies
To loose you from your miseries.

(GRETCHEN *throws herself beside him*)

GRETCHEN: Oh, let us call on the saints on bended knees!
Beneath these steps—but see—
Beneath this sill
The cauldron of Hell!
And within,
The Evil One in his fury
Raising a din!

FAUST: Gretchen! Gretchen!

GRETCHEN: That was my lover's voice!

(*She springs up: the chains fall off*)

I heard him calling. Where can he be?
No one shall stop me. I am free!
Quick! My arms round his neck!
And lie upon his bosom! Quick!
He called "Gretchen!" He stood at the door.
Through the whole of Hell's racket and roar,
Through the threats and jeers and from far beyond
I heard that voice so sweet, so fond.

FAUST: It is I!

GRETCHEN: It's you? Oh say so once again!

(*She clasps him*)

It is! It is! Where now is all my pain?
And where the anguish of my captivity?
It's you; you have come to rescue me!
I am saved!
The street is back with me straight away
Where I saw you that first day,
And the happy garden too
Where Martha and I awaited you.

   FAUST: Come! Come!

   GRETCHEN: Oh stay with me, oh do!
Where *you* stay, I would like to, too.

   FAUST: Hurry!
If you don't,
The penalty will be sore.

   GRETCHEN: What! Can you kiss no more?
So short an absence, dear, as this
And you've forgotten how to kiss!
Why do I feel so afraid, clasping your neck?
In the old days your words, your looks,
Were a heavenly flood I could not check
And you kissed me as if you would smother me—
Kiss me now!
Or I'll kiss you!

   (*She kisses him*)

Oh your lips are cold as stone!
And dumb!
What has become
Of your love?
Who has robbed me of my own?

   (*She turns away from him*)

   FAUST: Come! Follow me, my love! Be bold!
I will cherish you after a thousandfold.
Only follow me now! That is all I ask of you.

   GRETCHEN: And is it you then? Really? Is it true?

FAUST: It is! But come!

GRETCHEN: You are undoing each chain,
You take me to your arms again.
How comes it you are not afraid of me?
Do you know, my love, *whom* you are setting free?

FAUST: Come! The deep night is passing by and beyond.

GRETCHEN: My mother, I have murdered her;
I drowned my child in the pond.
Was it not a gift to you and me?
To you too—You! Are you what you seem?
Give me your hand! It is not a dream!
Your dear hand—but, oh, it's wet!
Wipe if off! I think
There is blood on it.
Oh God! What have you done?
Put up your sword,
I beg you to.

FAUST: Let what is gone be gone!
You are killing me.

GRETCHEN: No! *You* must live on!
I will tell you about the graves—
You must get them put right
At morning light;
Give the best place to my mother,
The one next door to my brother,
Me a shade to the side—
A gap—but not too wide.
And the little one on my right breast.
No one else shall share my rest.
When it was you, when I could clasp you,
That was a sweet, a lovely day!
But I no longer can attain it,
I feel I must use force to grasp you,
As if you were thrusting me away.
And yet it's you and you look so kind, so just.

FAUST: If you feel it's I, then come with me! You must!

GRETCHEN: Outside there?

FAUST: Into the air!

GRETCHEN: If the grave is there
And death on the watch, then come!
Hence to the final rest of the tomb
And not a step beyond—
You are going now? O Heinrich, if *I* could too!

FAUST: You can! The door is open. Only respond!

GRETCHEN: I dare not go out; for me there is no more
hope.
They are lying in wait for me; what use is flight?
To have to beg, it is so pitiable
And that with a conscience black as night!
So pitiable to tramp through foreign lands—
And in the end I must fall into their hands!

FAUST: I shall stay by you.

GRETCHEN: Be quick! Be quick!
Save your poor child!
Go! Straight up the path—
Along by the brook—
Over the bridge—
Into the wood—
Left where the plank is—
In the pond!
Catch hold of it quickly!
It's trying to rise,
It's kicking still!
Save it! Save it!

FAUST: Collect yourself!
One step—just one—and you are free.

GRETCHEN: If only we were past the hill!
There sits my mother on a stone—
My brain goes cold and dead—
There sits my mother on a stone—
And wags and wags her head.
No sign, no nod, her head is such a weight,
She'll wake no more, she slept so late.
She slept that we might sport and play.
What a time that was of holiday!

FAUST: If prayer and argument are no resource,
I will risk saving you by force.

GRETCHEN: No! I will have no violence! Let me go!
Don't seize me in that murderous grip!
I have done everything else for you, you know.

FAUST: My love! My love! The day is dawning!

GRETCHEN: Day! Yes, it's growing day! The last day
breaks on me!
My wedding day it was to be!
Tell no one you had been before with Gretchen.
Alas for my garland!
There's no more chance!
We shall meet again—
But not at the dance.
The people are thronging—but silently;
Street and square
Cannot hold them there.
The bell tolls—it tolls for *me*.
How they seize me, bind me, like a slave!
Already I'm swept away to the block,
Already there jabs at every neck,
The sharp blade which jabs at mine.
The world lies mute as the grave.

FAUST: I wish I had never been born!

(MEPHISTOPHELES *appears outside*)

MEPHISTOPHELES: Away! Or you are lost.
Futile wavering! Waiting and prating!
My horses are shivering,
The dawn's at the door.

GRETCHEN: What rises up from the floor?
It's he! Send him away! It's he!
What does he want in the holy place?
It is I he wants!

FAUST: You shall live!

GRETCHEN: Judgment of God! I have given myself to
Thee!

MEPHISTOPHELES (*to* FAUST): Come! Or I'll leave you
both in the lurch.

GRETCHEN: O Father, save me! I am Thine!
You angels! Hosts of the Heavenly Church,
Guard me, stand round in serried line!
Heinrich! I shudder to look at you.

MEPHISTOPHELES: She is condemned!

VOICE FROM ABOVE:　　　　　　　Redeemed!

MEPHISTOPHELES: Follow me!

(*He vanishes with* FAUST)

VOICE (*from within, dying away*): Heinrich, Heinrich!

❧

TRAVELS IN ITALY

TRANSLATED BY A. J. W. MORRISON AND
CHARLES NISBET

NAPLES, TUESDAY, MARCH 20, 1787

The news that an eruption of lava had just commenced, which, taking the direction of Ottajano, was invisible at Naples, tempted me to visit Vesuvius for the third time. Scarcely had I jumped out of my cabriolet,* at the foot of the mountain, when immediately appeared the two guides who had accompanied us on our previous ascent. I had no wish to do without either, but took one out of gratitude and custom, the other for reliance on his judgment—and the two for the greater convenience. Having reached the summit, the older guide remained with our cloaks and refreshment, while the younger followed me, and we boldly went straight toward a dense volume of smoke, which broke forth from the bottom of the funnel; then we quickly went downward by the side of it, till at last, under the clear heaven, we distinctly saw the lava emitted from the rolling clouds of smoke.

We may hear an object spoken of a thousand times, but its peculiar features will never be caught till we see it with our own eyes. The stream of lava was small, not broader perhaps than ten feet, but the way in which it flowed down a gentle and tolerably smooth plain was remarkable. As it flowed along, it cooled both on the sides and on the surface, so that it formed a sort of canal, the bed of which was continually raised in consequence of the molten mass congealing even beneath the fiery stream, which with uni-

* Zweiradigen einpferdigen Fuhrwerk.

form action precipitated right and left the scoria which was floating on its surface. In this way a regular dam was at length thrown up, in which the glowing stream flowed on as quietly as any millstream. We passed along the tolerably high dam, while the scoria rolled regularly off the sides at our feet. Some cracks in the canal afforded opportunity of looking at the living stream from below, and as it rushed onward, we observed it from above.

A very bright sun made the glowing lava look dull; but a moderate steam rose from it into the pure air. I felt a great desire to go nearer to the point where it broke out from the mountain; there, my guide averred, it at once formed vaults and roofs above itself, on which he had often stood. To see and experience this phenomenon, we again ascended the hill, in order to come from behind to this point. Fortunately at this moment the place was cleared by a pretty strong wind, but not entirely, for all round it the smoke eddied from a thousand crannies; and now at last we stood on the top of the solid roof (which looked like a hardened mass of twisted dough), but which, however, projected so far outward, that it was impossible to see the welling lava.

We ventured about twenty steps further, but the ground on which we stepped became hotter and hotter, while around us rolled an oppressive steam, which obscured and hid the sun; the guide, who was a few steps in advance of me, presently turned back, and seizing hold of me, hurried out of this Stygian exhalation.

After we had refreshed our eyes with the clear prospect, and washed our gums and throat with wine, we went round again to notice any other peculiarities which might characterize this peak of hell, thus rearing itself in the midst of a paradise. I again observed attentively some chasms, in appearance like so many Vulcanic forges, which emitted no smoke, but continually shot out a steam of hot glowing air. They were all tapestried, as it were, with a kind of stalactite, which covered the funnel to the top, with its knobs and chintz-like variation of colors. In consequence of this irregularity of the forges, I found many specimens of this sublimation hanging within reach, so that, with our staves and a little contrivance, we were able to hack off a few, and to secure them. In the shops of the dealers in lava I saw specimens labeled simply "Lava"; and I was delighted to have discovered that it was volcanic soot precipitated from the hot vapor, and distinctly exhibiting the sublimated mineral particles which it contained.

The most glorious of sunsets, a heavenly evening, refreshed me on my return; still I felt how all great contrasts confound the mind and senses. From the terrible to the beautiful—from the beautiful to the terrible; each destroys the other, and produces a feeling of indifference. Assuredly, the Neopolitan would be quite a different creature, did he not feel himself thus hemmed in between Elysium and Tartarus.

MORITZ AS ETYMOLOGIST

Long ago it was truly said by a wise man, "The person unable to cope with the necessary and useful likes to busy himself with the unnecessary and useless!" Many a one might perhaps be disposed to apply this remark to the following:—

Our comrade Moritz, though living in the midst of the highest art and the fairest scenes of nature, would not desist from puzzling and perplexing himself concerning the inward recesses of man, his structure and developments; applying himself principally to the generalities of languages.

At that time, in consequence of Herder's prize-writing, "On the Origin of Languages," and in conformity with the then-prevailing mode of thought, the idea had gained ground that the human race had not, as the offspring of one pair, spread itself from the higher regions of the East over the whole earth; but that at some remarkably productive period of the globe, after nature had in graduated scale produced the most varied animals, the human species in more or less complete structure came to birth in this or that place, in many favorable situations. In most intimate relation to his physical organs and his mental capacities, language developed as a constitutional faculty of man. There was, therefore, no need, as regards speech, either of supernatural direction or of transmission from one pair downward. In this sense it is we are to seek for a universal language, of which each autochthonic family has endeavored to give a manifestation. The affinity of all languages is rooted in the *unanimity of the idea* in conformity with which the creative power formed the human race and its organization. Hence it follows that, partly from inward impulse, partly from outward inducement, the very limited number of vowels and consonants was rightly or wrongly applied to the expression of feelings and ideas; for it was natural, nay, inevitable, that the most divergent autochthons should partly concur with, partly deviate from each other, and so in the future deprave or improve this or that language. What holds good with respect to the root words would then hold good also with respect to the derivations by which the relations to each other of particular conceptions and ideas are expressed and more precisely distinguished. All this might be so far well and good, and as something unsearchable, and never to be determined with certainty, left to itself.

On this subject I find the following items in my papers:

"It is pleasant to me that out of his state of brooding inertia, out of his dejection and self-distrust, Moritz should turn to some kind of activity; for in that case he becomes quite amiable. His whimsicalities then gain a true basis, his reveries purpose and meaning. He is now busy with an idea which I also have broached, and which gives us great entertainment. The idea is difficult to communicate, so crazy it seems to sound. Yet I will attempt it.

"He has invented an alphabet of the understanding and feeling, showing that the letters are not arbitrary, but have their basis in human nature, all referring to various parts of the inward sense which they respectively express. Languages may now be criticized according to this alphabet, and it is found that all peoples have attempted to express themselves in conformity with the inward sense, though by reason of arbitrariness and accident all have strayed from the right road. Consequently, in languages we have to search after those expressions which have most happily hit the mark; we find them now in this language, now in that. We then alter the expressions till they appear to us quite right, invent new expressions, and so on. Nay, if we will play the game rightly, we make names for men, examining whether his name suits this or that man, and so on.

"The etymological game already occupies many people, and so it gives us, too, a great deal to do by way of entertainment. As soon as we meet, it is produced like a game of chess, and a hundred kinds of combinations are attempted, so that anyone who happened to overhear us would necessarily take us for lunatics. I for my part would not like to entrust the secret to any but my most intimate friends. In short, it is the wittiest game in the world, and incredibly exercises the linguistic sense."

THE ROMAN CARNIVAL

In undertaking a description of the Roman Carnival, we cannot but fear the objection being raised that such a festival is a subject not properly admitting of description. So vast a throng of sensible objects would, it may be represented, require to pass in review immediately before the eye—would require to be personally seen and comprehended in his own way by each person wishing to obtain any idea of it.

This objection becomes all the more serious when we have ourselves to confess, that to the stranger viewing it for the first time, especially if he is disposed and qualified only to *see* it with his bodily eyes, the Roman Carnival affords neither an integral nor a joyous impression—is neither a particular gratification to the eye nor an exhilaration to the spirits.

The long and narrow street in which innumerable people lurch hither and thither, it is impossible to survey; it is

scarcely possible to distinguish anything within the limits
of the tumult which your eye can grasp. The movement
is monotonous, the noise stupefying, the days of the festival
close with no sense of satisfaction. These misgivings, however, are soon dissipated when we enter into a more minute
explanation, and indeed the reader will have to decide for
himself at the end whether our description justifies our
attempt.

The Roman Carnival is a festival which, in point of
fact, is not given to the people, but which the people give
themselves.

The state makes few preparations, and but a small con-
tribution to it. The merry round revolves of itself, and
the police regulate the spontaneous movement with but a
slack hand.

Here is no festival to dazzle the eyes of the spectator,
like the many Church festivals of Rome; here are no fire-
works affording the onlooker from St. Angelo a single
overwhelming spectacle; here is no illumination of St.
Peter's Church and dome, attracting and delighting a
great concourse of strangers from all lands; here is no
brilliant procession on whose approach the people are required to worship with awe. On the contrary, all that is
here given is rather a simple sign that each man is at liberty
to go fooling to the top of his bent, and that all license is
permissible short of blows and stabs.

The difference between high and low seems for the
time being abolished, everyone makes up to everyone,
everyone treats with levity whatever he meets, and the
mutual license and wantonness is kept in balance only by
the universal good humor.

In these holidays the Roman exults, down to our times,
that the birth of Christ, though able indeed to postpone
it for some weeks, was not adequate to abolishing the
feast of the Saturnalia and its privileges.

It shall be our endeavor to bring the riot and merriment
of these days clearly before the imagination of our readers.
We flatter ourselves we shall be of service to such persons as have once been present at the Roman Carnival,
and would like to entertain themselves with a vivid re-

membrance of it, as also to those who still contemplate a
journey thither, and whom these few leaves may provide a
pleasing perspective of an over-thronged and tumultuous
merrymaking.

THE CORSO

The Roman Carnival collects in the Corso. This street
limits and determines the public celebration of these days.
Anywhere else it would be a different sort of festival, and
we have therefore first of all to describe the Corso.

Like several long streets of Italian towns, it derives its
name from the horse-races which conclude the entertainment of each Carnival evening, and with which too, in
other places, other festivals, such as that of the patron
saint or the consecration of a church, are ended.

The street runs in a straight line from the Piazza del
Popolo to the Piazza di Venezia; about three thousand
five hundred paces long, and enclosed by high, mostly
splendid buildings. Its breadth is not proportionate to its
length, nor to the height of its edifices. The pavements for
foot passengers take up on both sides from six to eight
feet. The space in the middle for carriages is at most places
from twelve to fourteen feet wide, and therefore, as will be
readily calculated, allows but three vehicles at the most
to drive abreast.

The obelisk on the Piazza del Popolo is, during the
Carnival, the extreme limit of this street at the lower end,
the Venetian Palace at the upper end.

DRIVING IN THE CORSO

On all Sundays and festival days of the year the Roman
Corso is a scene of animation. The Romans of wealth and
distinction take their drives here an hour or an hour and a
half before nightfall in a long continuous line. The carriages
start from the Venetian Palace, keeping the left side, and in
fine weather they pass the obelisk, drive through the gate,
on to the Flaminian way, sometimes as far as Ponte Molle.

On returning at an earlier or later hour, they keep the other side, so that the two lines of carriages pass each other in opposite directions in the best order.

Ambassadors have the right of driving up and down between the rows; this distinction was also allowed the Pretender, who stayed in Rome under the name of Duke of Albania.

The moment, however, the bells have sounded night this order is interrupted. Each one turns the way it pleases him, seeking his nearest road home, often to the inconvenience of many other equipages, which get impeded and stopped in the narrow space.

The evening drive, which is a brilliant affair in all great Italian towns, and is imitated in each small town, if only with a few coaches, attracts many foot passengers into the Corso; each one coming to see or to be seen.

The Carnival, as we may soon more particularly observe, is, in fact, but a continuation or rather the climax of the usual Sunday and festival-day recreations; it is nothing eccentric, nothing foreign, nothing unique, but attaches itself quite naturally to the general Roman style of living.

CLIMATE, CLERICAL DRESS

Seeing a multitude of masks in the open air will appear to us the less strange, because all the year through we are accustomed to seeing so many striking scenes of life in broad daylight.

On the occasion of every festival the outspread tapestries, the scattered flowers, the painted cloths stretched above your head, transform the streets into great salons and galleries.

No corpse is brought to the grave without the accompaniment of the masked fraternities. The many monks' dresses habituate the eye to strange and peculiar figures. It indeed looks like Carnival the whole year round, the abbots in their black dress appearing among the other clerical masks to represent the more noble tabarros (cloaks).

COMMENCEMENT

With the beginning of the new year the playhouses are opened, and the Carnival has taken its start. Here and there in the boxes you notice a beauty, in the character of an officer, displaying to the people her epaulettes with the greatest self-complacency. The driving in the Corso becomes more thronged. The general expectancy, however, is directed to the last eight days.

PREPARATIONS FOR THE CONCLUDING DAY

Many preparations announce to the public the approach of the paradisiacal hours.

The Corso, one of the few streets in Rome which are kept clean the whole year, is now more carefully swept and tidied up. People are busy seeing that the small basalt blocks, square-hewn, pretty and uniform, of which the beautiful pavement consists, are in proper trim, any which are in any degree worn being removed and replaced by new basalt wedges.

Besides this you observe living indications of the near-approaching event. Each Carnival evening, as we have noticed, closes with a horse race. The horses kept for racing are mostly little, and, on account of the foreign extraction of the best of them, are called *Barberi*.

A racing horse, in a covering of white linen, closely fitted to the head, neck, and body, and adorned with bright ribbons at the seams, is brought in front of the obelisk to the spot whence later on he is to start. He is trained to stand still for some time with his head directed to the Corso. He is next led gently along the street, and at the Venetian Palace is treated to some oats, to make him feel the greater inducement to speed swiftly to that place.

As this practice is repeated with most of the horses, to the number often of from fifteen to twenty, and this performance is always attended by a number of merry noisy boys, a foretaste is thus given to the inhabitants of the greater uproar and jubilee shortly to follow.

Formerly the first Roman houses kept race horses in their mews, and it was deemed an honor to a house for one of its horses to have carried off a prize. Bets were laid, and the victory celebrated by a feast. Latterly, however, this fancy has much declined, and the desire to acquire a reputation by horses has percolated down into the middle, nay into the lowest class of the people.

From those earlier times has been handed down the custom that a troop of riders, accompanied by trumpeters, go about through the whole of Rome exhibiting the prizes, and riding into the grounds of distinguished houses, where, after discoursing some trumpet air, they receive a gratuity.

This prize is called *Palio,* and as many days as the about three and a half ells long by not quite an ell broad, which, being attached to a piebald pole, is made to wave in the air. On its lower end is worked crosswise the picture of some running horses.

This prize is called *Palio,* and as many days as the Carnival lasts, so many of these quasi-standards are displayed by the procession just mentioned along the streets of Rome.

Meanwhile the Corso begins to alter its appearance. The obelisk now becomes the limit of the street. In front of it a grandstand is erected, with many rows of seats ranged above each other, and looking right into the Corso. Before this scaffold the lists are set up between which the horses must be brought out to run.

On both sides, moreover, great scaffolds are built, attached to the first houses of the Corso, the street in this way being continued into the square. On both sides of the lists stand small raised and covered boxes for the persons who are to regulate the running of the horses.

Up the Corso you see further scaffolds raised in front of many houses. The squares of St. Carlo and of the Antoninus Column are separated by palings from the street, and everything sufficiently betokens that the whole celebration shall and will be confined within the long and narrow Corso.

Lastly the middle of the street is strewn with *puzzolane,* that the competing horses may not so easily slip on the smooth hard street.

SIGNAL FOR THE COMPLETE CARNIVAL LICENSE

In this way expectation is every day fed and kept on the strain till at last a bell from the Capitol, shortly after noon, announces that people are now at full liberty to go fooling under the bright heavens.

Immediately on hearing it the serious Roman, who has been watchful the whole year round against falling into any slip, doffs his earnestness and gravity.

The bricklayers, who have been thumping away up to the last minute, pack up their tools and make merry over the end of their labor. All balconies, all windows, are gradually hung with tapestries; on the raised pavements on both sides chairs are set out; the tenants of smaller houses and all the children are in the street, which now ceases to be a street, and resembles rather a large festive salon, a vast adorned gallery.

SUPERINTENDENCE

While the Corso grows ever more animated, and among the many persons walking in their usual dresses a Punchinello here and there shows himself, the military have mustered in front of the Porta del Popolo. Led by the general on horseback, in good order and new uniform, with clanging music, they march up the Corso, and at once occupy all the entrances to it, appoint a couple of guards to the principal places, and assume the oversight of the whole festivity.

The lenders of chairs and scaffolds now call diligently to the passers-by, "Luoghi! Luoghi, padroni! Luoghi!" ("Places, gentlemen, places!")

MASKS

The masks begin to multiply. Young men, dressed in the holiday attire of the women of the lowest class, exposing an open breast and displaying an impudent self-complacency, are mostly the first to be seen. They caress the men they meet, allow themselves all familiarities with the women they encounter, as being persons the same as themselves, and for the rest do whatever humor, wit, or wantonness suggests.

Among other things, we remember a young man, who played excellently the part of a passionate, brawling, untamable shrew, who went scolding the whole way along the Corso, railing at every one she came across, while those accompanying her took all manner of pains to reduce her to quietness.

Here comes a Punchinello, running with a large horn attached to bright cords dangling about his haunches. By a slight motion, while entertaining himself with the women, he contrives to assume the impudent shape of the old god of the gardens in holy Rome, and his insolence excites more mirth than indignation. Here comes another of like kidney, but more modest and placid, bringing his fair half along with him.

The women having just as much a mind to don the breeches as the men the petticoats, the fairer sex show no contempt for the favorite costume of Punchinello; and in this hermaphrodite figure, it must be allowed, they often show themselves in the highest degree charming.

With rapid steps, declaiming as before a court of justice, an advocate pushes through the crowd. He bawls up at the windows, lays hold of passers-by masked or unmasked, threatens every person with a process, impeaches this man in a long narration with ridiculous crimes, and specifies to another the list of his debts. He rates the women for their coquetries, the girls for the number of their lovers. He appeals by way of proof to a book he carries about with him, producing documents as well, and setting everything forth with a shrill voice and fluent tongue. It is his aim to expose and confound every one. When you fancy he is at an end he is only beginning, when you think he is leaving he turns back. He flies at one without addressing him, he seizes hold of another who is already past. Should he come across a brother of his profession, the folly rises to its height.

However, they cannot attract the attentions of the public for a long time at once. The maddest impression is swallowed up in repetition and multiplicity.

The quakers make if not so much noise, yet at least as great a sensation as the advocates. The quaker masks appear to have grown so general, on account of the easiness with which old-fashioned pieces of dress can be procured at the secondhand-goods stalls.

The main requirements in reference to these quaker masks is that the dress be old-fashioned, yet in good preservation and of fine silk. You seldom see one in other dress than velvet or silk, his vest being brocaded or laced, and, like the original, he must be of full body. His face is in full mask with puffed cheeks and small eyes; his wig has odd pigtails dangling to it; his hat is small and mostly bordered.

This figure, plainly, comes very near the *buffo caricato* of the comic operas, and as the latter mostly represents a silly, enamored gull, the quakers show themselves in the character of tasteless dandies. They hop about on their toes with great agility, and carry about large black rings without glass to serve them in the way of opera glasses, with which they peer into every carriage, and gaze up at all windows. Usually they make a stiff bow, and, especially on meeting each other, express their joy by hopping several times straight up in the air, uttering at the same time a shrill, piercing, inarticulate cry, in which the consonants "brr" prevail.

You may often hear this note of salutation sounded by a quaker, and taken up by those of his persuasion next him, till in a short time the whole Corso is rent by their screams.

Wanton boys, again, blow into large twisted shells, assailing the ear with intolerable sounds.

What with the narrowness of the space and the similarity

of the masks—for at all hours of the day there may be seen hundreds of Punchinellos and about a hundred quakers running up and down the Corso—you soon perceive that few can have the intention of exciting a sensation or attracting attention to themselves. Any bent on that object would have to appear at an early hour in the Corso. Each one is much more intent on amusing himself, on giving free vent to his follies, and enjoying to the full the license of these days.

The girls and women, in particular, devise methods of their own for merrymaking. Every one of them hates above everything to stay indoors, and, having but little money to expend on a mask, they are inventive enough to devise all sorts of ways for disguising rather than adorning themselves.

The masks of beggars, male and female, are very easy to assume; beautiful hair is the first requirement, then a perfectly white mask, an earthen pipkin held by a colored cord, a staff, and a hat in the hand. With humble demeanor they step under the windows, bow before each person, receiving for alms sweets, nuts, or other like dainty.

Others take it still easier, and wrapping themselves up in cloaks, or appearing in a nice housedress, their faces alone being masked, they go about for the most part without male attendants, carrying as their offensive and defensive weapon a small besom composed of cane branches in blossom, which they in part use to ward off pestilent fellows, in part to flourish wantonly in the faces of acquaintances and strangers whom they meet without masks.

When four or five girls have once caught a man on whom they have designs, there is no deliverance for him. The throng prevents his escape, and let him turn how he will the besom is under his nose. To defend himself in earnest against such provocations would be a very dangerous experiment, seeing the masks are inviolate and under the special protection of the watch.

In the same way the usual dresses of all the classes are made to serve as masks. Grooms with their big brushes fall to rubbing down any back they take a fancy to. Drivers offer their services with their usual importunity. Pretty, on the other hand, are the masks of the country girls, the Frascati maidens, fishers, Neapolitan watermen, Neapolitan bailiffs, and Greeks.

Occasionally a theatrical mask is imitated. Some people again take little trouble about a mask, folding themselves up in tapestry or linen cloths, which they tie over the head.

A white figure is in the habit of stepping in the road of others, and hopping before them, by way of representing a ghost. Others distinguish themselves by odd combinations. The tabarro, however, as being the least distinctive, is deemed the noblest mask.

Witty and satirical masks are very rare, for these have a particular purpose in view, and aim at being particularly noticed. Yet I once saw a Punchinello in the character of a cuckold. The horns were movable, the wearer being able to draw them out and in like those of a snail. When he stopped before the window of a newly married couple, and slipped out only the faint tip of one horn, or stepping up to another window shot out both horns to their utmost length, vigorously ringing the bells attached to their ends, the public in a moment gave merry attention and often laughed loudly.

A wizard mingles among the crowd, shows the people a book with numbers, and reminds them of their passion for lotteries.

One stands in the throng with two faces, so that you are at a loss to distinguish the front from the back of him, whether he is coming towards you or going from you.

Nor must the stranger feel any ill humor, should he in these days find himself made the subject of jest. The long clothes of the native of the North, his large buttons, his curious round hat, strike the fancy of the Romans, who therefore take the foreigner for a mask.

The foreign painters, particularly those given to the study of landscapes and buildings, who are to be found sitting everywhere in public places in Rome drawing, are studiously caricatured and show themselves very busy with large portfolios, long surtouts, and colossal pencils.

The German journeymen bakers in Rome, who are often

found drunk, are represented in their own or in a somewhat ornamental costume, staggering about with a bottle of wine.

We remember but one satirical mask. It had been proposed to raise an obelisk in front of the Church of Trinità dei Monti. The proposal, however, was not popular, partly because the place for its erection was very confined and partly because, for the sake of raising it to a certain height, it would be necessary to build a very high pedestal. It therefore occurred to one satirical wit to carry, by way of headpiece, an enormous white pedestal, crowned by an extremely small reddish obelisk. On the pedestal were large characters, the sense of which was guessed perhaps by only a few people.

CARRIAGES

While the masks are multiplying, the coaches gradually drive into the Corso in the order we have above described when speaking of the driving on Sundays and other holidays, with the difference only that the carriages coming from the Venetian Palace along the left-hand side of the street stop short at the point where the street now terminates, and then, turning, drive up on the other side.

We have already pointed out that, deducting the space appropriated for the foot pavements, the ground left in the middle of the Corso is at most places hardly more than the breadth of three carriages.

The foot pavements on each side are all blocked with scaffolds, or occupied with chairs, where many spectators are already seated. Alongside of the scaffolds and chairs there is a never-failing stream of carriages moving up or drifting down. The foot passengers are therefore restricted to the interval between the carriage lines, of eight feet at most. Each one pushes and elbows his way about as best he can, and from all the windows and balconies a thronged populace looks down on a thronged populace.

In the first days of the Carnival only the ordinary carriages are to be seen, each person reserving for the following days anything ornamental or magnificent he has

to bring out. Toward the end of the Carnival the more
open carriages make their appearance, seating some six
persons. Two ladies sit on raised seats opposite each other,
displaying their whole figures; four gentlemen occupy the
remaining four seats. Coachmen and servants are all in
masks, the horses, too, being arrayed in gauze and flowers.

You often see a beautiful white poodle dog decked in
rosy ribbons between the coachmen's feet, while bells
jingle from the horses' trappings; and the display rivets
the attention of the public for a few moments.

As may be readily supposed, only beautiful women will
mount a seat where they are so much in the eyes of the
whole world, and only the fairest of the fair will there
appear with unmasked face. When such a queen of beauty
takes the Corso, crowning the slow-paced carriage, she becomes the cynosure of all eyes, and from many sides she
may hear the words of admiration addressed to her, "O
quanto è bella!"

In earlier times, these equipages are said to have been
more numerous and more costly, being also rendered more
interesting by mythological and allegorical representations.
Lately, however, for whatever reason, the more distinguished folk appear to be lost in the mass, being more
intent on enjoyment than on showing themselves better
than others.

The more the Carnival advances toward its termination,
the more splendid do the equipages become.

Even seriously disposed people, who sit themselves
without masks in their carriages, permit their coachmen
and servants to wear them. The coachmen usually select
a female dress, and in the last days of the Carnival women
alone appear to drive the horses. They are often prettily,
nay charmingly, dressed. A squat ugly fellow, on the
other hand, in the tip-top of fashion, with high frisure and
feathers, makes a striking caricature, and as the beauties
above referred to have to hear their praises sounded, so
must he swallow the affront, when some one steps up to
him and shouts, "O fratello mio, che brutta puttana sei!"
(Oh, my brother, what an ugly drab you are!)

It is a common thing for the coachman, if he comes

across one or two of his female friends in the crowd, to lift them up on to the box. They sit beside him, generally in men's clothes, and then the little Punchinello legs, with small feet and high heels, often play antics with the heads of the passers-by.

The servants act in a similar style, taking up their male and female friends at the back of the carriage, and all that is left now is a place on the boot, as is the fashion in the case of English country coaches.

The masters and mistresses seem well pleased to see their carriages thoroughly packed; everything is permitted: everything is proper in these days.

CROWDS

Let us now glance at the long, narrow street, where from all balconies and windows thronged onlookers, standing above long dependent bright cloths, gaze down on scaffolds packed with spectators, and on long lines of chairs on both sides of the street. Between the two lines of chairs crawl two lines of carriages. Between the two carriage lines, again, is a space capable of accommodating a third line of carriages, but which is now wholly occupied by people not walking but elbowing and jostling hither and thither. All precautions are taken to keep the coaches a little apart from each other, to prevent collision in case of a block. Many of the passengers, however, for the sake of a little air, venture to slip out of the throng into the narrow spaces between the wheels of the preceding and the horses of the succeeding carriages, and the greater the danger and difficulty to the walkers, the more do their wantonness and boldness seem to increase.

Most of the foot passengers moving between the two carriage lines, to avoid danger to limbs and dress, carefully leave an interval between themselves and the wheels and axles of the coaches. Whoever, then, is tired of dragging along with the slow dense mass, and has courage to do so, may slip into the vacant line between the wheels and the foot passengers—between the danger and the avoider of it—and may thus in a short time speed over a long stretch of road, till he stumbles against some new obstacle.

Our narrative seems already to trespass the bounds of credibility, and we should scarcely venture any further were it not for the many people who have been present at the Carnival, and who can vouch for the perfect accuracy of our statements; and were the Carnival not a yearly festival which may in future be visited with our book in hand.

For what will our readers now say, when we assure them that all we have above related is but, as it were, the first stage of the throng, tumult, uproar, and riot?

PROCESSION OF THE GOVERNOR AND SENATOR

While the coaches push slowly forward, and at every block come to a standstill, the foot passengers have no few inconveniences to put up with.

The Pope's guard ride up and down individually among the throng to clear the occasional disorders and interruptions, and in endeavoring to get out of the way of the coach horses, the foot passenger only bobs up against the head of a saddle horse. That, however, is not the worst of it.

The Governor drives in a large state carriage with a retinue of several coaches along the interval between the two rows of other coaches. The Pope's guard and the servants who go in front warn the people to clear out of the way, this procession taking up for the moment the whole space shortly before occupied by the foot passengers. The people jam themselves as best they can between the other carriages, and by hook or crook contrive to get to one side or the other. And as water when a ship cuts through it is parted only for a moment, at once commingling again behind the rudder, so the mass of masked and other foot passengers at once reunites behind the procession. Soon again, however, the straitened crowd is disturbed by some new movement.

The Senator advances with a similar procession. His

great state carriage and the carriages of his retinue swim
as on the heads of the compressed crowd, and while every
man, be he native or foreigner, is captivated and enchanted by the amiability of the present Senator, Prince
Rezzonico, the Carnival is perhaps the only occasion when
people wish him well out of their sight.

While these two processions of the heads of justice and
police in Rome penetrated only the first day through the
Corso for the sake of formally opening the Carnival, the
Duke of Albania drove daily along the same route to
the great inconvenience of the crowd; reminding Rome, the
old ruler of kings, during a time of universal mummery, of
the farce of his kingly pretensions.

The ambassadors, who had the same privilege of driving
as he, used it sparingly and with humane discretion.

THE BEAU MONDE AT THE
RUSPOLI PALACE

The free circulation of the Corso is, however, liable to
interruptions and blocks other than those caused by these
processions. At the Ruspoli Palace and its neighborhood,
where the street is not wider but the foot pavements stand
higher than elsewhere, the *beau monde* have taken possession of all the chairs. The fairest ladies of the middle class
charmingly masked, and waited upon by their friends, display their graces to the inquisitive eye of the passers-by.
Whoever comes near them lingers to contemplate the fair
rows, and each one endeavors, among the many male figures arrayed there, to single out the female ones, and in a
pretty officer, perhaps, to discover the object of his longing.
At this spot the movement first comes to a stand; the
coaches stay as long as possible in this neighborhood, and
as one must come to a standstill at last, one prefers to remain in this pleasant society.

COMFITS

Hitherto our description has conveyed the idea of but a
straitened or distressed situation. Now, however, we must

relate how the compressed merriment is set in liveliest agitation by a petty warfare, carried on mostly in the way of jest, but often assuming an all too serious aspect.

Probably some time or other a fair one, to attract the notice of her passing friend amid all the hubbub and mummery, threw at him some sugared caraways, when, of course, nothing was more natural than that he should turn round and recognize his roguish fair one. This, at all events, has now grown a universal habit, and after a volley one often sees two friendly faces salute each other. Yet partly from economy, and partly from the abuse of the practice, genuine sweets are less used, and a cheaper and more plentiful stuff is demanded.

It has come to be a trade to carry about, among the crowd, for sale in large baskets gypsum tablets, made by means of a funnel, and having the appearance of sugar plums.

No man is safe from an attack; every one is, therefore, in a state of defense; and so, in wantonness or otherwise, there arises, now here, now there, a species of duel, skirmish, or battle. Foot passengers, coach drivers, spectators at windows, in stands, and on chairs, join in, reciprocally charging and defending.

The ladies have gilded and silver-plated little baskets full of these comfits, and their attendants stand sturdily to defend the fair ones. With their coach windows dropped down the inmates await an onset. People jest with their friends, and defend themselves obstinately against strangers.

Nowhere, however, is this combat more earnest and general than in the neighborhood of the Ruspoli Palace. All maskers who have places there are provided with baskets, bags, or handkerchiefs held by the four corners. They attack more than they are attacked. No coach passes with impunity, without suffering at the hands of some maskers or other. No foot passenger is secure from them. An abbot in black dress becomes a target for missiles on all hands; and seeing that gypsum and chalk always leave their mark wherever they alight, the abbot soon gets spotted all over with white and gray. Often these affrays grow serious and general, and with astonishment you see how envy and personal hatred vent themselves in this way.

All unobserved a masked figure slips up, and with a handful of comfits pelts one of the first beauties so violently and unerringly that the masked face rattles, and the fair neck is marked. Her attendants on both sides are kindled into fury; with the contents of their baskets and bags they storm impetuously on the assailant. He is, however, too well masked and harnessed to suffer from the repeated discharges. The more invulnerable he is, the more boldly he plies his onslaught. The defenders protect the lady with their tabarros. The assailant in the forefront of the battle assaults the neighbors too, and what with rudeness and violence generally offends every one, so that the surrounding people join issue and do not spare their comfits or the heavier ammunition, chiefly sugar almonds, that they have in reserve for such cases. At last, overpowered on all sides and with his shot all spent, the assailant is obliged to beat a retreat.

Usually, one does not commit himself to such an adventure without a second to reinforce him with ammunition. The men, too, who drive a trade with gypsum comfits, generally hasten to the scene of such an engagement, ready to weigh out shot from their baskets to any number of pounds.

We have ourselves witnessed a battle of this kind, when the combatants, from want of other ammunition, threw their gilt baskets at each other's heads, and could not be prevailed on by the watch, who suffered from the discharges, to desist from further warfare.

Assuredly, many of these frays would end in stabbings, did not the wound-up *corde,* the well-known instrument of Italian police, at several corners, remind people at all moments in the midst of their frolics how dangerous it would be for them to have recourse to dangerous weapons.

Innumerable are these frays, and generally more in the way of jest than earnest.

Here comes, for example, an open carriage, full of Punchinellos, toward Ruspoli. They intend while passing by the onlookers to hit them all one after the other. Unfortunately, however, the throng is too great, and the carriage is brought to a halt in the middle. All the surrounding people are at once animated by one purpose, and from all sides hail showers descend on the coach. The Punchinellos in the carriage spend all their ammunition, and for a long time are exposed to a cross fire from all sides, till in the end the coach looks all covered over with snow and hail, in which state, amid universal ridicule and cries of indignation, it slowly moves off.

DIALOGUE AT THE UPPER END OF THE CORSO

While in the middle of the Corso these lively and violent games occupy a large part of the fair sex, another part of the public finds at the upper end of the Corso another species of entertainment.

Not far from the French Academy appears, unexpectedly issuing from among the onlooking maskers on a scaffold, a so-called Capitano of the Italian Theater, in Spanish dress, with feathered hat and large gloves, and begins in emphatic tones to relate his great deeds by land and water. He does not proceed far in his narrative till another Punchinello takes up a position over against him, suggests doubts and objections in reference to his statements, and while appearing to take all in good faith, by the puns and platitudes he interjects he brings the great achievements of the hero into ridicule.

Here, too, each passer-by stands still to listen to the lively altercation.

KING OF THE PUNCHINELLOS

A new procession often increases the throng. A dozen Punchinellos choose a king, crown him, put a scepter in his hand, attend him with music, and, in an ornamental little carriage, lead him up the Corso amid loud cries. All Punchinellos spring up to it as the procession advances, increase the train, and with shouting and brandishing of hats make room for it.

You then observe for the first time how each one endeavors to diversify these universal masks. One wears a wig, the other a woman's hood over his black face, the third for a cap has a cage stuck on his head with a pair of birds in it, dressed as abbot and dame, hopping about on the perches.

SIDE STREETS

The frightful crush we have endeavored to the best of our ability to bring before the eyes of the readers drives, of course, a crowd of maskers out of the Corso into the neighboring streets. There lovers walk more quietly and confidentially together, while madcaps find more scope there for their escapades.

A body of men, in the Sunday dress of the common people, in short doublets with gold-laced vests under them, the hair gathered up in a long descending net, walk up and down with young men disguised as women. One of the women appears to be far advanced in the family way; they walk quietly up and down. All at once the men begin to quarrel; a lively exchange of words arises; the women thrust themselves into the affair; the brawl grows from bad to worse. At last the combatants draw large knives of silvered pasteboard and fall foul of each other. The women, with dreadful cries, rush in to keep them apart, one being pulled in this direction, another in that. The onlookers join in the affair as though it were all in earnest, and try to bring each party to reason.

Meanwhile, the woman who is far gone in the family way falls ill from the shock. A chair is brought. The other women run to her assistance. Her appearance is pitiable, and before you are aware of it, she brings to the world some unshapely brat, to the great merriment of the spectators. The play is over, and the troop move on to some other place to repeat the same, or produce another like farce.

The Roman, who is continually hearing stories of murder, is disposed on every occasion to play with ideas of

murder. The very children have a game they call *chiesa,*
corresponding with our "Frischauf in allen Ecken." Properly, however, it represents a murderer who seeks refuge
on the steps of a church. The others represent the con-
stables who in all ways endeavor to catch him without,
however, daring to touch the place of refuge.

In the side streets, especially the Strada Babuina, and
the Spanish Place, the mirth goes on with equal liveliness.

The quakers too come in flocks, the more freely to display their finery. They have a maneuver which makes
everyone laugh. They come marching, twelve at a time,
perfectly straight on tiptoe, in short and rapid steps, forming an entirely even front. When they come to a square,
wheeling to right or left, they all at once form a column
and now trip away behind each other. All at once, again,
with a right turn they are restored to their former order;
then, before you know where you are, again left turn. The
column is shoved as if on a spit into a doorway, and the
fools have disappeared.

EVENING

Now, evening approaches and everything that has life
presses ever more into the Corso. The coaches have already
been long at a standstill, nay, sometimes two hours before
nightfall no carriage can any longer move from the spot.

The Pope's guard and the watchmen are now busy getting all carriages as far as possible away from the middle,
and into a perfectly straight row, and with all the multi-
tudinous crowding no little disorder and irritation are
occasioned. Everywhere there is kicking, pushing, and pull-
ing. A horse kicking, those behind necessarily back out of
the way, and a carriage with its horses is fairly squeezed
into the middle. Straightway descend on the carriage op-
probrium of the guard, the curses and threatenings of the
watch.

No use for the unlucky coachman to accomplish apparent impossibilities; imprecations and threats assail him. If
he cannot fall in again he must without any fault of his

own away into the nearest side street. Ordinarily, the side streets are themselves chokeful of carriages which have arrived too late, and could no longer get into the line because the circulation was already stopped.

PREPARATIONS FOR THE RACE

The moment of the horse race is drawing ever nearer, a moment on which the minds of so many thousands of men are strained.

The lenders of chairs, the erectors of scaffolds are now more importunate than ever with their cries "Luoghi! Luoghi avanti! Luoghi nobili! Luoghi Padroni!" It is their pressing interest that in the last moments the places they have to dispose of be all taken even though at a lesser charge.

And fortunate it is that there is still a vacant chair here and there. For the General, with a part of the guard, now rides down the Corso between the two rows of coaches, sweeping away the foot passengers from the only space that yet remained to them. Each one then looks out for a chair, a place on a scaffold, on a coach, between the carriages, or at a friend's window, every one of which is now running over with spectators.

Meanwhile, the place in front of the obelisk is entirely cleared of the people, and affords perhaps one of the finest sights in the present world.

The three façades, hung with carpets, of the above described grandstands, enclose the place. Many thousands of heads look forth, ranged in row above row, giving the picture of an ancient amphitheater or circus. Above the central scaffold towers up in the air the whole height of the obelisk, the scaffold covering but the pedestal. Here you first become aware of its prodigious height, serving as it does by way of measure of the vast human mass. The open space gives the eye a refreshing sense of rest, and you look all expectation on the empty lists fronted by a rope.

The General now comes down the Corso, as a sign that the place is all cleared, and behind him the guard allow no man to step out of the row of the coaches. He takes a place in one of the boxes.

THE RACE

The order of the horses having been determined by lot, they are led by dressed-out grooms into the lists behind the rope. They have no covering of any kind on the body. Here and there spiked balls are attached to them by cords, and the place where they will be spurred is protected by leather till the moment of starting. Large sheets of tinsel are stuck over them. When brought into the lists they are, mostly, wild and impatient, and it needs all the grooms' strength and tact to keep them in.

Their eagerness for the race makes them intractable; the presence of so many people makes them shy. They often toss their heads over into the neighboring list and over the rope, and this movement and disorder intensify every moment the eager expectancy of the spectators.

The grooms are on the alert to the utmost degree, because at the moment of the start the skill of the man letting off the horse, as also accidental circumstances, tell greatly to the advantage of one horse or the other.

At last the rope falls, and the horses are off.

On the open square they endeavor to get ahead of each other, but once they come into the narrow space between the two rows of coaches nearly all competition is useless.

One pair is generally in front, straining every muscle. Notwithstanding the scattered gravel, fire strikes from the ground, the manes fly, the tinsel rustles, and you hardly catch a glance of them before they are again out of sight. The rest of the horses impede each other, pushing and driving; and sometimes one clears the cavalcade and away, though late, after the other two, the riven pieces of tinsel fluttering over the forsaken track. Soon the horses are all vanished, the people reunite from both sides and again fill up the race ground.

Other grooms await the arrival of the horses at the Venetian Palace. They contrive to catch and hold them fast at an enclosed place. The prize is awarded to the victor.

The holiday thus ends with an overpowering momentary sensation, swift as lightning; on which thousands of people have been strained for a considerable time, though most of them would be at a loss to explain the ground either of their expectation or of their gratification.

From the above description it may easily be inferred that this sport is apt to become dangerous for both animals and men. We will cite only a few instances. With the narrow passage between the carriages a back wheel may readily project a little outward, leaving, perhaps, a somewhat wider space behind it. In this case a horse racing past, and sore pressed by the other horses, will in all likelihood take advantage of the piece of ground left vacant, when almost inevitably he will stumble on the projecting wheel.

We have ourselves seen a case in which a horse in such a plight fell from the shock, the next three horses chasing up behind tumbled over the first, while the last horses happily cleared those that were fallen and continued their career.

A horse falling this way is often killed on the spot, and not seldom spectators also receive mortal injuries. A great mischief may also arise when the horses suddenly turn about.

It has sometimes happened that malignant, envious people, on seeing a horse a long way ahead of his competitors, have shaken their cloaks in his eyes, and by this action have caused him to turn about and run to one side. Still worse is it when the grooms at the Venetian Square have not succeeded in catching the horses. They, then, irresistibly face round, and, the racecourse being wholly refilled with the crowd, many accidents are occasioned that are either not heard of or unheeded.

AN END OF ORDER

The horses generally do not leave the ground till the night has set in. As soon as they have reached the Venetian Palace, little mortars are let off. This signal is repeated in the middle of the Corso, and given for the last time in the neighborhood of the obelisk.

At this moment the watch leave their posts, the order of the coaches is no longer kept, and assuredly even for the spectator who looks tranquilly on all from his window, this is an anxious and vexatious moment, and a few remarks regarding it will not be out of place.

We have already observed above that the fall of night, which is decisive of so much in Italy, breaks up the usual drives on Sundays and festival days. There are no watch and no guards, but it is an old custom, a universal convention, that people drive up and down in the order we have described. So soon, however, as Ave Maria is rung, no one will give up his right of turning about at any time and in any way he pleases. The driving during Carnival on the Corso being subject to the same laws, though the crowding and other circumstances make a great difference, no one will give up his right to abandon the established order.

When we look to the prodigious throng, and see the race-course, which had been cleared but for a moment, again inundated in a trice with people, it would seem only reasonable that each equipage should seek in due order the nearest side street and hasten home.

But as soon as the signal has been given, some carriages press into the middle of the street, jamming and confusing the foot passengers; and as the one coach fancies a drive-up, the other a drive-down, in the narrow space, the two block up each other's way, and often prevent the more reasonable people who have kept the rank from making the least progress.

Let a returning horse now come upon such a complication, and danger, mischief, and vexation increase on all sides.

210

NIGHT

And yet, later on, all this muddle and confusion are for the most part happily cleared up. Night has fallen, and each one wishes himself the happiness of a little rest.

THEATERS

All face masks are from this moment removed, and a great part of the public hasten to the theater. Only in the boxes you may still see tabarros and ladies in mask dresses. The whole pit appears again in ordinary costume.

The Aliberti and Argentina theaters give grave operas, with intercalated ballets; Valle and Capranica comedies and tragedies, with comic operas for interlude. Pace imitates them, though imperfectly; and so down to puppet shows and rope-dancing booths there is a wide range of subordinate theaters.

The great Tordenone theater, which was once burned down and on being rebuilt immediately fell in, unfortunately no longer entertains the people with its blood-and-thunder tragedies and other wondrous representations.

The passion of the Romans for the theater is great, and was formerly in the Carnival time still more ardent, because only at that season could it be gratified. At present there is at least one playhouse open in the summer and autumn as well as winter, and the public can in some measure satisfy its desires in this respect the greater part of the year.

It would lead us too far away from the purpose on hand were we to give a circumstantial description of the theaters and their idiosyncrasies. Our readers will remember our treatment of this subject at another place.

FESTINE

We shall, likewise, have little to relate about the so-called "Festine." They are great masked balls occasionally given in the beautifully illuminated Aliberti theater.

Here, too, tabarros have the reputation of being the

most becoming mask for both gentlemen and ladies, and the whole salon is filled with black figures, a few character masks being sprinkled among them.

All the greater curiosity, therefore, is excited when a few noble figures appear displaying what is a rather rare sight, masks taken from various art epochs and imitating in a masterly way various statues preserved in Rome. In this manner are shown Egyptian gods, priestesses, Bacchus and Ariadne, the Tragic Muse, the Historical Muse, a town, vestals, a consul; all being in accordance with the costume more or less happily carried out.

DANCES

The dances during these holidays are generally in long rows according to English fashion. The only difference is that in their few rounds they mostly express pantomimically some characteristic action or other. For example, two lovers have a falling out, then a reconciliation; they part and meet again.

The Romans, through these pantomimic ballets, are accustomed to strongly marked gesticulation. In their social dances, too, they love an expression which would appear to us exaggerated and affected. No one will readily engage in dancing who has not learned it artistically. The minuet, in particular, is looked upon as a work of art, and represented, so to say, by but a few couples. A couple doing a performance of this kind is quite enclosed by the rest of the company, who watch their movements with admiration, and at the end shower their applauses on them.

MORNING

If the fashionable world amuses itself in this fashion till morning, in the Corso people are busy at break of day cleaning and sorting it. Particular attention is paid to the equal and clean dispersion of the puzzolane in the middle of the street.

It is not long before the grooms bring the race horse which yesterday showed the worst behavior before the obelisk. A little boy is mounted on it and another rider with a whip lashes it from behind, making it speed to the goal at its swiftest pace.

About two o'clock in the afternoon, after the bell has rung out the signal, there begins anew each day the round of the festival as already described. The walkers direct their steps to the Corso; the watch march up; balconies, windows, scaffolds, are again hung with tapestries; the maskers multiply and give vent to their follies; the coaches drive up and down; the street is more or less thronged, according as the weather or other circumstances are favorable or unfavorable. Toward the end, the Carnival naturally increases in spectators, masks, carriages, dresses, and noise. Nothing, however, which precedes comes at all near to the throng and excesses of the last day and evening.

LAST DAY

Generally by two hours before nightfall the rows of coaches are entirely at a standstill. No carriage can any longer move from the spot, nor can any in the side streets squeeze in. The scaffolds and chairs are filled at an early hour, although the places are let out dearer. Every one seeks to secure a place at the earliest moment, and people await the running of the horses with more intense longing than ever.

At last this moment also flies by. The signal is given that the festival is at an end. Neither carriage, nor masker, nor spectator, however, shifts ground.

All is quiet, all hushed, while the dusk gently deepens.

MOCCOLI

Hardly have the shades of night crept over the narrow and lofty street when lights are seen shining forth here and there, at the windows, and on the scaffolds; in a short time the circulation of light has proceeded so far that the whole street is luminous with burning wax tapers. The balconies are adorned with transparent paper lanterns. Each person holds his taper out of the window; all scaffolds are illuminated. The inside of the coaches, from whose roofs hang down small crystal chandeliers shedding light on the company, are very pretty, while in other carriages ladies, with bright tapers in their hands, seem to invite outsiders to contemplate their beauty.

The servants stick little tapers on the edges of the coach roof. Open carriages appear with bright paper lanterns. Many of the foot passengers display high light-pyramids on their heads; others have their lights stuck on reeds fastened together, which often attain, with the rod, to a height of two or three stories.

It is now incumbent on everyone to carry a taper in his hand, and the favorite imprecation of the Romans, "Sia ammazzato!" (Be murdered!) is heard from all ends and corners. "Sia ammazzato chi non porta moccolo!" (Murder to him who does not carry a taper!) you hear one calling out to the other, while at the same time trying to blow out his neighbor's taper. What with kindling and blowing out lights and the uncontrollable cry "Sia ammazzato!" life and bustle and mutual interest pervade the prodigious crowd.

No matter whether the person next to you is an acquaintance or a stranger, you equally try to blow out his light, and on his rekindling it to blow it out again. And the stronger the bellowing, "Sia ammazzato!" reverberates from all sides, the more does the expression lose its dreadful meaning, the more you forget you are in Rome, in a place where for a trifle such an imprecation might speedily be given effect to.

In time the expression loses all trace of horror. And as in other languages curses and disparaging phrases are often used as interjections of admiration and joy, so in Italian you often hear this evening "Sia ammazzato!" employed as watch-word, as cry of joy, as refrain for all jests, banterings, and compliments.

Thus we hear jestingly, "Sia ammazzato il Signore Abbate che fa l'amore!" (Be murdered the abbot who is making love!) Or one calls to his intimate friend passing by, "Sia ammazzato il Signore Filippo!" Or in the way of

flattery and compliment, "Sia ammazzata la bella Princi-
pessa!" "Sia ammazzata la Signora Angelica, la prima
pittrice del secolo!" (Be murdered Signora Angelica, the
first painter of the age!)

All these phrases are sung out swiftly and impetuously,
with a long drawl on the penultimate or antepenultimate.
Amid all this never-ceasing cry the blowing out and kindling of tapers go on constantly. Whomsoever you meet in
the house, on the stairs, whether you are in a room with
company, or see your neighbor when looking out from
your window, you everywhere endeavor to get the advantage of him in blowing out his light.

All ages and classes contend furiously with each other.
They jump on the steps of each other's coaches. No pend-
ant light, hardly a lantern, is safe. The boy blows out his
father's flame and never ceases crying, "Sia ammazzato il
Signore Padre!" All in vain for the father to scold him
for his impudence; the boy asserts the freedom of the
evening, and only the more savagely murders his father.
The tumult, while growing fainter on both ends of the
Corso, becomes the more uncontrollable in the center, so
that at last there arises a crush past all conception; past
the powers of the liveliest memory to realize again.

No one dares to move from the place where he stands
or sits. The heat of such a throng of people, of so many
lights, the smoke of tapers ever blown out and ever re-
kindled, the infinitude of cries from so many men who
bellow the more the less they can move a limb—all this,
at last, makes the most robust senses giddy. It appears
impossible that many accidents should not happen; that
the coach horses should not get wild; that many persons
should not get crushed, squeezed, or otherwise hurt.

And yet, as each one ultimately longs more or less to
get away, striking into the nearest lane he can reach, or
seeking free air and relief in the nearest square, the mass
of people is gradually broken up, dissolving from the ends
of the street toward the middle, and this festival of general
unrestrained license, these modern Saturnalia close with
a universal stupefaction.

The common people now hasten to feast till midnight on

a well-prepared banquet of meat soon to be forbidden, while the more elegant world betakes itself to the play-houses to bid farewell to greatly curtailed pieces. At last the stroke of midnight puts an end to these pleasures also.

ASH WEDNESDAY

And so vanishes the extravagant festival like a dream, like a tale—leaving, perhaps, less trace in the soul of the actors than remains in the minds of our readers to whom we have presented the whole in its connection.

If during the course of these follies the rude Punchinello has reminded us, though unbecomingly, of the joys of love to which we owe our existence, if a Baubo on the open square has desecrated the secrets of woman in child-bearing, if so many kindled tapers have put us in mind of the end of the holiday, we may in the midst of so much nonsense have had our attention drawn by means of these symbols to the most important scenes in our life.

Still more does the narrow, long, densely packed street suggest to us the ways of the world, where each spectator and actor, with natural face or under mask, from balcony or scaffold, sees but a short distance before and around him, makes progress in coach or on foot only step by step, is rather pushed than walks, is detained more perforce than of free will, endeavors with all zeal to attain a better and less confined position only to find himself in new embarrassments, till at last he is crushed out of the way.

Might we continue a more serious style of speech than the subject seems to allow, we should remark that the intensest and highest pleasures appear to us like the fleeting coursers but for a moment, rustling past us and leaving hardly any trace on our mind; that freedom and equality can only be enjoyed in the tumult of folly; and that the greatest pleasure only powerfully allures when it trenches upon danger, and tempts us by the offer of bitter-sweet gratifications in its vicinity.

In this way, without premeditation, we should have concluded our Carnival, too, with Ash-Wednesday reflections. Not that we would cast any shade of sadness on our readers. On the contrary, seeing that life as a whole, like the Roman Carnival, stretches far beyond our ken, and is full of troubles and vexations, we would desire that everyone should with us be reminded by this careless crowd of maskers of the importance of every momentary, and often apparently trivial, enjoyment of life.

POEMS WITH CLASSICAL THEMES

THE GODLIKE

TRANSLATED BY VERNON WATKINS

Noble let man be,
Helpful and good;
For that alone
Distinguishes him
From all beings
That we know.

Hail to the unknown,
Loftier beings
Our minds prefigure!
Let man be like them;
His example teach us
To believe those.

For unfeeling,
Numb, is nature;
The sun shines
Upon bad and good,
And to the criminal
As to the best
The moon and the stars lend light.

Wind and rivers,
Thunder and hail
Rush on their way
And as they race
Headlong, take hold
One on the other.

So, too, chance
Gropes through the crowd,
And quickly snatches
The boy's curled innocence,
Quickly also
The guilty baldpate.

Following great, bronzen,
Ageless laws
All of us must
Fulfill the circles
Of our existence.

Yet man alone can
Achieve the impossible:
He distinguishes,
Chooses and judges;
He can give lasting
Life to the moment.

He alone should
Reward the good,
Punish the wicked,
Heal and save,
All erring and wandering
Usefully gather.

And we honor
Them, the immortals,
As though they were men,
Achieving in great ways
What the best in little
Achieves or longs to.

Let noble man
Be helpful and good,
Create unwearied
The useful, the just;
Be to us a pattern
Of those prefigured beings.

SONG OF THE SPIRITS OVER THE WATERS

TRANSLATED BY VERNON WATKINS

The soul of man
Is like the water:
From heaven it comes,
To heaven it rises,
And lifted, swiftly
To Earth it plunges,
Forever changing.

Where the clear jet
Streams from the high
Precipitous rock face,
In powdery drizzle
It hangs in cloud billows
On the smooth rock,
And lithely taken
Boils in water veils,
Softly roaring
Down to the deep.

Where rock crags rise
To meet the fall,
It foams in confusion,
Withdrawing gradually
To the abyss.

In the flat bed
It glides through the valley of pasture,
And in the smooth lake
Feed on their images
All constellations.

Wind is the ripple's
Favorite lover;
Wind from the ground swell
Stirs up the foam waves.

Soul of man,
How you seem like the water!
Fortune of man,
How you seem like the wind!

LIMITS OF HUMAN NATURE

TRANSLATED BY VERNON WATKINS

When the primeval,
Holy Father
With temperate hand
From thundering cloud forms
Over Earth scatters
Lightnings of blessing,
I kiss the lowest
Hem of his garment,
Childlike awe throbbing
True in my breast.

For with gods
No man should ever
Dare to be measured.
If he uplifts himself
And bestirs
The stars with his cranium,
Nowhere then cleave
His uncertain footsoles,
And with him play
The clouds and the winds.

If he stands firm with
Marrowy bones
On the deep-founded,
Enduring Earth,
Then he aspires not,
Save to the oak tree
Or to the vine
Himself to liken.

What then distinguishes
Gods from men?
That many waves
Before them move,
An eternal stream:
Us the wave gathers,
Us the wave swallows,
And we sink.

A little ring
Confines our life,
And many generations
Link up, enduring
On their existence's
Endless chain.

PROMETHEUS

TRANSLATED BY MICHAEL HAMBURGER

Cover your heaven, Zeus,
With cloudy vapors
And like a boy
Beheading thistles
Practice on oaks and mountain peaks—
Still you must leave
My earth intact
And my small hovel, which you did not build,
And this my hearth
Whose glowing heat
You envy me.

I know of nothing more wretched
Under the sun than you gods!
Meagerly you nourish
Your majesty
On dues of sacrifice
And breath of prayer
And would suffer want
But for children and beggars,
Poor hopeful fools.

Once too, a child,
Not knowing where to turn,
I raised bewildered eyes
Up to the sun, as if above there were

An ear to hear my complaint,
A heart like mine
To take pity on the oppressed.

Who helped me
Against the Titans' arrogance?
Who rescued me from death,
From slavery?
Did not my holy and glowing heart,
Unaided, accomplish all?
And did it not, young and good,
Cheated, glow thankfulness
For its safety to him, to the sleeper above?

I pay homage to you? For what?
Have you ever assuaged
Have you ever relieved
The burdened man's anguish?
The frightened man's tears?
Was it not omnipotent Time
That forged me into manhood,
And eternal Fate,
My masters and yours?

Or did you think perhaps
That I should hate this life,
Flee into deserts
Because not all
The blossom of dream grew ripe?

Here I sit, forming men
In my image,
A race to resemble me:
To suffer, to weep,
To enjoy, to be glad—
And never to heed you,
Like me!

A WINTER JOURNEY IN THE HARZ

TRANSLATED BY CHRISTOPHER MIDDLETON

As the buzzard aloft
On heavy daybreak cloud
With easy pinion rests
Searching for prey,
May my song hover.

For a god has
Duly to each
His path prefixed,
And the fortunate man
Runs fast and joyfully
To his journey's end;
But he whose heart
Misfortune constricted
Struggles in vain
To break from the bonds
Of the brazen thread
Which the shears, so bitter still,
Cut once alone.

Into grisly thickets
The rough beasts run,
And with the sparrows
The rich long since have
Sunk in their swamps.

Easy it is to follow that car
Which Fortune steers,
Like the leisurely troop that rides
The fine highroads
Behind the array of the Prince.

But who is it stands aloof?
His path is lost in the brake,
Behind him the shrubs
Close and he's gone,

Grass grows straight again,
The emptiness swallows him.

O who shall heal his agony then
In whom each balm turned poison,
Who drank hatred of man
From the very fullness of love?
First held now holding in contempt,
In secret he consumes
His own particular good
In selfhood unsated.

If in your book of songs,
Father of love, there sounds
One note his ear can hear,
Refresh with it then his heart!
Open his clouded gaze
To the thousand fountainheads
About him as he thirsts
In the desert!

You who give joys that are manifold,
To each his overflowing share,
Bless the companions that hunt
On the spoor of the beasts
With young exuberance
Of glad desire to kill,
Tardy avengers of outrage
For so long repelled in vain
By the cudgeling countryman.

But hide the solitary man
In your sheer gold cloud!
Till roses flower again
Surround with winter-green
The moistened hair,
O love, of your poet!

With your lantern glowing
You light his way

Over the fords by night,
On impassable tracks
Through the void countryside;
With daybreak thousand-hued
Into his heart you laugh;
With the mordant storm
You bear him aloft;
Winter streams plunge from the crag
Into his songs,
And his altar of sweetest thanks
Is the snow-hung brow
Of the terrible peak
People in their imaginings crowned
With spirit dances.

You stand with heart unplumbed
Mysteriously revealed
Above the marveling world
And you look from clouds
On the kingdoms and magnificence
Which from your brothers' veins beside you
With streams you water.

From ROMAN ELEGIES

TRANSLATED BY MICHAEL HAMBURGER

I

Speak to me, stones, and you, high palaces also,
   Streets, now say but one word! Genius, will you not stir?
True, all is living yet within your sanctified precincts,
   Timeless Rome; only me all still in silence receives.
O, who will whisper to me, at what small window, revealing
   Her, the dear one, whose glance, searing, will quicken
     my blood?

Can I not guess on what roads, forever coming and going,
    Only for her sake I'll spend all my invaluable time?
Still I'm seeing the sights, the churches, the ruins, the
       columns,
    As a serious man ought to and does use his days.
That, however, will pass; quite soon no more than one
       temple,
    Amor's temple alone the votary's zeal shall seek out.
True, this Rome's a whole world; but without love the
       whole world would
    Not be the whole world at all, neither would Rome
    still be Rome.

II

Honor whomever you please! But I at last am in safety!
    Beautiful ladies, and you, men of the elegant world,
Ask about uncles and aunts and second cousins and
      great-aunts,
    Then, after talk that's prescribed, start the wearisome
      game.
And the rest of you too, farewell, in large and in little
    Circles, who more than once brought me close to
    despair.
Pointless, politic, repeat every current opinion
    Which across Europe incensed hounds the lone
    wanderer's track.
So once the ditty *Malbrough* pursued the traveling Briton,
    First from Paris to Leghorn, then from Livorno to
    Rome,
Thence on to Naples; and though he now were to sail
    off to Smyrna,
    "Malbrough" would welcome him there! "Malbrough"
    ring out on the quay.
And no differently I wherever I went had to hear the
    People scold and complain, curse the corruption of
    kings.
Now in vain you will try to find me, secure in the refuge
    Which to Amor the prince, royal protection, I owe.
Here with his wings he conceals, covers his guest; the
    belovèd,

Roman in thought, does not fear Gauls in their
    thundering rage.
Never yet she's inquired for news and rumors, but rather,
    Watchful, attends to the man, learns all his wishes
        and needs.
She delights in her friend, the vigorous, liberal stranger
    Who can tell her of snow, mountains, and timber-built
        house;
Shares the flames and the glow which she has awakened
    within him,
    Pleased that he does not stint gold as a Roman
        would do.
Richer now is her table; dresses and gowns are not lacking,
    Nor a carriage that waits close to the opera's door.
Mother and daughter alike are glad of the Northerner's
    presence.
    Roman bosom and limbs yield to barbarian rule.

III

Happy now I can feel the classical climate inspire me,
    Past and present at last clearly, more vividly speak.
Here I take their advice, perusing the works of the ancients
    With industrious care, pleasure that grows every day.
But throughout the nights by Amor I'm differently busied,
    If only half improved, doubly delighted instead.
Also, am I not learning when at the shape of her bosom,
    Graceful lines I can glance, guide a light hand down
        her hips?
Only thus I appreciate marble; reflecting, comparing,
    See with an eye that can feel, feel with a hand that
        can see.
True, the loved one besides may claim a few hours of
        the daytime,
    But in nighttime hours too makes full amends for
        the loss.
For not always we're kissing; often hold sensible converse.
    When she succumbs to sleep, pondering, long I lie still.
Often too in her arms I've lain composing a poem,
    Gently with fingering hand count the hexameter's beat

Out on her back; she breathes, so lovely and calm in
    her sleeping,
    That her breath to the inmost depth, glowing, transfuses
      my breast.
Amor meanwhile refuels the lamp and remembers
    How his great triumvirs too likewise he once had
      obliged.

ANACREON'S GRAVE

TRANSLATED BY MICHAEL HAMBURGER

Where the rose is in flower, where vines interlace with
    the laurel,
    Where the turtle-dove calls, where the small cricket
      delights,
What a grave is this, which all the gods have embellished,
    Graced and planted with life? It is Anacreon's rest.
Springtime, summer, and autumn blessed the fortunate
    poet:
    And from winter the mound kept him secure in the end.

ELECTIVE AFFINITIES

(From *Novels and Tales*)

TRANSLATED BY JAMES ANTHONY FROUDE AND
R. DILLON BOYLAN

Charlotte's tact, in whatever circle she might be, large or small, was remarkable, and she was able to set aside disagreeable or excited expressions without appearing to notice them. When a conversation grew tedious, she knew how to interrupt it; when it halted, she could set it going. And this time her good gift did not forsake her.

"I am sure you will forgive me my fault," she said, "when I tell you what it was this moment which came over me. I heard you reading something about affinities, and I thought directly of some relations of mine, two of whom are just now occupying me a great deal. Then my attention went back to the book. I found it was not about living things at all, and I looked over to get the thread of it right again."

"It was the comparison which led you wrong and confused you," said Edward. "The subject is nothing but earths and minerals. But man is a true Narcissus; he delights to see his own image everywhere; and he spreads himself underneath the universe, like the amalgam behind the glass."

"Quite true," continued the Captain. "That is the way in which he treats everything external to himself. His wisdom and his folly, his will and his caprice, he attributes alike to the animal, the plant, the elements, and the gods."

"Would you," said Charlotte, "if it is not taking you away too much from the immediate subject, tell me briefly what is meant here by affinities?"

"I shall be very glad indeed," replied the Captain, to whom Charlotte had addressed herself. "That is, I will tell you as well as I can. My ideas on the subject date ten years back; whether the scientific world continues to think the same about it, I cannot tell."

"It is most disagreeable," cried Edward, "that one cannot nowadays learn a thing once for all, and have done with it. Our forefathers could keep to what they were taught when they were young; but we have, every five years, to make revolutions with them, if we do not wish to drop altogether out of fashion."

"We women need not be so particular," said Charlòtte; "and to speak the truth, I only want to know the meaning of the word. There is nothing more ridiculous in society than to misuse a strange technical word; and I only wish you to tell me in what sense the expression is made use of in connection with these things. What its scientific application is, I am quite content to leave to the learned; who, by the way, as far as I have been able to observe, do not find it easy to agree among themselves."

"Where shall we begin," said Edward, after a pause, to the Captain, "to come most quickly to the point?"

The latter, after thinking a little while, replied shortly, "You must let me make what will seem a wide sweep; we shall be on our subject almost immediately."

Charlotte settled her work at her side, promising the fullest attention.

The Captain began:

"In all natural objects with which we are acquainted, we observe immediately that they have a certain relation to themselves. It may sound ridiculous to be asserting what is obvious to every one; but it is only by coming to a clear understanding together about what we know, that we can advance to what we do not know."

"I think," interrupted Edward, "we can make the thing more clear to her, and to ourselves, with examples; conceive water, or oil, or quicksilver; among these you will see a certain oneness, a certain connection of their parts; and this oneness is never lost, except through force or some other determining cause. Let the cause cease to operate, and at once the parts unite again."

"Unquestionably," said Charlotte, "that is plain; raindrops readily unite and form streams; and when we were children, it was our delight to play with quicksilver, and wonder at the little globules splitting and parting and running into one another."

"And here," said the Captain, "let me just cursorily mention one remarkable thing, I mean, that the full, complete correlation of parts which the fluid state makes possible, shows itself distinctly and universally in the globular form. The falling water-drop is round; you yourself spoke of the globules of quicksilver; and a drop of melted lead let fall, if it has time to harden before it reaches the ground, is found at the bottom in the shape of a ball."

"Let me try and see," said Charlotte, "whether I can understand where you are bringing me. As everything has a reference to itself, so it must have some relation to others."

"And that," interrupted Edward, "will be different according to the natural differences of the things themselves. Sometimes they will meet like friends and old acquaintances; they will come rapidly together, and unite without either having to alter itself at all—as wine mixes with water. Others, again, will remain as strangers side by side, and no amount of mechanical mixing or forcing will succeed in combining them. Oil and water may be shaken up together, and the next moment they are separate again, each by itself."

"One can almost fancy," said Charlotte, "that in these simple forms one sees people that one is acquainted with; one has met with just such things in the societies among which one has lived; and the strangest likenesses of all with these soulless creatures are in the masses in which men stand divided one against the other, in their classes and professions; the nobility and the third estate, for instance, or soldiers and civilians."

"Then again," replied Edward, "as these are united together under common laws and customs, so there are intermediate members in our chemical world, which will combine elements that are mutually repulsive."

"Oil, for instance," said the Captain, "we make combine with water with the help of alkalis—"

"Do not go on too fast with your lesson," said Charlotte. "Let me see that I keep step with you. Are we not here arrived among the affinities?"

"Exactly," replied the Captain; "we are on the point of apprehending them in all their power and distinctness; such natures as, when they come in contact, at once lay hold of each other, and mutually affect one another, we speak of as having an affinity one for the other. With the alkalis and acids, for instance, the affinities are strikingly marked. They are of opposite natures; very likely their being of opposite natures is the secret of their effect on one another—they seek one another out eagerly, lay hold of each other, modify each other's character, and form in connection an entirely new substance. There is lime, you remember, which shows the strongest inclination for all sorts of acids—a distinct desire of combining with them. As soon as our chemical chest arrives, we can show you a number of entertaining experiments, which will give you a clearer idea than words, and names, and technical expressions."

"It appears to me," said Charlotte, "that if you choose to call these strange creatures of yours related, the relationship is not so much a relationship of blood, as of soul or of spirit. It is the way in which we see all really deep friendships arise among men; opposite peculiarities of disposition being what best makes internal union possible. But I will wait to see what you can really show me of these mysterious proceedings; and for the present," she added, turning to Edward, "I will promise not to disturb you any more in your reading. You have taught me enough of what it is about to enable me to attend to it."

"No, no," replied Edward, "now that you have once stirred the thing, you shall not get off so easily. It is just the most complicated cases which are the most interesting. In these you come first to see the degrees of the affinities, to watch them as their power of attraction is weaker or stronger, nearer or more remote. Affinities only begin really to interest when they bring about separations."

"What!" cried Charlotte, "is that miserable word, which unhappily we hear so often nowadays in the world; is that to be found in nature's lessons too?"

"Most certainly," answered Edward; "the title with which chemists were supposed to be most honorably distinguished was, artists of separation."

"It is not so any more," replied Charlotte; "and it is well that it is not. It is a higher art, and it is a higher merit, to unite. An artist of union is what we should welcome in every province of the universe. However, as we are on the subject again, give me an instance or two of what you mean."

"We had better keep," said the Captain, "to the same instances of which we have already been speaking. Thus what we call limestone is a more or less pure calcareous earth in combination with a delicate acid, which is familiar to us in the form of gas. Now, if we place a piece of this stone in diluted sulphuric acid, this will take possession of the lime, and appear with it in the form of gypsum, the gaseous acid at the same time going off in vapor. Here is a case of separation; a combination arises, and we believe ourselves now justified in applying to it the words 'Elective Affinity.' It really looks as if one relation had been deliberately chosen in preference to another."

"Forgive me," said Charlotte, "as I forgive the natural philosopher. I cannot see any choice in this. I see a natural necessity rather, and scarcely that. After all, it is perhaps merely a case of opportunity. Opportunity makes relations as it makes thieves; and as long as the talk is of natural substances, the choice to me appears to be altogether in the hands of the chemist who brings the creatures together. Once, however, let them be brought together, and then God have mercy on them. In the present case, I cannot help being sorry for the poor acid gas, which is driven out up and down infinity again."

"The acid's business," answered the Captain, "is now to get connected with water, and so serve as a mineral fountain for the refreshing of sound or disordered mankind."

"That is very well for the gypsum to say," said Edward, smiling, "if there be not some little *arrière pensée* behind this. Confess your wickedness! You mean me by your lime; the lime is laid hold of by the Captain, in the form of sulphuric acid, torn away from your agreeable society, and metamorphosed into a refractory gypsum."

"If your conscience prompts you to make such a reflection," replied Charlotte, "I certainly need not distress myself. These comparisons are pleasant and entertaining; and who is there that does not like playing with analogies? But man is raised very many steps above these elements; and if he has been somewhat liberal with such fine words as Election and Elective Affinities, he will do well to turn back again into himself, and take the opportunity of considering carefully the value and meaning of such expressions. Unhappily, we know cases enough where a connection apparently indissoluble between two persons, has, by the accidental introduction of a third, been utterly destroyed, and one or other of the once happily united pair been driven out into the wilderness."

"Then you see how much more gallant the chemists are," said Edward. "They at once add a fourth, that neither may go away empty."

"Quite so," replied the Captain. "And those are the cases which are really most important and remarkable—cases where this attraction, this affinity, this separating and combining, can be exhibited, the two pairs severally crossing each other; where four creatures, connected previously, as two and two, are brought into contact, and at once forsake their first combination to form into a second. In this forsaking and embracing, this seeking and flying, we believe that we are indeed observing the effects of some higher determination; we attribute a sort of will and choice to such creatures, and feel really justified in using technical words, and speaking of 'Elective Affinities.' "

"Give me one instance of this," said Charlotte.

"One should not spoil such things with words," replied the Captain. "As I said before, as soon as I can show you the experiment, I can make it all intelligible and pleasant for you. For the present, I can give you nothing but horrible scientific expressions, which at the same time will give you no idea about the matter. You ought yourself to see these creatures, which seem so dead, and which are yet so full of inward energy and force, at work before your eyes. You should observe them with real personal interest. Now they seek each other out, attract each other, seize, crush, devour, destroy each other, and then suddenly reappear again out of their combinations, and come forward in fresh, renovated, unexpected form; thus you will comprehend how we attribute to them a sort of immortality—how we speak of them as having sense and understanding; because we feel our own senses to be insufficient to observe them adequately, and our reason too weak to follow them."

"I quite agree," said Edward, "that the strange scientific nomenclature, to persons who have not been reconciled to it by a direct acquaintance with or understanding of its object, must seem unpleasant, even ridiculous; but we can easily, just for once, contrive with symbols to illustrate what we are speaking of."

"If you do not think it looks pedantic," answered the Captain, "I can put my meaning together with letters. Suppose an A connected so closely with a B, that all sorts of means, even violence, have been made use of to separate them, without effect. Then suppose a C in exactly the same position with respect to D. Bring the two pairs into contact; A will fling himself on D, C on B, without its being possible to say which had first left its first connection, or made the first move toward the second."

"Now then," interposed Edward, "till we see all this with our eyes, we will look upon the formula as an analogy, out of which we can devise a lesson for immediate use. You stand for A, Charlotte, and I am your B; really and truly I cling to you, I depend on you, and follow you, just as B does with A. C is obviously the

Captain, who at present is in some degree withdrawing me from you. So now it is only just that if you are not to be left to solitude, a D should be found for you, and that is unquestionably the amiable little lady, Ottilie. You will not hesitate any longer to send and fetch her."

"Good," replied Charlotte; "although the example does not, in my opinion, exactly fit our case. However, we have been fortunate, at any rate, in today for once having met all together; and these natural or elective affinities have served to unite us more intimately. I will tell you that since this afternoon I have made up my mind to send for Ottilie. My faithful housekeeper, on whom I have hitherto depended for everything, is going to leave me shortly, to be married. (It was done at my own suggestion, I believe, to please me.) What it is that has decided me about Ottilie, you shall read to me. I will not look over the pages again. Indeed, the contents of them are already known to me. Only read, read!"

With these words, she produced a letter, and handed it to Edward.

❧

NOVELLE

TRANSLATED BY CHRISTOPHER MIDDLETON

The thick mist of early autumn day was still lying over the expanse of the courtyard at the Prince's palace as the eye discerned, through its gradually dispersing veil, the whole turmoil of the hunt on horseback and on foot. One could recognize the activities of the nearest hurrying figures: stirrups were being lengthened and shortened, guns and cartridge bags passed from hand to hand, and satchels of badger skin were being straightened, while the hounds pulled impatiently at the leash, almost throwing off balance the men who held them. Here and there, too, a horse would make a quick movement, excited by the fire of its own nature, or by the spur of its rider, who, even here in the half-light, could not suppress a certain vain ambition to announce his presence. However, all were waiting for the Prince, whose farewells to his young wife had already occasioned overmuch delay.

Not long married, these two now knew the joy of hearts whose feelings are as one; both were of lively and active character, each took pleasure in sharing the other's aims and inclinations. The Prince's father had lived to see, and to turn to good use, the day when it became clear that all members of the state should be equally industrious, and that each person, in such employ as suited his talents, should first earn and then enjoy his living.

The success this policy had achieved could be measured during these days when the great market gathered—a market which might well be called a trade fair. Yesterday the Prince had led his wife on horseback through the maze of stacked wares, and had drawn her attention to the happy interchanging here of mountainous and plain country; he had carefully pointed out to her, here at their very center, the activities of the lands he governed.

Though the Prince was occupied during these days with such pressing matters, in almost uninterrupted conference with his advisers, and particularly with his minister of finance, the master of the hunt also upheld his right to attention, and to his mind it was impossible to resist the temptation to arrange, as was apt for these autumn days, a hunt, already once postponed, such as would provide for the court and the numerous visitors from other parts a special and unusual festive occasion.

The Princess was reluctant to stay behind; but it had been decided to penetrate far into the mountains, and to surprise the peaceable folk in the forests there with an unexpected invasion.

As he took his leave, the Prince did not omit to suggest to his wife that she might herself go riding with Prince Friedrich, his uncle. "I shall leave you Honorio, too," he said, "the young squire here at court, who attends to the stables, and he will look after everything." And, implementing these words, he gave as he descended the stairs the necessary instructions to a young man of handsome appearance, and then left with his guests and his retinue.

The Princess, who had waved her handkerchief to her husband as he appeared in the courtyard below, now proceeded into the rooms on the other side of the palace, which commanded toward the mountains an open prospect that was all the more beautiful since the palace stood at some height above the river, and so offered to the front and to the rear a variety of interesting views. She found the telescope still in the position in which it had been set the previous evening, when the conversation had turned upon the lofty ruins of the old family castle which could be seen over woodland, hill, and treetop and which had emerged with remarkable clarity in the evening light; for it was then that the masses of light and shade enabled the beholder to obtain the clearest possible impression of this

striking old monument. Also this morning there appeared
through the lenses most vividly the autumn coloring of
the various species of tree which, unchecked and undisturbed over the long years, had grown up between the
distant walls. The lovely lady directed the telescope, however, somewhat lower, toward an empty and stony space
over which the hunt must pass; she waited patiently, and
she had not been in error: for the clarity and magnifying
power of the glass enabled her bright eye to pick out
beyond question the Prince and the master of horse; and
she could not restrain herself from waving once more
with her handkerchief, when it seemed to her (though
it need not have been so) that for an instant they drew rein
and looked back.

At this moment, the Prince's uncle, Friedrich, was announced. He came with his draftsman, who carried under
his arm a large portfolio. "Ah, my dear niece," said this
vigorous old gentleman, "we have brought the drawings of
the family castle, made especially to show, from various
different points of view, how the massive fortifications of
earlier times have resisted all weathers and all seasons,
and how nevertheless the walls have weakened at points,
and have here and there fallen into decay. Recently we
have done a good deal to make this wilderness more easily
penetrable, for, as it now stands, it will astonish and delight every traveler and every visitor."

As he discussed the drawings one by one, the old
prince continued: "Here, where we arrive at the castle itself, after walking up the defile through the outer ring-
walls, there confronts us a crag, which is one of the most
solid in the whole mountain range; at the top of it a tower
is built, but here it is well-nigh impossible to tell where
nature ends and art and craftsmanship begin. Also we see
walls adjoining on each side, and outer defense walls
built terracewise down the slope. But that is not quite
accurate, for it is actually the forest which surrounds this
very ancient stronghold; for a hundred and fifty years, no
ax has been heard here, and everywhere huge trees have
grown; as you push your way through to the walls, smooth
maple, rough oak, slim fir, obstruct you with trunk and

root, and we have to wind our way round these, and choose
our path wisely. Look, how excellently the draftsman has
reproduced the distinctive detail on the page, how conspicuous are the various species of trunk and root which
entwine the walls, and the thick branches winding through
the gaps. It is a wilderness without equal, unique in its
fortuitous creation, where the old signatures of long-van-
ished human power can be seen struggling with the ever-
living and ever-advancing forces of nature."

Then, producing another drawing, he went on: "Now,
I wonder what you will think of the castle courtyard,
which, owing to the collapse of the old gate tower, has
not been entered for countless years. We tried to reach it
from the side, we forced a way through walls, and broke
down arches, and thus opened an easy, though hidden access. Inside, no clearing was necessary, for here there is
a naturally level space at the top of the crag, even though
at points huge trees have joyfully seized the opportunity to
take root; gently, but with resolve, they have grown up,
and now their branches extend right up into the galleries,
along which the old knight used to pace to and fro, yes,
they have even pushed their way through doorways and
through windows into the vaulted halls, from which we
really have no wish to expel them; they are the masters
now, and they may remain so. When we removed the deep
deposits of leaves, we found the courtyard quite smooth
and level, most extraordinary, perhaps there is no place
in the world quite like it.

"But, in addition to all this, it is remarkable—and it
should be seen at the place itself—that on the staircase,
which leads up to the main tower, a maple should have
taken root, and have grown into so huge a tree that one
can circumvent it only with difficulty, in order to mount
up to the battlements, from which an uninterrupted view
may be enjoyed. But up here, too, one can stay comfort-
ably in the shade, for this tree ascends wonderfully high
into the air over all things.

"We must be grateful to our good artist here, who, in
his various drawings, most laudably makes us feel that
we are in the very presence of these things; he has spent
the best hours of the day and of the season on his work,

and he has studied these objects for many weeks. In this corner a little house was built for him, and for the custodian whom we appointed to assist him. You will never believe me, my dear, when I tell you what a beautiful view and prospect he enjoys from here, over countryside and toward the courtyard and the walls. Now that he has prepared these sketches with such clarity and care for the distinctive detail, he can complete his work down here at his ease. These pictures might grace the walls of our conservatory, then nobody will be able to let his eye wander over the symmetrical designs of our flowerbeds, arbors, and shady walks, without wishing to confront and meditate up in the castle itself both old things and new, that which is rigid, obdurate, and indestructible, and that which is vigorous, pliant, and irresistible."

Honorio came in and announced that the horses were ready; the Princess, turning to her husband's uncle, said: "Let us ride up to the castle, so that I can see in reality what you have shown me in these drawings. Ever since I came here I have heard of this enterprise; but not until this moment have I felt so eager to see with my own eyes what seemed impossible, when I heard accounts of it, and what remains to me incredible, though shown here in these pictures."

"Not yet, my dear," the old Prince replied. "What you have just seen represents what it can be and will be. At the moment we have still to overcome some initial obstacles; art must first make perfect, if it is not to be put to shame by nature."

"But at least we can ride up in that direction, even if only to the foot of the crag; today I very much want to see the wide world."

"Just as you wish," was the old prince's answer.

"But let us ride out through the town," the Princess went on, "over the great market square, where all the countless booths have been erected, making a little town, an encampment, all of their own. It is as if the needs and occupations of all the families in the land around have been brought to light, gathered in this central point, and laid out for all to see; for here, if one looks carefully enough, one can see everything that people do and require, one thinks for a moment that no money is needed, that all business is being done by barter; and that is just how it is, at root. Since the Prince gave me to consider these things yesterday, I have been delighted by the thought of how here, at the juncture of mountain and plain, both evince so clearly their needs and their desires. As the high-lander turns the wood of his forests into a hundred forms and shapes, and molds his iron to serve a variety of pur-poses, so does the plainsman meet him here with wares so diverse that one can often hardly recognize the materials of which they are made, or the purposes to which they should be put."

"I know that my nephew is most attentive to these mat-ters," the old prince answered; "for, particularly at this season of the year, it is important to receive more than one gives; to achieve this end is ultimately the sum of our whole state economy, as it is also of the economy of the tiniest household. But forgive me, my dear, I never like to ride through the market when the fair is in progress: at every step one is obstructed and halted, and then in my imagination there flares up again that appalling disaster which seems to have been branded upon my very eyes ever since I saw just such a mass of goods and merchandise go up in flames. I had hardly—"

"Let us not waste these lovely morning hours," the Prin-cess interrupted, for he had several times frightened her by describing that catastrophe in detail, how once on a long journey he had in the evening gone to bed in the best hotel that overlooked the market place, which a fair filled to overflowing, and had been waked up that night, terrified by the clamor and flames that surged toward his lodging.

The Princess now made haste to mount her favorite horse, and led her reluctantly willing companion not through the rear gate of the palace and up the hill, but downhill through the front gate; for who would not have been glad to ride beside her, who would not have willingly followed her? And Honorio, too, had without reluctance abstained from joining the hunt to which he had for so long looked forward, in order to devote his services entirely to her.

As foreseen, when they reached the market they could only ride at a walking pace; but the lovely and good-natured Princess enlivened every delay with intelligent observations. "I am reviewing yesterday's lesson," she said, "since necessity does after all wish to prove our patience." And indeed the whole crowd pressed the riders so close that they could make their way forward only slowly. The countryfolk were overjoyed to see the young lady and many smiling faces betokened decisively the delight with which they discovered that the first lady in the land was also the most beautiful and most graceful.

Here were mountain people from quiet farms cultivated among crags, fir trees and pine, commingling with plainsfolk from the hills, from meads and pastures, tradespeople too from the small towns, and everyone who had assembled here. The Princess surveyed them all unspeaking, and then observed to her companion how all these people, wherever they came from, used for their clothing more material than was necessary, more cloth and linen, more ribbon for braiding. "It is," she said, "as if the women could not pad themselves enough, the men puff themselves out enough, for their satisfaction."

"And that is their right," the old gentleman replied; "any lavishing of what is available in plenty, in whatever direction, makes people happy, and most happy of all when they lavish it upon their own dress and adornment." The lovely Princess conveyed with a nod that she agreed.

Thus they had slowly proceeded, to arrive at an open square, near the outskirts of the town, and here, where the many market booths and stalls came to an end, stood a conspicuous building made of wooden planks; and hardly had this come into view when a deafening roar met their ears. The feeding time for the wild animals on display there seemed to have come; it was the lion's roar that they heard, the voice of the jungle and of the desert; the horses shied; and one could hardly fail to observe how terribly indeed the king of the waste spaces announced his presence in the midst of the civilized world's peaceful existence. As they came nearer to the building, it was impossible for them to miss seeing the gaudy and colossal painting which represented in strong colors and vigorous images those strange animals for the sight of which the

peaceable citizen was supposed to feel an insuperable desire. The fierce, prodigious tiger sprang at a blackamoor,
and was about to tear him to pieces; a lion stood, gravely
majestic, as if he could see before him no prey that was
worthy of his consideration; beside this great one, other
singular and colorful creatures deserved less attention.

"On our return," the Princess remarked, "let us dismount and take a closer look at our uncommon guests."

"It is extraordinary," the old prince replied, "how
people always like to be excited by what is terrifying. In
there, the tiger will be lying quietly in his cage; and out
here he must fiercely attack a blackamoor, so that people
may believe that they will see something of that sort inside
also; as if there were not already enough murder and
killing, fire and perdition, in the world; the ballad-mongers
have to repeat it all at every street corner. The good people
want to be intimidated, so that they can afterwards feel
all the more keenly how pleasant it is to draw breath at
one's ease."

But whatever feelings of fear may have accrued to them
at the sight of such terrifying pictures, these were all at
once extinguished as they passed through the gates of the
town and rode out into the serenest countryside beyond.
Their path led them first along the river, which was narrow
here, with room only for light craft, but which, some
distance further down its course, as a great waterway, acquired a name, and brought life to distant lands. Then
they gradually ascended through well-stocked orchards and
parklands, and they continued further still, and saw about
them an open region, with pleasant homesteads, until
first a copse, then a small forest, absorbed them, and the
most charming localities restricted and enlivened their
view. They were welcomed by an ascending vale of meadows, recently mown for the second time, like velvet to the
eye, and watered by a lively stream which poured in abundance from a sudden source above, and they rode on,
toward a higher and more open viewpoint, which they
reached, emerging from the forest, after a lively ascent,
to see before them, still some distance ahead beyond
further groups of trees, the old castle, objective of their

pilgrimage, high aloft, the topmost point of a wooded
crag. But behind them—and nobody arrived at this juncture without looking back—they descried through fortuitous gaps in the tall trees the Prince's palace to the left,
lit by the morning sun, the symmetrical upper portion of
the town, swathed in light clouds of smoke, and, continuing to the right, the lower town, the river with its several
bends, its meads and mills; beyond this, a broad and
fertile region.

After they had gazed their fill, or rather, as usually
happens when we look about us from so high a position,
beginning only now to long for a wider, less restricted
view, they rode across a broad and stony space, over
against them the massive ruin like a green-crowned peak,
with a few ancient trees deep down at its foot; they
penetrated further, and then found themselves confronted
by its most precipitous and unsurmountable flank. Here
from time immemorial stood massive crags, untouched
by change, solid, firmly rooted at the jutting base, and
so towering up aloft; rock which had fallen in the course
of time lay tumbled below in massive irregular slabs and
fragments, and seemed to forbid even the boldest advance. But what is steep and precipitous seems to appeal
to young people; young bodies delight to dare, to attack,
to conquer such obstacles. The Princess indicated that
she was eager to make the attempt, Honorio too beside
her; the old prince, though more cautious, agreed, being
reluctant to evince any lack of vigor. The horses, it was
decided, should remain below, beneath the trees; and
they aimed to ascend to a certain point at which a massive promontory offered a level space whence one surveyed
a prospect which, though it was near to being such as
might be seen from above by the eye of a bird, nevertheless receded, as in the perspective of a painting, deep
into the distance.

The sun, now near its highest point, shed a brilliant
light: the Prince's palace, with its various portions, main
buildings, wings, domes, and towers, looked very magnificent; the upper part of the town spread out to its full
extent; also one could easily see into the lower part and,

through the telescope, the market and even the market booths. Honorio usually carried one of these useful instruments slung over his shoulder; they gazed up and down the river, at the fertile land which on the near side was broken into terraced heights, and on the far side flowed away in level country alternating with moderate hills; countless villages, for it had long been customary to argue how many could be discerned from up here.

Over the great expanse lay a serene stillness, such as is wont to fall at the noon hour, when Pan sleeps, so the Ancients said, and all nature holds its breath for fear of awakening him.

"This is not the first time," said the Princess, "that I have observed from a high point, whence one can see so far into the distance, how pure and peaceful the clear landscape of nature looks, giving the impression that there can be nothing ugly in the world; and then, when one returns once more among human habitations, however lofty or low, wide or narrow they may be, there is always something to combat, to dispute, to settle, and to put in order."

Honorio, who had meantime been looking through the telescope at the town, shouted, "Look! Look! there's a fire starting in the market place!" They looked and saw smoke, but the brightness of the sun subdued that of any flames. "The fire is spreading!" cried Honorio, still looking through the glass; and the mischief became evident also to the naked eye of the Princess; one could discern a red spasmodic glare of flames, smoke rose up, and the old prince said: "We must go back; this is bad; I always feared that I might see such a calamity a second time." When they had descended and were approaching the horses, the Princess addressed the old gentleman: "You ride back, quickly, and take the groom; leave Honorio with me, we shall follow at once." The old prince realized at once the wisdom, indeed the urgency of her instructions, and he rode down the waste and stony slope as quickly as the ground would allow.

When the Princess had mounted her horse, Honorio said: "Ride slowly, I implore you, Your Highness! In the town and at the palace, everything for fighting fires is in the best possible order, and nobody will be disconcerted by such an unexpected and remarkable outbreak. But here the ground is rough, small stones and short grass, to ride fast is unsafe; in any case, by the time we arrive, the fire will have been put down." The Princess did not believe him; she saw the smoke spreading, thought she saw a brilliant flash, thought she heard an explosion; and now there moved in her mind all those terrifying images which repeated descriptions by the excellent old prince of the market fire experienced by him had impressed upon her, alas, all too deeply.

That incident had indeed been terrible, unforeseen and deeply affecting enough to bequeath to the imagination for life a fearful foreboding of its recurrence. At night on the broad market square, packed as it was with booths, a sudden conflagration had seized stall after stall, even before the people who were sleeping in and on these flimsy erections had been shaken from their dreams; the old prince himself, a travel-weary stranger, having only just fallen asleep, leapt to the window, saw everything illuminated in a most terrifying fashion, and flame upon flame, overleaping one another, to the right and to the left, licking toward him. The houses overlooking the market square, reddened by the reflection, seemed to glow already, threatening to catch fire at any moment, and to burst into flames; below, the invincible element raged, planks crashed to the ground, laths cracked and split, sheets of canvas blazed, and their shreds, dark, with jagged flaming edges, flew round in the air, as if evil spirits, changing and rechanging their shapes, were consuming themselves in a wild dance, and sought to emerge here and there from the flames again. But then with shrill cries, people began to save whatever they could lay their hands on; servants and hired men struggled to extract bales of cloth which were already on fire, and to haul out unharmed parts of burning wooden trestles, then to pack these in boxes which they were finally compelled to abandon as prey to the swiftly advancing flames. Many persons indeed must have longed for the crackling fire's approach to be halted, for only a moment even, and, as they considered what to do, have been swallowed up with all their possessions; what blazed and glowed on the one side stood on the other side as yet in dark night. Resolute men and strong-willed persons fiercely fought the fierce enemy, and saved some things, though they lost their eyebrows and hair. Alas, this wild confusion was now re-enacted in the lovely mind of the Princess; the serene morning prospect now seemed clouded over, her eyes seemed darkened, forest and field took on a strangely anxious aspect.

They rode into the peaceful valley, oblivious of its refreshing coolness, and were only a few paces below the lively source of the stream which flowed nearby, when the Princess saw beneath them, in the bushes at the far end of the valley, something strange, which she quickly realized was the tiger; it came leaping toward her, just as she had recently seen it in the paintings; and the sight of it, added to the terrible images which had occupied her mind not long before, made a singular impression upon her. "Ride back! Princess," Honorio cried, "ride back!" She turned her horse to face the steep slope which they had just descended. But the young man rode on toward the beast, drew his pistol, and, when he thought that he was near enough to it, fired; but unluckily his shot missed, the tiger sprang sideways, Honorio's horse shied, and the enraged animal continued on its way, upward, straight for the Princess. The Princess hastened as quickly as her mount would allow, up the steep and stony incline, hardly expecting that the gentle creature, unaccustomed to such efforts, would be able to endure the ascent. Her horse exerted all its strength, urged on by its threatened rider, time and again its hoofs struck against the small boulders which littered the slope, and finally, after a great effort, it fell exhausted to the ground. The lovely lady, resolute and agile, was not slow to scramble to her feet; the horse too stood up again; but the tiger was coming nearer, though less quickly now; the rough ground, the sharp stones, seemed to hinder its advance, and only Honorio's rapid approach from behind seemed to spur it on, and to inflame it afresh. Racing toward the place where the Princess stood with her horse, both arrived simultaneously; Honorio leaned forward, aimed with his second pistol, and shot the beast through the head, so that it fell at once, and, as it lay there full length, they could see for the first time its tremendous power, of which now only the physical shell remained. Honorio had leaped from his horse, and was already kneeling on the animal; he smothered its last movements, and held his drawn hunting knife ready in his hand. A handsome young man, he had galloped his horse in just such a way as the Princess had seen him do when he took part in games of jousting and tilting. In just this way as he passed on the racetrack his bullet struck the Turk's head mounted on the stake right under the turban, full in the forehead; in just such a way he had galloped swiftly forward and plucked the blackamoor's head from the ground with his naked saber. In all such arts he was skilled and fortunate; and now both these qualities had come to his aid.

"You must kill him," said the Princess; "I am afraid that he may hurt you with his claws."

"Forgive me," the young man replied, "he is already dead enough, and I do not wish to spoil the skin; it will look so splendid on your sledge in the winter."

"You must not laugh," said the Princess; "at such moments as this, from the depths of the heart there surge up all the godly feelings that dwell in it."

"And mine too!" Honorio exclaimed; "never have I known such godly feelings as I do now; and that is why my thoughts were most glad; I only see this skin as something which will go where you go, and give you joy."

"It would always remind me of this dreadful moment," she replied.

"But," the young man said, and his cheeks glowed, "but it is a trophy more innocent than the weapons of conquered enemies that used in earlier times to be carried on display before a conqueror."

"It will remind me then of your courage and skill, and need I add that you can count on my gratitude and on the Prince's good will as long as you live. But do stand

up! The beast has no more life in it; let us think what
we must do next. But first, stand up!"

"Since I am kneeling before you now," the young man
answered, "since I find myself in an attitude which would
be forbidden to me in any other circumstances, then let
me ask to be now, at this moment, to be assured of the
favors and of the grace which you bestow upon me. I
have often asked his Highness your husband for the privilege of leave to go abroad on a journey. Whoever has
the good fortune to sit at your table, whomsoever you
honor with the privilege of enjoying your society, must
have seen the world. Travelers come here from all parts,
and if mention is made of a town, or of any important
place in the world, the members of your court are always
asked if they have been there themselves. Nobody is
credited with intelligence who has not seen all these things;
it is as if one had much to learn, only for the benefit
of others!"

"Stand up!" the Princess repeated; "I would not like
to voice any wish or request which would oppose my
husband's convictions; but, unless I am mistaken, the
cause of his retaining you until now will soon be removed.
His intention was to see that you matured into an independent nobleman, who would, when abroad as hitherto
at court, do honor both to himself and to the Prince;
and I cannot but believe that your action today has provided you with as good a passport as any young man
could take with him into the world."

The Princess had no time to notice that a certain sorrow
replaced the youthful joy of his expression, nor did he
have time to yield to his feelings; for, hastening up the
hill, holding a boy by the hand, a woman now ran toward
the group that we know so well; and hardly had Honorio
risen pensively to his feet, when she threw herself, weeping and lamenting, over the body of the tiger, and showed
by this action, as well as by her gaudy and unusual,
though neat and appropriate, dress, that she was the
mistress and keeper of the creature that lay there; and
likewise the dark-eyed boy, with his curly black hair, and
with a flute in his hand, weeping like his mother, less

unrestrainedly, but also with deep feeling, knelt down beside her.

This unhappy woman's overwhelming outbreak of passion was followed by a stream of words, disjointed and fitful, flowing like a brook that leaps from rock to rock. A natural language, with short and abrupt sentences, it touched the heart; it would be vain to try to translate it into any dialect that we know; but let us not omit to give the gist of what she said: "They have killed you, poor beast, killed you, when there was no need of it. You were tame and you would have quietly sat down and waited for us; for your pads hurt you, and your claws had no strength left in them. You missed the hot sun, which would have made them grow strong. You were the finest of your kind; no man ever saw a royal tiger laid out to sleep so splendidly as you lie now, dead, never to rise again. When you awoke in the early light of morning, and opened your maw, and put out your red tongue, you seemed to smile at us, and, even if you roared, you playfully took your food from the hands of a woman, from the fingers of a child! How long we traveled with you on your journeys, how long was your company needful and profitable to us! Yes, profitable! For indeed out of the eater came our meat, and out of the strong came our sweet refreshment. Oh, and now never, never again!"

Her lament had not yet finished when, down the slope from halfway up toward the castle, horsemen came galloping, soon recognizable as the Prince's hunt, with the Prince himself in the fore. Hunting in the mountains beyond, they had seen the smoke clouds rising from the fire, and had ridden as in full cry, drawn by these melancholy signs, over the direct path through vales and gorges. As they raced over the stony clear ground, the horses shied and stopped, and they now saw ahead of them the unexpected group of persons standing out with remarkable clarity on the empty clearing it occupied. After this initial recognition, nobody spoke, and, when they had somewhat recovered from the surprise, a few words sufficed to explain whatever details the scene itself did not make obvious. Thus the Prince stood confronted with the strange and amazing event, around him a circle of horsemen and of men who had hurried after him on foot. There was no question of having to deliberate what should be done; and the Prince was engaged in issuing orders and directing affairs when suddenly into the circle a tall man forced his way, dressed in strange and gaudy clothes like the woman and the child. And now the whole family showed its grief and astonishment. But the man, calm, stood at a respectful distance before the Prince, and said: "This is no time for mourning; my lord, mighty hunter, the lion too is at large, he too has come to these hills, but spare him, have pity, let him not die as this good beast has died."

"The lion?" asked the Prince: "Have you found his tracks?"

"Yes, sir! A countryman down there, who, without any need to do so, had taken refuge in a tree, directed me to go up there, to the left; but I saw this crowd of men and horses, and, being curious and in need of help, I hurried here."

"Good, then," the Prince commanded, "the hunt shall cover that side; load your guns, go cautiously to work, it will do no harm if you drive him into the deep woods; but, in the end, good man, we shall not be able to spare this creature of yours; why were you so careless as to let him escape?"

"The fire broke out," answered the other, "we did not move, we waited tensely, it spread fast, but was far from us; we had enough water for our protection, but some gunpowder exploded and blew fragments of burning stuff towards us, and over us; we were not quick enough, and now we are disconsolate."

The Prince was still issuing instructions, but for a moment there seemed to be some delay, when a man was seen running down from the castle; it was soon possible to recognize in him the custodian who was employed to watch over the painter's workshop, in which he lived as foreman in charge of the laborers. He arrived out of breath, but told in a few words his story: up there, behind the upper ring-wall, the lion was quietly lying in the sunshine, at the foot of a century-old beech tree. But angrily the man concluded: "Why did I take my gun into the town yesterday to have it cleaned! If I had had it with me, that lion would never have stood up again; the skin would have been mine, and I would have had every right to boast about it to the end of my days!"

The Prince, whose military experience came here also to his aid, for he had found himself before now in situations where ineluctable trouble threatened on several sides, said to the other man on hearing this: "If I spare your lion, what pledge can you give me that it will do no harm to my people in the country around?"

"My wife and my child," said the man quickly, "offer to tame the lion and to keep him quiet until I bring up the great box with the iron clasps, and then we shall take him back again, harmless and unharmed."

The boy raised his flute, as if he was about to play it; it was the type of instrument which is usually called the *flute douce,* and had a short mouthpiece, like a pipe; a good player could charm the most graceful music from it. Meanwhile the Prince had inquired of the custodian how the lion had reached the castle. And the latter replied: "Along the defile, with its sides of hewn stone, which has always been the only approach, and should remain so; two footpaths, which used to lead up there, we have so defaced that no person can penetrate, save by that original narrow access, to the magic castle, for it is as such that Prince Friedrich's mind and taste conceive of it."

The Prince considered for a moment, turning to the child, who had continued to play softly a kind of prelude upon his flute, and then, addressing Honorio, he said: "You have done much today, now finish your good day's work. Man the narrow defile, have your guns ready, but do not fire unless you can see no other means of driving the creature back; if needs be, light a fire, for that will frighten it, if it tries to escape down the hill. This man and his wife will do the rest." Honorio quickly set about executing these orders.

The child continued to play his melody, though it was none, a sequence of notes without pattern, and perhaps for this very reason so touching to the heart; the bystanders were as bewitched by the movement of this songlike music, and at this moment the child's father began, with proper enthusiasm, to speak, and continued thus:

"God has given the Prince wisdom and the knowledge that all God's works are wise, each according to its kind. Behold the crag, how firm it stands, unmoving, defying the tempest and the heat of the sun; ancient trees adorn its brow, and thus crowned it gazes far into the distance around; but if one part of it plunges down from aloft, it has no will to remain what it was, but falls, broken in many fragments, and covers the slope's flanks. But here too the fragments will not remain, they leap headlong down into the depth below, the stream takes them and bears them onward to the great river. Not resisting, being not angular and obstinate, no, but smooth and rounded, they travel all the more swiftly on their way, and pass from river to river, arriving at the sea, where the giants move in their squadrons, and the dwarfs teem in the depths.

"But who will glorify the Lord, whom the stars praise from eternity to eternity! Why do you look about yourselves, into distant places? Consider the bee here, late in autumn still he gathers pollen, and builds his house, foursquare, his own mason, his own laborer. See here the ant, he knows his way and does not lose it, he builds his dwelling of grass, of crumbs of earth, of pine needles, he builds it up and roofs it over; but his labor is in vain, for the horse stamps his hoof and breaks the house in pieces; look! he crushes the beams and scatters the planks, snorts impatiently, brooking no impediment; for the Lord has made the horse the companion of the storm, that he may carry his rider wherever his rider may wish to go, and the woman, wherever she may wish to go. But in the jungle of palm trees he appeared, the lion, with grave step he traversed the desert, where he reigns over all other beasts, and nothing withstands him. Yet man knows how to tame him, and the cruelest of the creatures is in

awe before him who is made in the image of God, as
the angels too are made, who serve the Lord and His
servants. For in the lion's den Daniel was not afraid;
he stood firm, and was comforted, and the wild beast's
roar did not stop his godly song."

This speech, with its accents of natural enthusiasm,
the child accompanied with occasional graceful notes
upon his flute; but when his father had finished, the child
began to sing, with clear-throated notes, a bright voice,
in agile cadences, whereupon the father took the flute,
and played in harmony with the song, as the child sang:

> In the pit, but out of it,
> I hear the Prophet's holy psalm;
> Wings of angels overhead
> Cool his brow and keep off harm.
> Round him nestle prowling lion,
> Lion and prowling lioness;
> See, this miracle is done
> By gentle songs of godliness.

As the father continued to accompany the words on
the flute, the mother joined in, from time to time, to sing
the descant.

But it was particularly moving when the child now
changed the order of the lines in the verse, which, though
it did not add new meaning, yet made the feeling em-
bodied in the lines more keen and more rich.

> Angels flying up and down
> Refresh with song from overhead;
> Sweet and heavenly their psalm.
> In the pit, but out of it,
> They shall keep the child from harm.
> Gentle songs of godliness
> Shield from danger, shield from pain;
> Angels that fly here shall bless,
> And their blessing now is done.

And hereupon the three together began to sing, with full and exalted voice:

> Over earth and over sea
> Eternally the Lord commands.
> Fatling and lion together lie,
> And the heaped flood upright stands.
> Faith and hope their power shall prove;
> The bright knife freezes in mid-air;
> This miracle is done by love,
> By love revealed in loving prayer.

Everyone was quiet, heard, listened, and now as the music faded one could notice its impression, and, possibly, ponder it. Everyone seemed to be soothed by it, each in his own way was touched. The Prince, as if he could only now see the end of the danger which had just threatened, looked down to his wife, who, as she leaned against him, took out her small embroidered handkerchief and raised it to her eyes. Her young heart was happy that it had been relieved of the burden which had lain the last hour upon it. Complete stillness lay over the crowd, and everyone seemed to have forgotten the perils around them: the fire below, and, from above, the presence of a suspiciously tranquil lion.

A gesture from the Prince, ordering the horses to be brought nearer, set the group in motion again; then he turned to the woman and said: "Do you think, then, that you can soothe the escaped lion, where you find it, with your singing, and with this child's singing, and with the help of this flute's music, and that you can bring it to its cage, harmless and unharmed?" They assured him affirmatively that they could do this; the custodian went with them as guide. Now the Prince left quickly with a few men, and the Princess followed more slowly with the others; but the mother and her son, accompanied by the custodian, who had meanwhile acquired a gun, climbed up the steeper slope.

At the entrance to the defile, where the access to the castle opened, they found the huntsmen busy heaping up dry twigs, so that they could if necessary light a large fire.

"It will not be necessary," said the woman; "all will be well."

Further on, they saw Honorio sitting on part of the wall, his double-barreled gun across his knees, at his post, prepared for any eventuality. But he hardly seemed to notice them as they advanced, he sat as if plunged deep in meditation, he looked about him, as if his thoughts were elsewhere. The woman spoke to him and asked him not to let the men light the fire, but he seemed hardly to notice what she said; she spoke animatedly again, and said: "My fine young man, you have killed my tiger—I do not curse you; spare my lion, my good young man—I shall bless you."

Honorio was gazing straight ahead, at the sun, which was beginning to go down. "You look westward," the woman said, "and that is well, for much must be done there; only make haste, do not delay, and you will conquer. But first conquer yourself." At this, Honorio seemed to smile; the woman continued the ascent, but could not restrain herself from looking back once more at the young man behind her; the sun shed a reddish light over his face, and she thought that she had never seen a better-looking young man.

"If your child," the custodian now said, "can inveigle and quiet the lion with his flute and song, as you believe he can, then we shall easily be able to master him, for the great beast has lain down very close to the broken vault, through which, since the main gate has collapsed, we have made an entrance to the castle courtyard. If the child can persuade the lion to enter there, I can close the opening without much difficulty, and the boy, if he thinks the plan is good, can slip away over one of the small winding staircases which he will find in the corner. We ourselves ought to hide, but I shall take up a position from which my gun will be able at any moment to come to the child's aid."

"None of these complications are necessary; God and art, godliness and good fortune, must do their best."

"So be it," the custodian replied, "but I know my duty.

First I shall guide you along a difficult path up to the wall, just opposite the entrance which I mentioned; the child can climb down then, as into the arena of a theater, and inveigle the beast to enter there, when he has soothed it."

This was done; the custodian and the mother hid, and saw from above the boy, who had climbed down the winding staircase, appearing in the open courtyard, and then vanishing again through the dark opening opposite; but he at once began to play on his flute, whose music gradually faded, and then stopped. There came a pause, full of mystery; the old huntsman, for all his acquaintance with danger, was oppressed by this strange human event. He thought that he would have preferred to confront the dangerous beast himself; but the mother, her face serene, bent forward, listening, showed not the smallest sign of unrest.

At last they heard the flute again; with bright and gratified eyes the child stepped out of the hollow, the lion walking behind him, but slowly and, it seemed, with some difficulty. Now and then it apparently made as if to lie down, but the boy led it round in a semicircle among the trees, which were still thick with bright-colored foliage, until finally in the last rays of the sun, which shone through a gap in the ruins, he sat down as if transfigured, and began once more his soothing song, which we may here repeat.

> In the pit, but out of it,
> I hear the prophet's holy psalm;
> Wings of angels overhead
> Cool his brow and keep off harm.
> Round him nestle prowling lion,
> Lion and prowling lioness;
> See, this miracle is done
> By gentle songs of godliness.

While the child was singing, the lion had sat down close to him, and had placed in his lap its heavy right forepaw, which the child gently stroked as he continued to sing, noticing soon that a sharp thorn had pierced the flesh between the pads. Carefully he drew out the painful point, and smiled as he took his bright silken scarf from his neck, to bandage the dreadful paw, so that his mother for joy leant backwards with outstretched arms, and would perhaps from habit have shouted applause and clapped, had not the rough hand of the custodian gripped her, reminding her that the danger had not yet passed.

After playing some notes in prelude on his flute, triumphantly the child sang:

> Over earth and over sea
> Eternally the Lord commands.
> Fatling and lion together lie,
> And the heaped flood upright stands.
> Faith and hope their power shall prove;
> The bright knife freezes in mid-air;
> This miracle is done by love,
> By love revealed in loving prayer.

If it is at all possible to think that, on the features of such a fierce creature, the forest king, the despot of the animal realm, an expression of friendliness, of grateful satisfaction, could be discerned, then here it was so; and truly the child in his transfiguration looked like a great and victorious conqueror, and the lion, though he did not look like a defeated being, for his power still lay hidden within him, did yet have the appearance of a being tamed, of a being that had surrendered to its own peaceful will. The child played, and sang on, interlacing the lines of his song, as was his way, and also adding new lines:

> Angels in their bliss consort
> With every child, if he be good;
> Shield from wicked will and thought;
> Help to do the noble deed.
> By incantation and a child
> Enchanted was the forest king;
> Made gentle he that once was wild
> By godly songs that children sing.

POEMS: MIDDLE AND LATE

HARPIST

TRANSLATED BY VERNON WATKINS

I

Who never ate his bread with tears,
Who never through the long night hours
Sat weeping on his bed of fears,
He knows you not, you heavenly powers.

Into our life you lead us in,
The wretch's guilt you bring to birth,
Then bring affliction down on sin,
For all guilt takes revenge on Earth.

II

Who gives himself to loneliness,
Ah, he is soon alone;
Each lives, each loves, and comfortless
Leaves him to pine alone.

Yes, leave me to my bane,
And if but once I can
Make solitude my own,
Then I am not alone.

There steals a lover listening light
To find if his girl is alone.
So past me steals by day and night
In solitude this woe,
In solitude this bane.
Ah, if at length I can
Be in the grave, my own,
They'll leave me there alone!

HOPE

TRANSLATED BY VERNON WATKINS

You have deprived of honor all who have witnessed
      against you;
  Yet to the martyr, late, doubly sublime it returns.

MIGNON II

TRANSLATED BY MICHAEL HAMBURGER

None but whom loss has rent
Knows what I suffer.
In lonely banishment,
Dead to all pleasure,
I search the sky, intent
On one direction.
Oh! but far off he went
Who loves and knows me.
I reel; hot pangs torment
My heart and entrails.
None but whom loss has rent
Knows what I suffer.

HEGIRA

TRANSLATED BY MICHAEL HAMBURGER

North and West and South are breaking,
Thrones are bursting, kingdoms shaking:
Flee, then, to the essential East,
Where on patriarch's air you'll feast!
There to love and drink and sing,
Drawing youth from Khizr's spring.

Pure and righteous there I'll trace
To its source the human race,
Prime of nations, when to each
Heavenly truth in earthly speech
Still by God himself was given,
Human brains not racked and riven.

When they honored ancestors,
To strange doctrine closed their doors.
Youthful bounds shall be my pride,
My thought narrow, my faith wide.
And I'll find the token word,
Dear because a spoken word.

Mix with goatherds in dry places,
Seek refreshment in oases
When with caravans I fare,
Coffee, shawls, and musk my ware;
Every road and path explore,
Desert, cities and seashore;

Dangerous track, through rock and scree:
Hafiz, there you'll comfort me
When the guide, enchanted, tells
On the mule's back, your ghazels,
Sings them for the stars to hear,
Robber bands to quail with fear.

Holy Hafiz, you in all
Baths and taverns I'll recall,
When the loved one lifts her veil,
Ambergris her locks exhale.
More: the poet's love song must
Melt the houris, move their lust.

Now, should you begrudge him this,
Even long to spoil such bliss,
Poets' words, I'd have you know,
Round the gate of Eden flow,
Gently knocking without rest,
Everlasting life their quest.

PLEDGES OF BLESSING

TRANSLATED BY STEPHEN SPENDER

To believers, talisman
Brings luck and wealth, when of cornelian.
If it stand on ground of onyx
Consecrated lips there fix!
All things ill it drives away,
Protects you, protects where you stay.
If the engraven word proclaim
With pure intention Allah's name,
To love and act it will inflame.
And so, especially, women can

Construct their hopes on talisman.
Amulets are likewise signs
On paper, with their written lines.
Though here one does not suffer duress
Of the rare gem's narrowness,
And here the pious souls can use
Longer verses, as they choose.
Men string around their necks these papers
Devoutly, as with scapulars.

Behind the inscription nothing else lies hid,
It is itself, must tell you everything,
And after reading it, you cry with feeling,
Delightedly: "Mine! Mine! That's what I said!"

Abraxas I bring but seldom.
Here the ambiguous creation
Of a darkened aberration
Would pass itself as highest wisdom.
If I tell some absurd things,
Think, it is Abraxas he brings.

A signet ring—hard to inscribe it:
Most sense in narrowest space confined;
If here you know to make a genuine thought fit,
The word stays buried, unconscious in the mind.

TALISMANS

TRANSLATED BY STEPHEN SPENDER

I

To God belongs the Orient!
To God belongs the Occident!
Northern lands and Southern lands
Rest in quiet of his hands.

II

He who is the only just one
Wills justice for everyone.
Of his hundred names, be then
This most highly praised. Amen!

III

By error I must entangled be:
Yet thou canst disentangle me.
In what I invent in what I act
Show my way thou doest direct.

IV

Though my thought and feeling be earth
These lead to gains of higher worth.
The spirit, not scattered like dust, can move,
Driven back onto itself, above.

V

In breathing air, there are two kinds of graces:
Air one takes in, and air that one releases;
That one is effort, this other one revives:
So wonderful the mixing in our lives.
Thank God then, thou, each time he presses thee,
And thank him next when he releases thee.

BLESSED LONGING

TRANSLATED BY MICHAEL HAMBURGER

Tell it only to the wise,
For the crowd at once will jeer:
That which is alive I praise,
That which longs for death by fire.

Cooled by passionate love at night,
Procreated, procreating,
You have known the alien feeling
In the calm of candlelight;

Gloom-embraced will lie no more,
By the flickering shades obscured,
But are seized by new desire,
To a higher union lured.

Then no distance holds you fast;
Winged, enchanted, on you fly,
Light your longing, and at last,
Moth, you meet the flame and die.

Never prompted to that quest:
Die and dare rebirth!
You remain a dreary guest
On our gloomy earth.

SONNET

TRANSLATED BY MICHAEL HAMBURGER

Nature, it seems, must always clash with Art,
And yet, before we know it, both are one;
I too have learned: their enmity is none,
Since each compels me, and in equal part.

Hard, honest work counts most! And once we start
To measure out the hours and never shun
Art's daily labor till our task is done,
Nature once more freely may move the heart.

So too all growth and ripening of the mind:
To the pure heights of ultimate consummation
In vain the unbound spirit seeks to flee.

Who seeks great gain leaves easy gain behind.
None proves a master but by limitation
And only law can give us liberty.

HATEM TO ZULEIKA

TRANSLATED BY MICHAEL HAMBURGER

No longer on sheets of silk
Symmetrical rhymes I paint,
No longer frame them
In golden arabesques;
Imprinted on mobile dust
They are swept by the wind, but their
       power endures,
As far as the center of Earth,
Riveted, bound to the soil.
And the wanderer will come,
The lover. If he enters
This place, all his limbs
Will feel the thrill.
"Here, before me, the lover loved.
Was it Medjun, the tender?
Farhad, the strong? Was it Djemil,
       the obstinate?
Or one of a thousand other
Happy, unhappy men?
He loved! I love as he loved.

I avenge him!"
But you, Zuleika, rest
On the delicate cushion
That I prepared for you and embellished.
And your limbs too, roused from their
            languor, thrill.
"It is he who calls me, Hatem,
And I call to you, O Hatem, Hatem!"

THE BRIDEGROOM

(*1828*)

TRANSLATED BY MICHAEL HAMBURGER

At midnight, I was sleeping, in my breast
My fond heart lay awake, as though it were day;
Day broke: as though by falling night oppressed
I thought: what's day to me, bring what it may?

Since she was lacking; all my toil and strife
For her alone patiently I'd withstood
Throughout the hot noon hours. What quickening life
In the cool evening! Blessed it was, and good.

The sun went down; and hand to dear hand wedded
We took our leave of him, watched the last ray burn,
And the eye said, eye to clear eye threaded:
But hope, and from the East he will return.

At midnight! Led by starlight through the gloom,
Dream-wrapt, I go to where she lies at rest.
Oh, may I lie at last in that same room!
Life's good, though worst befall us, life is blessed.

TRUE ENOUGH

To the Physicist

(1820)

TRANSLATED BY MICHAEL HAMBURGER

"Into the core of Nature"—
O Philistine—
"No earthly mind can enter."
The maxim is fine;
But have the grace
To spare the dissenter,
Me and my kind.
We think: in every place
We're at the center.
"Happy the mortal creature
To whom she shows no more
Than the outer rind,"
For sixty years I've heard your sort announce.
It makes me swear, though quietly;
To myself a thousand times I say:
All things she grants, gladly and lavishly;
Nature has neither core
Nor outer rind,
Being all things at once.
It's yourself you should scrutinize to see
Whether you're center or periphery.

IN LIVING AS IN KNOWING . . .

TRANSLATED BY MICHAEL HAMBURGER

In living as in knowing, be
Intent upon the purest way;
When gale and current push you, pull you,
Yet they'll never overrule you;

Compass and pole-star, chronometer
And sun and moon you'll read the better,
With quiet joy, in your own fashion
Will reach the proper destination.
Especially if you don't despair
Because the course is circular:
A circumnavigator, hail
The harbor whence you first set sail.

SICILIAN SONG

(*1811*)

TRANSLATED BY MICHAEL HAMBURGER

Eyes bright and cherry-black,
If you but blink
The tallest houses crack,
Whole cities fall;
And do you think perhaps
This cob wall of my heart,
Mere straw and clay and gravel,
Will not collapse?

REFLECTIONS AND MAXIMS

TRANSLATED BY W. B. RÖNNFELDT

General ideas and great conceit are always in a fair way to cause terrible mischief.

The most insignificant man can be complete if he keeps within the limits of his capacities and attainments. But even fine talents are obscured, rendered useless and destroyed, if that constantly requisite proportion is wanting. This is an evil which will often manifest itself in modern times; for who is there that will be able to satisfy the demands of an age so full and intense as the present, and one, too, that moves with such rapidity?

It is a great mistake to fancy oneself greater than one is, and to value oneself at less than one is worth.

As little as you can stifle a steam engine, so little can you do so in a moral sphere either. The activity of commerce, the continual rustle of paper—money, the accumulation of debts in order to pay debts—all these form the monstrous elements to which a young man is nowadays exposed. Well is it for him if he is endowed by nature with a calm and temperate mind, so as neither to make disproportionate claims upon the world, nor yet leave his position to be determined by the world.

The dignity of art appears to the greatest advantage perhaps in music, because that art contains no material to be deducted. It is wholly form and intrinsic value, and it elevates and ennobles everything which it expresses.

An historical sense is one which is so formed that, in seeking to estimate contemporary merits and deserts, it knows how to take account also of the past.

The best that history has to give us is the enthusiasm which it arouses.

When a man is old, he should do more than when he was young.

He who is satisfied with pure experience and acts in accordance with it, has sufficient truth. The growing child is wise in this sense.

The history of knowledge is a great fugue in which the voices of the various nations appear one after the other.

If a man is to accomplish all that is demanded of him, he must deem himself greater than he is. So long as he does not carry this to an absurd length, we readily put up with it.

Work makes the companion.

Certain books seem to have been written, not in order to afford us any instruction, but merely for the purpose of letting us know that their authors knew something.

If I err, everyone can notice it, but not if I lie.

Generosity will win favor for anyone, especially when it is accompanied by humility.

The writing of history is a method of getting rid of the past.

No nation acquires the power of judgment unless it can pass judgment upon itself. But to this great privilege it can only attain at a very late stage.

Instead of contradicting my words, men should act in my spirit.

The novel is a subjective epopee, in which the author asks to be allowed to treat of the world after his own method. The only question, therefore, is whether he has any method of his own; the rest will come of itself.

Each one of us has his peculiarities, of which he is unable to divest himself. And yet many a man is brought to destruction by his peculiarities, and those, too, of the most innocent kind.

I feel pity for those persons who make so much ado about the transitoriness of all things and lose themselves in the contemplation of earthly vanity. Why, we are here for the very purpose of making the transitory imperishable, and this can be done only if we know how to appreciate both conditions.

Faith is private capital, stored in one's own house. It is like a public savings bank or loan office, from which individuals receive assistance in their days of need; but here the creditor quietly takes his interest for himself.

I see no error made which I might not have committed myself.

There are persons whom I wish well, and would that I could wish better.

There is something magical in rhythm; it even makes us believe that the sublime lies within our reach.

Dilettantism, treated seriously, and knowledge, pursued mechanically, lead to pedantry.

We all of us live upon the past, and through the past we are destroyed.

The world of empirical morality consists for the most part of nothing but ill will and envy.

Superstition is the poetry of life; the poet, therefore, suffers no harm from being superstitious.

The man who discloses my failings to others is my master, even though he be my servant.

Ingratitude is always a form of weakness. I have never known a man of real ability to be ungrateful.

It is really the errors of a man that make him lovable.

There are men who love their like and seek it; and others, again, who love their opposite and are attracted by it.

Translators may be compared to busy matchmakers who extol the charms of some half-veiled beauty to us as though she were most lovable; they arouse an irresistible longing for the original.

The whole art of living consists in giving up our existence in order to exist.

You must keep Beauty and Genius at a distance, if you would avoid becoming their slave.

An old man is deprived of one of the greatest privileges of humanity: he is no longer judged by his equals.

In regard to a slight point of difference which once formed a subject for discussion between us, and of which I am reminded by a passage in one of his letters, I made the following observations:

It matters a great deal whether the poet is seeking the particular for the universal, or seeing the universal in the particular. The former process gives rise to allegory, in which the particular serves only as an instance or example of the universal; the latter, on the other hand, is the true nature of poetry, it gives expression to the particular without in any way thinking of, or referring to, the universal.

And he who vividly grasps the particular will at the same time also grasp the universal, and will either not become aware of it at all, or will only do so long afterward.

We are never so far removed from our desires as when we imagine that we possess that which we desire.

The greatest men are always linked to their age by some weakness or other.

There is no surer method of evading the world than by following Art, and no surer method of linking oneself to it than by Art.

To behold difficult objects lightly handled gives us the impression of the impossible.

The ridiculous arises from a moral contrast which is innocently placed before the senses.

The intelligent man finds almost everything ridiculous, the sensible man hardly anything.

Our passions are true phoenixes. As soon as the old one is consumed, the new one rises forth from its ashes.

The secret places in the path of life may not and cannot be revealed; there are stumbling blocks over which every wanderer must fall. But the poet points to where they are.

It rarely happens that anyone of advanced age becomes historical to himself or that his contemporaries become historical to him, so that he neither cares nor is able to argue with anyone.

Various maxims of the ancients, which we are in the habit of repeating time after time, bore an entirely different signification from that which is generally attached to them in modern times.

Upon examining the matter more closely, it will be found that even the historian does not easily look upon history as something historical: for the individual historian, to whatever age he may belong, always writes as though he had himself been present at the time of which he treats; he is not content with simply relating the facts and movements of that time. Even the mere chronicler only points more or less to the limitations and peculiarities of his town or monastery or age.

The older we grow, the greater will the ordeals become.

It will perhaps be urged that, although poetry is held to be an art, it is not mechanical. But I deny that it is an art; nor is it a science. Arts and sciences are attained through reflection; but not so poetry, for this is an inspiration; it was infused into the soul when first it manifested itself. It should, consequently, be called neither art nor science, but genius.

There are many thoughts which come only from general culture, like buds from green branches. When roses are in bloom, you find them blooming everywhere.

Great talents are the finest means of conciliation.

The incurable evil of these religious disputes consists in the fact that the one side tries to trace back the highest interest of mankind to fables and empty words, while the other would give it a basis with which no one is satisfied.

Let no man imagine that people have waited for him as for the Savior.

There is no sadder sight than a person directly striving after the unconditioned in this thoroughly conditioned world; this, in the year 1830, is perhaps more out of place than ever.

Before the revolution all was *effort;* afterwards it was all changed to *demand.*

The classical is health; and the romantic, disease.

Ovid remained classical even in exile; he sought misfortune, not in himself, but in his banishment from the capital of the world.

In the Greeks, whose poetry and rhetoric were simple and positive, we encounter expressions of approval oftener than of disapproval. With the Romans, on the other hand, the contrary holds good; and the more corrupted poetry and rhetoric become, the more will censure grow and praise diminish.

The translator must proceed until he reaches the untranslatable; then, and not till then, will he gain an idea of a foreign tongue.

Of the most important matters of feeling as of reason, of experience as of reflection, we should treat only by word of mouth. The spoken word dies at once, unless another, suited to the hearer, immediately follows it and keeps it alive. Observe what takes place in social converse. If the word is not already dead by the time it reaches the listener, he murders it at once by a contradiction, a stipulation, a condition, a digression, a prevarication, and all the thousand artifices of conversation. In the case of the written word the evil is still greater. No one cares to read anything but that to which he is already in a certain measure accustomed; it is the known and the familiar which he demands in an altered form. Yet the written word has this advantage: it endures and can abide the time when it may be allowed to bear fruit.

The public should be treated like women; we must tell them absolutely nothing but that which they would like to hear.

The Germans—and herein they do not stand alone—possess the gift of rendering the sciences inaccessible.

TWO POEMS

NIGHT THOUGHTS

TRANSLATED BY MICHAEL HAMBURGER

You I pity, twice unhappy stars,
Being lovely, blessed with bright effulgence,
Gladly shedding light for ships in danger,
Yet by gods and mortals unrewarded:
Love you cannot, never yet knew love!
But incessantly eternal hours
Move your ranks through vast celestial spaces.
O, what distant journeys you've completed
Since, reposing in my loved one's arms,
You and midnight wholly I forgot.

ALL THINGS . . .

TRANSLATED BY MICHAEL HAMBURGER

All things the gods bestow, the infinite ones,
On their darlings completely,
All the joys, the infinite ones,
All the pains, the infinite ones, completely.

The Mentor Religious Classics

THE HOLY BIBLE IN BRIEF *edited by James Reeves*

The basic story of the Old and New Testaments told as one clear, continuous narrative. (#MD116—50¢)

THE PAPAL ENCYCLICALS in Their Historical Context *edited by Anne Fremantle*

The most important pronouncements of the Popes through the ages, as expressed in their official letters.

(#MQ533—95¢)

THE MEANING OF THE GLORIOUS KORAN: An Explanatory Translation *by Mohammed Marmaduke Pickthall*

The complete sacred book of Mohammedanism, translated with reverence and scholarship. (#MQ375—95¢)

THE SONG OF GOD: Bhagavad-Gita

The Hindu epic translated by Swami Prabhavananda and Christopher Isherwood. (#MT711—75¢)

THE WAY OF LIFE: Tao Tê Ching *by Lao Tzu*

A new translation by R. B. Blakney of a masterpiece of ancient Chinese wisdom. (#MP416—60¢)

THE SAYINGS OF CONFUCIUS *translated by James R. Ware*

The wise teachings of the ancient Chinese sage in a new translation. (#MP497—60¢)

THE TEACHINGS OF THE COMPASSIONATE BUDDHA *edited by E. A. Burtt*

The basic texts, early discourses, the Dhammapada, and later writings of Buddhism. (#MT637—75¢)

THE UPANISHADS: Breath of the Eternal

The wisdom of the Hindu mystics, translated by Swami Prabhavananda and Frederick Manchester.

(#MP386—60¢)

THE LIVING TALMUD: The Wisdom of the Fathers and Its Classical Commentaries, selected and translated *by Judah Goldin*

A new translation, with an illuminating essay on the place of the Talmud in Jewish life and religion.

(#MT286—75¢)

MENTOR Books of Special Interest

Great Dialogues of Plato *translated by W. H. D. Rouse.* New translations of "The Republic" and other works.

(#MQ672—95¢)

The Iliad of Homer *translated by W. H. D. Rouse.* A brilliant prose translation of the epic of the Trojan War.

(#MT650—75¢)

The Odyssey of Homer *translated by W. H. D. Rouse.* The travels of Ulysses told in modern prose. (#MT677—75¢)

Life Stories of Men Who Shaped History from Plutarch's Lives (abridged) *edited by Eduard C. Lindeman.*

(#MP397—60¢)

On Love, The Family and the Good Life: Selected Essays of Plutarch *translated with introduction by Moses Hadas.*

(#MD202—50¢)

The Anvil of Civilization *by Leonard Cottrell.* A fascinating history of the ancient Mediterranean civilizations.

(#MT649—75¢)

The Prince *by Niccolo Machiavelli.* The classic work on statesmanship and power, and techniques of control.

(#MP417—60¢)

The Inferno by Dante *translated by John Ciardi.* A masterpiece in a new translation by a celebrated poet.

(#MQ705—95¢)